"Jim voices loudly and with great effectiveness the clarion call to parents that Biblical, sound parenting lies at the heart of family, community, and social stability. Through his addressing of roles and personal responsibility-folded over love- he shows that parents are intended to be the primary influencers in God's plan for children and family. In a day and time when "love" has been distilled to "what feels good" and "what children 'want'", Jim's message stands as the right medicine for parents today."

K. Duane Hammack, licensed professional counselor
Member-Care Consultant at a Non-Profit Christian Agency

"We have only a few short years to be the guiding influence in our child's life. If we miss this target of opportunity they will spend the rest of their lives trying to catch up. The Two Sides of Parenting puts you in the driver's seat right beside your child during this critical phase of their life journey. Being a parent is like flying a kite; you must let the string out ever so slowly while maintaining shuttle tension until they can soar on their own. Mr. Wunderle will help you become a master kite maker!"

Chuck Burklow
President / CEO
Sterling Yard, Inc.

The Two Sides of Parenting

The Two Sides of Parenting

**BECOMING AN INTENTIONAL PARENT
THROUGH CHALLENGE AND SUPPORT**

Jim Wunderle

Copyright © 2015 Jim Wunderle
All rights reserved.

ISBN: 150846412X
ISBN 13: 9781508464129
Library of Congress Control Number: 2015902579
CreateSpace Independent Publishing Platform
North Charleston, South Carolina

This book is dedicated to my five children:

Brittney, Rachel, Meredith, Marty, and Chad.

You raised me right.

Contents

Preface xv
Acknowledgments xvii
Introduction xix

Chapter 1   Challenge and Support 1
    Support and Challenge with Children 2
    Low Challenge, Low Support 4
    Low Challenge, High Support 5
    High Challenge, Low Support 9
    Chapter One Discussion Questions: 12

Chapter 2   What is the Difference? 17
    High Challenge and High Support 18
    Final Cautions 20
    Chapter Two Discussion Questions: 24

Chapter 3   Modeling 27
    Modeling and the Culture 28
    Can Modeling Be Used Constructively? 30
    Parents as Models 31

    Jesus as our Model 32

    Parental Perfection? 34

    Recommendations 37

    Chapter Three Discussion Questions: 38

Chapter 4   Close Relationships 41

    Reasons for an Inadequate Parent-Child Bond 42

    What is the Big Deal? What is so Important About Relationships? 43

    Rebellion-Relationship Link 44

    Research on Bonding 45

    Benefits of the Relationship 46

    What Does A Relationship With My Child Look Like? 47

    Communication 48

    Physical Contact 51

    Examples of Effective Physical Touch: 52

    Shared Activities 52

    Relational Credits 55

    A Natural Desire To Obey?   Seriously?? 56

    Small Investments are the Best 57

    Yelling 58

    Stubborn Cases 60

    Chapter Four Discussion Questions: 60

Chapter 5   Supervision and Feedback 63

    Why Parents Do Not Supervise their Children 63

    A Biblical Example 65

    What is Supervision? 66

A Case Study..68

Is a High Level of Supervision Unrealistic?...69

Let's Get Specific...71

Supervision Stratagies..75

Not Oppression..79

Feedback...79

Is Feedback the Same as Criticism?...81

Tacet Approval...81

Feedback from Children...82

Overparenting..84

Chapter Five Discussion Questions:..85

Chapter 6 Guidance...87

Elements of Child Guidance...88

Structure..90

Sibling Rivalry..91

Arguing..93

Assumptions in Arguing..94

Avoid the Prime Causes of Arguments...95

Specific Stratagies to Stop Childish Arguing..97

Manipulation..99

General Strategies to Decrease Manipulation......................................100

Thirty Most Popular Manipulation Practices by Children.....................101

Parent Responses that Make Manipulation Worse...............................110

Parent Stratagies to End Manipulation...111

A Final Word..112

Chapter Six Discussion Questions:...113

Chapter 7	Limit Cultural Influences	115
	What are the limits?	116
	A Different Direction	118
	A Word About Movie Ratings	119
	Frantic Romantic	121
	Other Aspects of the Culture to Regulate	123
	Chapter Seven Discussion Questions:	123
Chapter 8	Independence	125
	Enmeshment	128
	The Problem with Enmeshment	131
	Encouraging Unhealthy Dependence	139
	Independence Versus Rebellion	140
	Rescuing	141
	Chapter Eight Discussion Questions:	144
Chapter 9	Obedience	147
	Permissive Parenting	148
	Clear Instructions	149
	Never Bluff	151
	Too Much Explaining!	152
	Consequences	153
	Consequence Tool #1: Positive Reinforcement	156
	Consequence Tool #2: Extinction	158
	Consequence Tool #3: Punishment	161
	Using Timeouts Effectively	164
	The Infamous Chart	166

	Redirection	169
	Spanking	169
	The Strong-Willed Child	173
	Chapter Nine Discussion Questions:	175
Chapter 10	Respect	177
	Why Should Children Respect Parents?	178
	Why Children Do Not Respect Parents	179
	How to Recognize Disrespect	180
	Firm Versus Harsh	181
	Two-Way Respect	183
	Dealing With Disrespect	184
	Chapter Ten Discussion Questions:	185
Chapter 11	Responsibility and Accountability	187
	Who Should Children Answer To?	189
	Taking Responsibility	190
	Earned Not Given	191
	Allowances	191
	Performance Versus Value	192
	Self-Soothing	194
	Children Sleeping With Parents	196
	Children and Power	198
	Tools of Power	199
	Cell Phones and Children	200
	Stratagies for Dealing With Lying	201
	Chapter Eleven Discussion Questions:	203

Chapter 12	Self-Development	205
	Guaranteed Results	205
	Security In Children	206
	What Consitutes a Secure Home?	207
	An Insecure Home	208
	Associations	210
	Indicators of Insecurity	211
	The Cycle	214
	Damaging to Development	215
	Breaking the Cycle	216
	Drama!	217
	Mothers and Sons	220
	To Tattoo.....or Not to Tattoo	221
	An Eschewed Perspective	222
	Chapter Twelve Discussion Questions:	223

Chapter 13	Putting It All Together	225
	The Cost of Waiting	228
	New Challenges	228
	Misdirected Goals	229
	Small Changes Can Make a Big Difference	231
	Grace is a Wonderful Thing	232
	Chapter Thirteen Discussion Questions:	233

	Appendix	235
	What Wrong with Children and Cell Phones?	235

Preface

The Two Sides of Parenting actually started as brief parenting tips sent via email to parents of young children at Travis Avenue Baptist Church in Fort Worth in the mid 90's. I recognized a need, at the time, for bite-sized parenting ideas that I had learned both as a parent and licensed counselor. Writing those tips for several years each week also forced me to refine and think through my own parenting ideas. I later had the opportunity to observe the link between styles of parenting, and behavioral and emotional outcomes while working on the adolescent unit at a psychiatric hospital. That two-year stint proved invaluable in defining discipline strategies in a concrete way. Several years later I developed a successful 3-hour parenting workshop I took to various churches. I later had the opportunity to work with the court system working with parents whose children had been removed by the state in the area of counseling and parent education. Most of these parents, I discovered, were also court-ordered to attend a parenting class. After hearing of learners who either slept or texted through the class they took, I did some research on available courses. Upon investigation I found that most of the courses offered were impractical and taught by unqualified individuals who often wasted the student's time. Sure the students received a certificate and checked off a box, but what did they learn? One client told me that a 30-minute Cosby episode was shown in each of the six one-hour classes. While entertaining, a 30-minute sitcom investment has little or no educational value for parents. I saw this as an opportunity and personal challenge to take the three-hour course and develop a longer, more detailed version: a course that was highly practical, easy to understand, and would convey ideas that would engage the most easily bored learner. Hence, an 8-hour parenting course was born including workbook and 200+ slide PowerPoint presentation. The ideas from that course then became the foundation of this book.

Acknowledgments

I wish to thank Mary Sue Rawls, Duane Hammack, and Jill Wunderle for their many hours of the reading this manuscript. Their helpful suggestions were immeasurable in the honing of parenting ideas and grammatical expression. I also want to thank Melissa Church…your writing expertise rescued me more than once.

Introduction

It was love at first sight. Nothing had ever compared to it and nothing ever could again. "Holding that newborn felt blissful, almost like I'd reached heaven already" the mother recounted. She spent hours holding her new son, and when she was not holding him she was gazing at him in awe. The new mother radiated with pride as she fed him from her breast; even the diaper changings were a joy. The father, though not as emotionally moved as Mom, expressed how proud he was to have his name passed on to the next generation. He envisioned going fishing together, building a backyard fort, and cheering his son on at the Friday night football game. "I could not wait to buy him his first tool box," the father smiled and remembered, "I might even pass my plumbing business on to him." With such hopes, how could this now 17 year-old boy's life be in such a chaos? Every judge, probation officer, policeman, social worker, and school counselor in town knew of this young man. He had made a name for himself, but not in a good way. His dad knew that raising a child would be expensive, and he was okay with that. Little did these parents realize the thousands they would be spending on this boy in medical doctors, counselors, court costs, treatment facilities, and attorney fees before he was even an adult. Not to mention the enormous time these parents had spent away from work addressing the latest crisis. But there was an even greater cost: that of the emotional turmoil to Mom and Dad. They were fatigued and battle scarred. Now these parents were court-ordered to attend family therapy in my counseling office as a last resort measure just months before Junior would be a legal adult- at which time this teenager would have all the freedom he had wanted for years. These parents had loved their son deeply! So what went wrong? I was glad they were seeking help, but dare I tell them that because of their parenting flaws they may have set a life-long course for their son?

INTRODUCTION

The problem with these parents is the same that I see often in families: they had underestimated their own power to guide their son, and had substituted activities and goals for instilling moral fiber. While the outcome in this family is more serious than in most families, as we will see in the next chapter, there is surprising commonality in the flawed approach of parents. This mom and dad assumed that the combination of school and other agencies, along with their son's desire to do the right thing would be enough. They also had their son participate in many sports and several school clubs which they assumed would do a good job of guiding him. Armed only with hope, they had become unintentional parents with no plan and no specific goal as to what they wanted their child to become. Like a pilot who becomes too comfortable, they had naively put their parenting on "automatic" anticipating the best. Their optimistic dreams had now let them down. With little cooperation from this teen that was months from being a legal adult and no incentive for him to change, we all struggled to find hope as we met.

Parenting is clearly the most difficult task anyone will ever undertake. And yet so few moms and dads equip themselves, get a clear understanding of the job, devise a strategy, and carry out their plan. For the most part we wing-it, stomp out fires as they appear, and hope for the best. We would never employ such a doomed plan to any other task, including our career. If we did many of us would quickly be fired from our jobs for lack of focus. But, this is often the approach parents take toward the most important mission of their lives.

What if parents had a deeper understanding of their role? What if they were better equipped with new tools for the job? What if parents took the power they have and channeled it? What if, after being re-tooled, understanding their role more clearly, and recognizing the power they have had all along, parents then became more confident? And more intentional?

This book seeks to do that very thing. We will begin with a clear understanding of parent-child relationships. We will see examples of ineffective methods and contrast it with a productive approach that works. A new mode of operating and the rationale behind it will be explained in simple terms that will make sense to mothers and fathers, and unify their discipline techniques. I invite the reader not to abandon their hope, but to put feet on that hope as we define your role as a parent and establish concrete methods with which to be successful at the most daunting task you will ever undertake.

I tend to be very practical. I am a bit theoretical also because it helps to know the foundational reasons behind something. Mostly I want to know that something works. I want specific instructions and details about something that helps me reach my goals in an efficient way. That efficiency includes effective use of my resources both short and long-term. Consequently, this book will be a little theoretical and a lot practical.

I also like tools. In my garage is every tool known to man…or at least as much as my budget allows. I often go to one of those massive home do-it-yourself stores. I get weak-kneed when I enter the store, and my wallet automatically gets lighter. I usually go for a specific item: paint, sandpaper, or an occasional specialty light bulb. But I always browse in the tool section. The reason I like tools so much is that they enable me to effectively do the repairs and projects I need to do- not only the repairs I now have, but the ones I *will* have. Without those tools it would be difficult or impossible to accomplish my goal.

This book is for every parent who barely has time to clean the kitchen or retrieve the newspaper from the front lawn, let alone ponder the theories behind child discipline. It is a very practical, hands-on, book of tools. It is a book of specific actions parents can take to accomplish the goal of raising their children.

The foundation of this book will rest on three themes:

1. *The Selfish Nature of Children:* Children are selfish and immature. And all readers express a collective "DUH!" In development terms children are egocentric, in clinical terms they are narcissistic, and in theological terms they possess a sin nature. Children want what they want and right now. If it hurts another person getting it, so be it. Yet, we often have unrealistic expectations of our children. We expect adult levels of maturity and responsibility from our kids. Children are not little adults, and it is unrealistic to expect that of them. We are also naïve or surprised when children put their own safety in danger, make poor choices, are deceptive toward parents, or act in a way that seeks their own interests at the expense of others. We should NOT be surprised at any of this. In fact, we should EXPECT it. It is in their nature! The testing of limits from our children is inevitable! Once we realize this we can prepare for it, teach against it, and maybe even prevent it.

INTRODUCTION

John Locke decades ago believed that children were a blank slate. In other words, children begin at ground zero in every aspect of who they are to become. Few who work with children believe this today. Both research and casual observation confirms certain tendencies in personality, talent, and skill very early on in most all children. Moreover, this selfish nature in children I believe to be universal.

Some in the educational and counseling community discount this selfish nature. As such they believe that if given a chance, children will make the right choice. This requires, as they say, to give children an opportunity to guide themselves. This permissive, naïve style of parenting has proven itself false. The immature and self-centered nature is extremely strong, and compels children to do the thing that pleases them, is the easiest path, and makes them happy in the moment, all at others' expense.

It is interesting that we never have to teach children to act badly...they do so automatically. We *do* have to teach children to act appropriately.

2. *Character Trumps Everything*: As a parent you may not have thought through your objective or have full clarity concerning what you are trying to achieve. Let me suggest that you make *instilling character* paramount. As many adults have clearly shown, the lack of character will undercut other areas your child may excel in. Bernie Madoff, Lance Armstrong, John Edwards, Arnold Schwarzenegger, and Ted Haggard are names we are familiar with. These are brilliant, talented, gifted individuals whose abilities were undermined by a lack of character. In some cases these individuals never regained the respect and opportunities they once held. Moreover, they caused their families and others incredible pain.

Character as it relates to this book will be defined as a set of high moral principles by which a person conducts his life. Many parents have children who are smart, talented, or gifted. They may be able to run fast, write poetry, play the flute, earn straight A's, or paint a picture. But, without self-control, respect for others, and integrity, their abilities will be undermined both now and into adulthood. Above everything, we must teach character, which includes ensuring that every aspect of our child's life promotes that same character.

3. *Parents Have Power in Determining who Their Children Become:* More than once I have heard a parent state, "It does not matter how you raise them, children are going to do what they want to anyway." This fatalistic approach to parenting promotes passiveness that almost guarantees failure. The fact is that, to the greatest extent, we as parents determine who and what our children will become. I do not mean a career or physical characteristics. I refer to the child's character, his philosophies of life, his faith, his integrity, his work ethic, his thoughts on the family, and many other attitudes and behaviors. In some cases there is a direct link between a parent's influence and a child's misbehavior. This is not a popular notion since occasionally parents must take sincere responsibility for their child's bad behavior. No, it is not a hundred percent predictable or controllable. There is not a 1:1 ratio between the parenting a child receives and his adult behavioral outcome since at some point children can choose a direction away from what we have taught, but the link is very high and very powerful. We all know of exceptions where derelict parents have produced a stable wholesome child, or solid parents have a rebellious wayward child, but this is rare. To the greatest degree, the quality of parenting will produce the quality of the child. This should give comfort to the reader, as this gives clear indication as to just how much power and influence we have.

   Most parents do not recognize the amount of influence they have to guide their child. Consequently, they may wait too late to apply that power at a point when the child, too, has power that is a struggle to control. We must recognize from the start that we have tremendous power to guide every aspect of our child. Unlike other fields, there are no guarantees in human behavior. In chemistry two chemicals are mixed with a certain results. If these same two chemicals are combined a thousand times the result will be the same. Other hard science fields such as physics and biology operate in the same predictable way. Not so in parenting. Nonetheless, we must be intentional, well-thought-out parents with a plan of action and an anticipation and high assurance of success.

Let me be clear…the goal is not to have perfect children. Children have imperfect parents (you and I) who create imperfect offspring. Perfection in parenting is neither achievable nor is it the goal!

INTRODUCTION

Excellence is the goal! It is about taking these few short years and giving it everything we have to be the best parents possible.

Good parenting is not:

- *Having perfect children.* Remember this does not exist. The absence of perfection as a goal does not de-obligate us to strong effort.
- *The absence of family issues.* All families have issues…even the most stable and wholesome of families. Most families have more problems than we think; they just hide it well through their recent social media post or good acting skills. It is these issues that give parents additional opportunities to teach children problem solving and high character.
- *Children who always obey.* No child does. In fact, some absence of compliance can be a good sign. It may mean the child has tenacity and a mind of his own that will manifest itself as leadership in the coming years. It may also mean he will be able to withstand future pressure to confirm to other's behavior or yield to temptations.
- *Never having a frustrating moment.* Parenting is VERY frustrating!
- *Having all the answers.* No one does.

CHAPTER 1
Challenge and Support

All human interactions can be characterized in one of two ways: challenge or support. Whether it is to give a command, to insult another person, to stop an action, or to convey warmth, all interactions fall into one of these two categories. When we say "good morning" to someone, we have just given of ourselves to them and therefore supported them. When we compliment someone we have built them up emotionally and therefore supported them. However, when we ask something of someone we have then challenged them. When we confront someone we have just challenged them into a different action. However, challenge and support do not have to be verbal.

When we smile at someone we support them. When we pat someone on the back, give them a high five, give a friendly wave, or hug someone we have just supported them. Likewise, a stern look, an accusing finger, a stuck out tongue, or a disgusted facial expression all challenge others. This challenge and support can also be written in the form of a letter, an organizational policy, or family rules.

Challenge, therefore, can be described as requiring, demanding, inciting, compelling, confronting, provoking, or commanding another into action or change. In each of these words we *want something of another person*. Since we have not been promoted to behavior police, it is not often that we legitimately or appropriately find ourselves commanding or provoking others into action. If, however, we are in a managerial position at work, in charge of a volunteer group, or are responsible for someone, we *are* likely to have to challenge another person. Or, if we occasionally find ourselves confronting the irresponsible effects of another's behavior on us, challenge can be appropriate.

Support, on the other hand, can be described as promoting, upholding, advocating, providing for, maintaining, backing, or instructing another person. In each of these words there is a sense of *giving something to another person*. We may give materially, but most often it involves some kind of emotional giving. Unlike challenge, support can be toward anyone at any time and is not as connected to a particular position or task. We can give a friendly nod to anyone, but we cannot appropriately command those around us without legitimate authority.

Support is generally well-received as most everyone enjoys a pleasant greeting, a compliment, or a door held for us. The world it seems has a shortage of givers and an abundant supply of takers. Supporting others makes both the giver and the receiver feel good.

Support and Challenge with Children

Every day we engage in a variety of exchanges with our children. Some of these interactions we initiate, and some our children initiate as we as parents respond to them. But in every case, and like the previous examples, our every encounter can be categorized by either challenge or support. We tell them to put on their coats. We give them a kiss as they walk out the door. We tell them to wipe their feet before they come in the house. We teach them to say please and thank you. We require them to eat their vegetables before they have dessert. We insist they do chores. We buy them the things they need in life. We command that they finish their homework before they go out and play. All of these examples and countless others illustrate the challenge and support decisions we must make as parents to help our children grow to be spiritually and emotionally stable adults. How is it then that parents are confused, make glaring mistakes, or in some cases become neglectful and under-parent? In short, it is because of the misapplication of either challenge or support.

Effective parenting is defined as the application of either challenge or support in the correct situation guided by a deliberate plan such that the child grows, develops, and reaches his full potential. It is the correct response to a particular situation in the correct dosage. That response is not impulsive, reactionary, off the cuff, or spontaneous. In fact it may not even be natural, but it *is* based on a well thought-out plan. That plan may include coaching, preparation, strategizing, self-control, education, intentionality, a clear purpose, training, periodic maintenance, practice, and regular prayer. However, even the best, most well-prepared parents are caught off guard at times, and the uniqueness of a situation may not have a clear answer. Moreover, the emotional state of even the best parents can take over at times- something we will discuss later.

Where do parents get their parenting ideas? The source of their approach can include tradition, instincts, learned responses, family customs, folklore, our own emotional issues, or the latest trend conveyed through the culture. My experience has indicated that the majority of our parenting ideas come from our own family of origin. More times than I care to count I have heard a sentence begin with, "The way I was raised…" or "That's the way we did it when I was growing up." Whether effective or ineffective, there is an unrecognized but deeply embedded programing that comes from the environment in which we grew up, and that programming has a strong tendency to repeat itself in the next generation.

Several years ago we had an old standard shift pickup truck. As my older son earned his learner's permit at age fifteen, this was the vehicle on which he would cut his teeth. To my surprise he jumped in and began driving as if he had been doing it for years. He not only quickly got the hang of the steering and braking aspect, but he shifted gears like a pro. He was a natural! One of my daughters on the other hand had great difficulty. Despite learning to drive on a compact automatic, that child (who will remain anonymous) required many trials, repeated instruction, and lots of patience to achieve a moderate level of driving competency.

Parenting is very similar. Some just seem to have a knack for appropriate discipline while others struggle to learn the simplest concepts. The problem is that the stakes are high- the comprehensive functioning of our children hangs in the balance. We *cannot* leave this to chance. We must get it right. And we must do whatever it takes to get it right.

Parenting is a skill like any other skill that typically takes instruction and practice. This instruction can come in the form of reading a book, taking a class, or verbal instruction from a older parent or mentor type. It is important to note that while the way our parents did it might be helpful, we cannot put our evaluation skills on the shelf. As competent parents we must think through our discipline decisions, not put our brains in automatic. Nor can we assume "the way we've always done it" is the optimum way.

Now that we understand challenge and support we will take this idea to the next level. If we think about high and low levels of both challenge and support we find ourselves with four combination possibilities: 1) low challenge low support, 2) low challenge high support, 3) high challenge low support, and 4) high challenge high support. Each of these scenarios involves different parental decisions and behavior, and each result in a different child outcome. The lesser three possibilities will be described first. The high challenge high support will alternative will be explained in greater detail in the next chapter.

Low Challenge, Low Support

A parent who provides little challenge and little support is typically a neglectful parent. This involves not attending to the reasonable needs of the child. It might include things like not providing adequate levels of emotional support, love, physical contact, communication, instruction, and supervision. In extreme cases it can involve inadequate food, shelter, clothing, and sanitary conditions. This usually produces a child who is completely unprepared for adulthood. The child often has poor hygiene and poor social skills. Since children depend on external value messages, he is likely to display a host of depressive symptoms due to the understood message that he is unimportant and unworthy. Those messages then become internalized and their hurtful impact becomes overwhelming.

In most cases this parent is low functioning, has not focused on self-development, and can be an alcohol or drug abuser. They usually have significant emotional issues themselves and are unable to provide or care for a child.

While this child usually spirals downward, the opposite reaction to this parenting style can occur. In an ironic and twisted sense, this child can thrive, become the hope of the family, and in some cases reverse roles with his parents. This child who is uncared for by his own parents can feel obligated to take care of not only himself, but the very parents who should be supporting him. He can even become a parentified child, taking on the role of care-taker, organizer, and primary support source for the family. This child's development is then thwarted as he is required to grow up too fast and take on adult responsibilities he is not ready for.

One of the commonalities among gang members is that of having no family. Yes, they have a biological family including a biological mother and a biological father. They also almost always have siblings.

But, typically they have no care, no supervision, no limits on their behavior, no one to hug them, and no one with which to have a heart-felt conversation. These children may even have to fend for their food, be creative in keeping themselves warm at night, and get themselves up and dressed in the morning and ready for school. Essentially they have no family and adopt an equally neglected and dysfunctional set of young adults as their new family- the gang. Here they have a protective alliance and a purpose- something missing at home.

Though most teenagers will not join a gang, **it is very common for an adolescent to form an emotional dependency and family-like bond with a friend that makes the friend the priority because their biological family bond is weak or absent.** As we will discover, this bond is the tool with which parents guide and protect their children. Without it, *friends* guide children- friends who are as immature and confused as they are. But, with a high level of peer support the child becomes confident- confident in ways of thinking and behaving that are often very flawed.

In the subsequent years of non-gang individuals this child is likely to become co-dependent, always looking for a poor dysfunctional soul to take care of. He will feel responsible for the happiness of those around him and may engage in compromising or extreme perspectives or behavior in order to make others happy. In order to compensate for no one being there when he needed it, he will be there for everyone whenever *they* need it. He is likely to have poor boundaries, accept the bad behavior of others, and perpetually strive to "fix" others, allowing dysfunctional people into his life that will ultimately be detrimental to him. At best this child will become a nurse, social worker, or clergy where he can make a career out of giving to individuals but retain some emotional issues with which to resolve. At worst this child will affix himself/herself to one drunk, addict, reprobate, or criminal after another while being dragged down by all of them and having numerous children with them.

Low Challenge, High Support

A parent who provides low challenge and high support is one who does little correction and minimal stimulating. In fact, very little will be required of this child by his parents since Mom or Dad see no benefit in burdening the child with things like rules or chores. The academic criteria is usually very low in this home, but this can be the one area where standards run higher because of the effect of social expectations on the parents and child. These parents rarely confront this child with his irresponsible behavior and see childhood as a time to enjoy all the good things in life. At the same time, this parent will provide all the material necessities in life and will typically be very loving and emotionally connected. It is here is that the problem lies.

Material possessions, privileges, favors, money, and the niceties of life with no sense of having earned or deserving them results in a whole host of difficulties and character flaws. They run the gambit including problems in attitudes, behavior, thought processes, relational difficulties, and emotional issues. This approach to parenting also results in an emotionally weak and dependent individual. Consider this...

If an individual desires to become more physically strong, then he will lift heavy weights, and therefore tax his muscles. The result is a hardened, tough physical body. Conversely, if an individual were to use his muscles little or none at all, the muscles would deteriorate, his physical capabilities would diminish, and his physical body would become soft and weak. In much the same way, requiring little of a child will ultimately make him soft emotionally, mentally, and morally. Overindulging a child will not toughen and prepare him for the problems, obstacles, and competitiveness that is characteristic of adult life. While a child, the effects of the lack of challenge may show up minimally. In the teenage years, however, problems will kick in as expectations have been created that Mom and Dad will take care of all my problems, provide me with everything I need (and possibly more?) without strings. In fact, "they owe me" the child will typically think. Now an entitled outlook has set in and Junior *deserves* a laundry list of material items as he now defines himself by his possessions. What has also probably gone unchallenged is his level of power. **It is not uncommon in this home for a young teenager to be dictating rules to his parents, manipulating them into various privileges, and demanding increasingly high dollar items.** This is immaturity run amuck. Since so little has been required of him and many aspects of good character have been omitted, this youth is now impulsive, irresponsible, lazy, unmotivated, disrespectful, and rude. With no moral compass imposed upon him, his immature and sexual impulses will rule him and he is likely to make many mistakes, possibly big ones. But, since support is so high, the parents may bail him out, compensate for his irresponsibility, and enable his poor choices.

My Super Sweet Sixteen was a popular television show several years ago where teenagers turn sixteen years old and have a birthday party thrown for them by their parent, but not just any party. These parties are over the top, exclusive, hedonistic events in which hundreds of thousands of dollars are spent on elaborate entertainment, outrageous themes, extravagant decorations, and usually topped with a birthday present fit for a sultan. These adolescents delight in focusing on their own superior status and strongly emphasize that only certain "special" people who receive their own invitation may attend the party. The show is complete with a demanding, unappreciative, narcissistic, spoiled, and melodramatic teen. The evening is typically capped off with a sickening display of the youth sulking because the party was not big enough or that the new Corvette was sky blue rather than royal blue. Despite the fact that these families have all of the resources imaginable (high support), requiring these teenagers to develop their strength of character is virtually non-existent (low challenge). These parents will hear the words "coddled" and "spoiled" whispered by other parents in reference to their child, but they will attribute it to their jealousy. Family income has only minimal effect on spoiling a child. It is the overall parenting approach that truly indulges.

One may think that children in poverty cannot be spoiled. It is true that a family in financial depravity will never throw a sweet sixteen party as described, or give their teenager a new Mercedes. Because of this, there may be some small advantage in character building toward these children. Income level is only a part of inadequate challenge. These low income families may not have the finances to give monetarily to their children, but excessive privileges and freedoms remain an option, as well as the lack of correction of spontaneous behavior problems throughout childhood. Further, it is often the case that low income families somehow still find the money for expensive items with which to materially spoil their children.

While the typical low challenge high support child may demand and threaten when he is not satisfied, he usually remains emotionally immature and dependent on his parents. This is because parental emotional support is present, but may be excessive, misplaced, or at least out of balance with the level of challenge. Consequently, though he will come to resent the limits that his parents and society will eventually place on him, he will also remain emotionally soft and vulnerable. He will cower at marginal obstacles from the world and remain an underachiever. He will now operate out of fear and the world will be viewed as a threatening place in which he is internally a child. His immaturity may cause him to have little self-restraint and he may function out of a focus on immediate gratification and pleasure that are often satisfied with food and/or sex.

Decision making will be difficult for this individual. If he *can* make decisions, he will have perpetual self-doubts and flaws in his judgments since there was never the opportunity to practice making decisions while under the safety net of his parents. This person may also have spikes of over-confidence and make unrealistic decisions. A 19 year-old son, for example, who has an inconsistent work history and performed poorly in college now announces that he wants to become a doctor. While he realizes the elevated status of an MD and the high and admirable aspirations this decision represents, he is clueless concerning the discipline, sacrifice, and persistent hard work that will be required.

This individual as an adult will also have a strained relationship with his parents for several reasons. First, there is a subtle, perhaps unconscious acknowledgement that his parents erred. There is an unspoken understanding that the parents were too high on support and too low on challenge. There has always been a strong relational bond that is part of the support characteristic. Now that bond is threatened by the realization that a gross imbalance has been in place. It becomes the "elephant in the living room" that everyone recognizes but no one talks about. It is now the issue that we actually exert effort in *avoiding* an issue that continually enters everyone's mind. It is not openly discussed but may slip out in a moment of anger on either the parent's or child's part. In that moment a dart is fired that blames or accuses the other. It is this rarely acknowledged flaw that is one source of a strained relationship.

A second source of eventual strain is the assumptions by this adult child that others are responsible for him and his decisions. Even as an adult he will often look to his parents for a high level of emotional support. It may also include everyday sustenance such as food and shelter, and even general caretaking. Efforts that appear to symbolize growth and progress may result in self-sabotage and failure. He may even unconsciously engineer bad outcomes out of fear, or display a self-fulfilling prophecy in which he believes so strongly that he is a failure that it actually comes to pass. For example, this young adult may enroll in college because there is unspoken social pressure to do so, but both the self-doubts and the lack of preparedness will plague him. It will also be necessary to save face and absolve himself of responsibility when he fails. Consequently, he may procrastinate and turn in assignments late, conveniently forget to set his alarm and miss classes, or fill his life with (sometimes beneficial or legitimate) activities that crowd out school work.

A third reason for this parent-child resentment is that the adult or teenage child will resent the very dependency that he enjoys but from which he cannot pull away. **Both the benefits of another taking care of him and the fear of a threatening world perpetuate his dependency on his parents.** He is ambivalent toward relinquishing the very thing that binds him, and it will take much courage, anger, or therapeutic intervention to sever this umbilical cord. This child may marry, but have little structure or goals. It will be likely that his over-dependency upon his parents will now transfer to his spouse, or even his children.

High Challenge, Low Support

While the low challenge, high support parent described in the last section provides an abundance of encouragement, assistance, and backing with little required of the child, this parent takes the opposite approach. Everything in the last set of parents is absent in these parents, and everything that was absent is now present. Josh McDowell has said that rules without a relationship lead to rebellion; it is this idea that characterizes this parent-child relationship.[1] This parent is all about structure, accountability, organization, productivity, and responsibility. Upon reading this last sentence you may be thinking, "So what's the problem?" The problem is, once again, one of excess, balance, or misplacement of these otherwise positive traits. The opposite is also a problem- a relationship without rules is chaos. This is why we must strive for "two sides of parenting."

Anyone who has ever been under the authority of another person has at some point been subject to an individual who barks out orders, is harsh and demanding, has unrealistic expectations, and who is unaccommodating and unappreciative. Misguided workplace supervisors often operate in this manner. Though we may expect some amount of encouragement as an employee, more than moderate levels of support in the work place are beyond the nature of this relationship. A child, however, must have the backing of an adult in order to develop properly. It must be an integral part of this relationship.

---

1 http://www.goodreads.com/quotes/264719-rules-without-relationship-leads-to-rebellion

This parent has rules for everything. Moreover, the home is well-ordered, neat, and maintained. The children are as regimented as any military base in the country. Homework is completed, chores are done, and there is a strong sense in which children answer to parents. All time is accounted for both at home and away, and the children's whereabouts are always known. The problem is there is no love, or more accurately, there is no demonstrated love. Similar to the employee-employer scenario, but even more so, this child does what he is told. Instead of feeling unappreciated, however, he feels unloved.

The Sound of Music is one of the most beloved movies of all time. In it, a seafaring captain whose wife has died is left with seven children. The father's military orientation combined with his repressed grief results in a home that is managed like a military base complete with the children standing in ranks and receiving orders from a whistle. While the children all follow orders well (or at least in Dad's presence), the home is empty and sterile. The children are not energetic and playful, but lifeless and emotionally blank. At one point in the film, play clothes are made to encourage fun and recreation in the children, but the stern, high challenge low support father objects. Lifeless himself, the captain sees no value in play or relationships.

Ironically, if asked, "Do you love your children?" These parents would scoff and be insulted. How dare anyone suggest their children are not loved? Dad works hard and financially cares for his family. He even tells his children he loves them on a rare occasion or when they say it first. But ask these children if they *feel* loved, and you are likely to get a more accurate picture.

As an infant, this child, like all children, longs for a relationship with his parents since children have an innate need for a warm, loving attachment. He makes attempts by holding his hands out, whimpering for attention, and gazing longingly into Mom and Dad's eyes…but no response. As a small child he wants to be held, inordinately so since he now must compensate for the self-doubt that has already begun. "Reassure me!" he conveys daily, but his parents do not get it. Like a zoo-keeper, they believe that all that is needed is feeding and watering. He asks questions, but his parents wrongly assume it is all about wanting information. He tells stories and yearns for someone to listen. This child is prone to attention-seeking behavior, including acting up and being mischievous.

As the years go on this parent may occasionally play recreational games with his child, but it is merely for the purpose of developing a skill. Physical touch is nonexistent. Dad and son fish together occasionally, but only for the purpose of catching fish and little conversation takes place. Talking is only for arguing anyway. The entire family operates in a mechanical manner, focused on tasks, going about their business, and disconnected from all other family members. Other than the couple of daily orders Dad barks out, no one much hears from him. Besides, all the children quit paying him any attention long ago.

As with the previous parenting approach, the child may keep a low profile while young, but there is an undercurrent of hostility brewing. As this child senses his relational deficit and as he better grasps reality through maturity, resentment sets in. This child grows angrier each year, and by mid-teens he will likely be enraged. He will curse at his father and tell him, "You do not care about me," but his father will be puzzled since he recently provided a car for him. The son will act tough and have a chip on his shoulder that will likely stay there for years. He will resent authority since it is authority that has betrayed him.

If the child is a male he will be characterized as angry, guarded, with constricted emotions. As a teen he will express this rejection of dictatorship as rebellion, bitterness, and oppositional behavior that may include violence and vandalism as he displaces his anger onto other things and other people. If, however, this teen is a female the same lack of connectedness with her parents will most often result in promiscuity. In either case it will result in a rejection of his/her parent's values including religious faith. It is very common even for pastors who love the Lord, embrace their church, and love their ministry, to have an inadequate relationship with their children as a result of an imbalance toward their ministerial calling. In these cases, children will either have a marginal faith, see God in the same distant or rejecting manner they see their father, or reject the faith all together.

Whether male or female, as an adult this child may achieve success at work as both a distraction from his inadequacies and an attempt to disprove his/her continuing self-doubt. But this child will have little relief from his insecurities even from his spouse. While they will be happy while dating, this son will present a facade of connectedness in which his girlfriend will trust and invest. Once they are married, however, the extent of their intimacy will be his requesting sex occasionally since emotional closeness to another person is foreign to him.

While he cried out and reached for adult connection earlier, as an older child and adolescent he has an attitude of "I don't need you anymore" as a preemptive rejection. By doing this he also covers up his hurt and decreases his vulnerability. Now, both in his marriage and in other relationships, he has long since given up, and in fact repels those who attempt to connect. He no longer wants to *feel* since feeling hurts. **Unless re-taught and re-programed he will be out of touch with all feeling except anger since this is the only acceptable emotion in his macho world, and since anger does a nice job of pushing others away.** Ironically, he is every bit as needy as when he was a small child. It is just that now we have hurt, disappointment, frustration, and rejection added to the neediness. His emotional needs are inordinately high but he does not know how, or is afraid to get his legitimate needs met.

In adult females that pushing away can result in a slightly different push-pull relationship. While recognizing that a legitimate emotional need exists in the form of a human connection, she will only let an individual become superficially close. A friend or potential boyfriend may be initially welcome. There may even be a sharing of information and camaraderie. But this self-disclosure will quickly be shut down, especially if it is a male. Not only will she shun relationship initiations, but she may not even know how quality relationships proceed since this is something she has never experienced before. What is strangely inconsistent is that she will often be sexual and give away the most precious thing she owns while being emotionally distant or unavailable. **Having sex with someone will provide a temporary anesthesia from the pain, and create the illusion of closeness, but end up being unsatisfying and empty in the end.**

It is also common that these children incorporate a performance-based sense of self-worth. Since it is only what the child *does* that is valuable and not that he *is*, the child and eventual adult will view him/herself solely in terms of their achievement. Consequently he will long for approval but rarely feel approved of since his emotional deficiency is so extreme.

Chapter One Discussion Questions:

1. In what ways do you generally 'support" others? Be specific.
2. To what extent do you practice a lifestyle of affirming others?
3. What one word describes each of the concepts of challenge and support?
4. Describe challenge as it relates to parenting?

5. Describe support as it relates to parenting?
6. What effect did your family of origin have on your parenting?
7. How has the style you choose in #6 affected you personally? How has it affected your parenting?
8. What beneficial things did you take from the family in which you grew up?
9. What dysfunctional or unproductive things did you take from your family of origin?
10. Look back over the three styles of parenting described in this chapter. Which style most closely resembles the family in which you grew up? How?
11. Does God support and challenge us? How?

CHAPTER 2
What is the Difference?

The three styles of parenting described in the previous chapter have been presented in slightly exaggerated scenarios. We have all seen these children. What is more common is less exaggerated examples of these children with only slightly more balanced parents. The reader may have even seen himself in the descriptions, linking his own personal outcome and family type. But how do the three previous scenarios compare with our last option of high challenge and high support?

With the first three unproductive alternatives having now been described, this fourth alternative will present a picture that is unmistakably superior. Like those who are trained to spot counterfeit dollar bills, having now had the bogus described, the authentic will be obvious. The high challenge high support parents approach their duty with a well-balanced, intentional, and effective manner.

High challenge high support parenting is different in several ways. First, parents as the name implies, guide their children through high levels of both challenge and support. They provide the intentional instruction, teaching, and modeling, and insist on responsible behavior. They encourage and assist their child in an age-appropriate manner, but also require a high level of a variety of actions on the part of the child. These parents give to the child, but fully expect him to give back relative to his age. These parents are also different in that this mom and dad are focused on the *placement* of challenge and support. These parents avoid excess and focus on the optimum balance between challenge and support.

In the three previous styles not only did parents not provide what the child needed, they also gave him/her what they did not need. When the child needed to be challenged because of an inappropriate behavior, the parents supported. For example, 8 year-old John is hitting the wall with a wooden bat. Instead of correcting, this mother smiles and goes about her business. When 14 year-old Linda is neglecting her homework by talking on the phone for the last two hours, Dad asks her if she had dinner yet. They may also err by providing challenge when support is needed. For example, a twelve year-old little leaguer is despondent because he loses a ballgame, but Dad tells him to quit whining. A daughter's meticulously fashioned cake flops and Mom's response is to convey disappointment in the daughter and apathy. This backward approach to child rearing encourages increased levels of inappropriate behavior, as well as decreased levels of appropriate and beneficial behavior. Moreover, anxiety and confusion levels in the child are guaranteed to ramp up and cause many different issues in behavior, thought, attitude, and overall development.

Consequently, as well as high levels of both challenge and support, it is imperative that these two components of parenting be placed in the correct situation. Let's return briefly to our definition of high-quality parenting. It is the application of either challenge or support *in the correct situation* guided by a *deliberate plan* such that the child grows, develops, and reaches his full potential. Good parenting is using that challenge or support in the appropriate circumstances to optimize effectiveness, guided by a purposeful, premeditated plan (thinking, planning, reading this book), and God Almighty (believe me, you'll need Him), to raise your child in the most emotionally and spiritually healthy way possible.

High Challenge and High Support

High challenge high support parents recognize that their children need high levels of correction and guidance, as well as much love and care. These parents are very attentive to their children's needs, and are occasionally even intuitive in that they accurately recognize signs of both good and bad directions of their child. They quickly attack problems and are quick to lend support to their child, which means they have the emotional resources and stability to do so. Several words apply when considering the idea of challenge such as require, demand, incite, compel, confront, provoke, command. But how do these specifically relate to child rearing?

These parents challenge their children in numerous ways. They generally require much of them relative to the child's age and abilities. When asked to do a job, it must be done correctly. In school, nothing less than the child's best is acceptable. This is not to be confused with perfectionism. Perfectionism is a relentless pursuit of a standard that does not exist. It creates anxiety in the child and instills the idea that he can never be good enough. It also instills the notion that one's self worth is tied to one's performance. Many adults today struggle with a performance-based self-concept that can be linked to expectations of perfectionism in childhood. These high challenge high support parents strive, not for perfection, but for excellence.

These children are also given commands that are specific, clear, and ultimately benefit the child. When he is told to empty the dish washer, he completes a task that helps the family. More importantly, it teaches the child a skill, moves him toward independence, and instills in him a sense of teamwork.

At times this child must be confronted with his irresponsible behavior, and these parents are not afraid to do this. They do, however, do it in a loving manner that conveys disapproval of the behavior, not the child. Consequently these parents understand the integration of challenge and support and the effective marriage of the two. However, these parents can let challenge or support stand alone as well.

Support involves words like promote, uphold, advocate, provide for, maintain, back, and instruct. All of these words in essence *give* to the child. There is an innate sense in children that they cannot provide for themselves. Despite some overconfidence that can emerge in adolescence, children instinctively know that they do not have the physical size and strength, the power, the knowledge, or the wherewithal to survive without a high level of parental sustenance. They are extremely and comprehensively dependent on adults for growth- especially character and emotional growth. Some development and independence will happen naturally as the child's normal inquisitiveness and observation teaches him. However, there is still a wide deficit if parents do not intentionally invest in their child through constant instruction, and this is where the support comes into play.

Support also makes a child feel secure and loved. Whereas challenge says to a child there is someone who cares about me enough to stop me from bad choices, support says to a child that there is someone who cares enough to teach and protect me beyond my ability to teach and protect myself. This begins with providing the basic physical needs of children: food, water, shelter, and clothing. Beyond this, he will be provided an education both formal and worldly. He will be taught certain skills such as how to throw a football, how to buy a pair of jeans, and how to have a conversation. The child will also need emotional support when he feels dejected, when he fails, or when he is verbally attacked by another. In some cases he will even need to be advocated for in areas where he does not yet have the ability to do it himself. Therefore, support is giving a child the tools to eventually function in the world, as well as the confidence from that loving adult to make it possible for the child to use those tools. Children who are raised with a proper balance of challenge and support are secure in their view of the world, self-motivated, self-confident, feel empathy and other positive emotions, develop normally, are able to give and receive love, are less emotionally needy, and develop a proper balance of dependence and independence

Final Cautions

By now you should have grasped the idea that the most effective parenting disseminates high levels of both challenge and support. This is extremely important since a lack of one (challenge or support) can undermine the efforts of the other. For example, a child may have much emotional, financial, and material backing such that he is overconfident, has a car, cell phone, and money, but lack in any sense of self-restraint. This child is consequently likely to misuse the possessions and be puzzled as to the bad outcome. Or, a child may have much self-imposed structure in his life, but have perpetual self-doubts and toward his worthiness and competence since his childhood included little emotional support.

Disciplining out of one side of parenting presents an imbalance that is common is families. That is why there are "two sides of parenting." It is the general tendency of fathers to lack support and mothers to lack challenge. Consequently, parenting must work together to provide balanced discipline for their children. As you dads have begun reading this book you may have thought, "Emotional support my eye, what they need is to toughen them up with a good swift kick in the pants." Similarly, you mothers may have resisted the idea of challenge and thought, "I know I can just love and nurture my child into behaving." Despite an individual's gender or general tendency, both notions are wrong, or more accurately, not effective in every circumstance. Consequently, it is not the particular parent or their own personality that should dictate what approach will work best, but the correct *placement* of the challenge or support that is crucial. It is this *matching* of approach to corresponding circumstance that will be what this book attempts to do.

In Galatians 6:2 we are told, "Carry one another's burdens, and in this way you will fulfill the law of Christ." Does this sound like support to you? According to this verse we should support others in the problems and difficulties they have. In the same way that Christians share the load of one another's burdens, parents must share the burden of the immaturity and inexperience of being a child. It is a parent's duty, responsibility, and obligation to remove or avoid a burden on their child that is too heavy and will stifle their development.

After having mandated that we carry one another's burdens, just three verses later in Galatians 6:5 Paul tells us, "For each one should carry his own load." Some would see this as a contradiction with verse two. But more accurately this represents a paradox that addresses the very topic of this book- that we must provide *both* challenge and support to our children and in doing so we will enable them to lead productive, responsible, emotionally stable and spiritually grounded lives.

This can present a possible obstacle for single parents since they may favor challenge or support and not provide the balance that two parents often provide. This makes it not just preferable, but *necessary* for single parents to occasionally solicit the feedback of other parents, as well as expose their child to opposite-gender adults. On the positive side, a single parent will not have to fight a partner's opposing tendency.

High challenge high support parents also start early and never let up. Even in utero, these parents provide prenatal care and are cautious in Mom's lifestyle decisions. After the birth these parents focus on safety, nutrition, and stimulation of the child while considering the disciplinarian role they will soon face. They know that there is nothing to challenge yet since their baby is now in need of pure support.

Lastly, **because children are always getting older the challenge/support balance is always changing.** Consider a six month-old child sitting on a parent's lap. The parent would place their hand on the child's back and front. The child's head might also be strategically supported as the child may not yet be able to hold his own head up. In this scenario the parent is giving tremendous support because that is what it needs. At this age the child is incapable of giving much of anything (challenge) and must be supported virtually one hundred percent. Jump ahead to when this child is a strapping 17 year-old. At this age he should be managing most of his life and making most of his own good decisions. But, what if the 17 year-old should sit on Mom's lap as in years before, and Mom were to place her hands back and front as before including support of his head. The word picture is an absurd one, but many parents do the emotional and practical equivalent of this scenario, sometimes when the child is well into adulthood.

Throughout the years we as parents must slowly transition out of support and into challenge in order to prepare our children for adulthood. While the ratio of support to challenge might be 95:5 as a toddler, it switches to 5:95 by late adolescence. This necessitates that we transition slowly but surely as the months and years of childhood go by.

Virtually all problems in parenting, therefore, are a result of:

- Inadequate support or challenge, or both.
- Applying challenge or support in the wrong situation.

Consequently, we as parents must analyze our challenge and support to our children, increase one or both, and ensure we are making application at the right moment or situation. Exactly what that looks like is explained in further chapters. Most parents need to increase one or the other, even if it is only slightly. Other more conflicted families may need to dramatically alter their emphasis by greatly expanding challenge or support.

An important point is that most people are naturally stronger in either challenge or support. This is usually tied to their personality or how they were raised, and may be the basis for their philosophy of parenting. A parent may have an especially kind-hearted personality that is the foundation of their lenient discipline, or the parent might possess very stern and strict temperament and approach his/her parenting in a similar way. Beyond their own upbringing, this emphasis in either challenge or support can also relate to unresolved personal issues, points of inadequacy, or trauma in their lives. A mother who was made fun of as a child because of her family's poverty and out-of-date clothing may now indulge her children to compensate, buying the children expensive, trendy clothes.

Moms and dads are sometimes not as thought-out in their parenting ideas as they should be. We often possess an opinion, personal experience, family-of-origin background, perspective, or belief, out of which we develop our philosophy of parenting. Competent parenting filters these adulterating ideas out and calmly processes an effective parenting philosophy, out of which come a myriad of appropriate discipline practices.

A second point is that **we often pair ourselves with a partner who is the opposite of us...sometimes dramatically so.** Consciously or unconsciously, we tend to compensate for our own inadequacies and are romantically attracted to our opposite. In some cases it is intentional, as an individual or single parent recognizes their discipline inadequacies and seeks out a strong parental figure as a mate. This can be especially true if mom is a single mother who is overwhelmed and feels that her children need a father to stabilize the home, or a single father who is uneasy concerning the girly aspects of his daughters. Either way, this means that a soft, passive male frequently is attracted to a rigid, no-nonsense female, and an overly sweet mother is drawn to a strong, firm male.

A third important point is that **this opposite tendency makes for inevitable conflict between moms and dads that must be resolved.** If the couple is dramatically different it can mean all-out war, with the children being the real losers. Especially in single parent situations, the early romantic feelings can mask any consideration of their opposite tendencies they must now address.

A competitive dynamic between parents can also emerge. The differences between mom and dad can start out small, but the more the mother sympathizes and coddles Junior, the more frustrated the father becomes. He now feels even more of a need to toughen up his son and takes vigorous action. Now mom becomes even more sympathetic...and the escalation continues. What were moderate differences in discipline styles initially has prompted parents to become more and more polar as each opts to compensate for the other's actions. Not only does this cause perpetual marital conflict, but the resulting confusion in the children is tremendous as they attempt to adhere to two different standards in the home.

The remainder of this book will focus on what high levels of both challenge and support look like, as well as the specific allocating of each at the right moment. We will focus on five aspects of challenge and five aspects of support that will clarify how this works. We will also focus on the ever-evolving balance as children grow older. Wherever possible this book will address age-appropriateness in relation to a specific recommendation or standard. The areas we will look at are:

Five areas of Support:

1. Modeling, 2. Close Relationships, 3. Supervision & Feedback, 4. Guidance, 5. Limiting Cultural Influences.

Five Areas of Challenge:

1. Independence, 2. Obedience, 3. Respect, 4. Responsibility and Accountability, 5. Self-Development

Chapter Two Discussion Questions:

1. Describe high support high challenge parenting. In what ways does this approach to parenting comprehensively meet the needs and teach children?
2. In what ways would a high challenge high support style of parenting decrease or minimize discipline problems?
3. As a parent, which are you naturally better at, challenge or support? Why do you think this is so?
4. To what extent are you and your spouse unified in your parenting? Do either of you ever compensate for the other's disciplinary actions?
5. What steps would you and your spouse need to take to fully accept one another's differences yet better achieve unity as parents?
6. Between you and your spouse, who needs to increase support? Who needs to increase challenge?
7. Explain the paradox between Galatians 6:2 and Galatians 6:5.

8. Why would a parent need to continually evolve in their implementation of challenge and support?
9. What does this chapter say is the cause of virtually all parenting problems? Can you think of some exceptions?

CHAPTER 3
Modeling

To remind the reader, to support is to promote, uphold, aide, advocate, provide for, maintain, back, instruct, bolster, sustain, or assist. The first aspect of support is modeling.

Years ago my family lived in Texas. It was in the heat of the summer when one of my sons was around 18 months old. He was waddling around the house in nothing but a diaper when I heard him chanting something from the other room. I drew closer and in better ear-shot to hear him crooning confidently, "I'm too sexy....I'm too sexy....I'm too sexy." A song from the 80's had been used in a television car commercial at that time, and having seen the ad several times my son had now picked up the mantra and paraded around in a diaper performing like a Chippendale tot. Most negative influences are much more momentous and not nearly so funny.

My son absorbing this song he heard on television is the essence of modeling. Modeling is defined as the process of observing and imitating another person's behavior. Chances are if you can shoot basketball, bake a cake, play the flute, or almost anything else, you first learned it by watching someone do it.

In the 1960's a man named Albert Bandura began to do research on how children mimic behavior. He showed children a film of two men playing with several toys. In the film, one man refused to share his toys and the other responded by clobbering him. Then the aggressive man takes all the toys and marches off in victory while the first man is seen sitting in a corner dejected with no toys. The children were then put in a room full of toys and left alone for the next 20 minutes while observers watched the children through a one-way mirror. The researchers found the children were significantly more aggressive than another group of children who had not seen the film. In fact, many of the children attacked their playmates in the *exact* same way they had just observed in the film. He later termed this observational learning, and, using a number of variations on the same theme, Bandura was able to duplicate these results many times over as one group of children after another imitated the bad behavior they had just witnessed.[1] The reader should feel as if he just stumbled upon gold as the implications here are huge! This makes the exposure, or lack of exposure, to a whole host of influences a key strategy in the shaping of our children's behavior.

In post-Bandura studies, it has been found that models with particularly high impact include those with high status, adults, aggressive males, and peers.[2] Is it any wonder that the negative behavior of angry, vulgar, rap and rock stars with lavish lifestyles are so frequently imitated by young males? In the 50 years since his research, could Bandura have imagined the influential power of the culture today?

Modeling and the Culture

Years ago individuals were generally well-mannered, polite, and civil toward one another. Today it is not only common, but popular to show one another up or curse out one another publicly and then boast about it. Bad behavior has always existed, but there was a sense of shame surrounding a lack of civility. Today, individuals engage in the worst, most perverted forms of behavior and are proud of it. To be an arrogant, self-centered, and vain public figure is an expected form of behavior that we barely notice any longer.

The next evolution of influences has now come onto the scene. Youth for many years delighted in sexually invigorating and rebellious lyrics in their music. This goes back to the original artists of the 50's and the Big Bopper who coined the term "rock and roll" as a euphemism for having sex. This, however, has given way to dark bands that focus on hopelessness, death, suicide, and anarchy. No one from the previous generation would have predicted that glorifying suicide and degrading women would sell gold records and make musicians millionaires, but that is where we find ourselves today. We as parents, however, must guard against an overabundance of negative influences on our children from society. And

---

[1] Bandura, A., Ross, D. & Ross, S.A. (1961). Transmission of aggression through imitation of aggressive models. *Journal of Abnormal and Social Psychology*, 63, 575-82.
[2] http://anopenparachute.blogspot.com/2011/08/social-learning-theory-and-aggression.html

while children and teenagers gravitate toward the most flamboyant, outlandish, and erotic musicians, as parents we must take a firm stand at times and say "no." or as Albert Bandura theorized, our children will blindly follow these artists into their own demise. But, it is not just musicians that parents must be wary of.

Seemingly at every turn there is a model whose behavior we abhor. While I am not in favor of separatism, it is easy to see how parents might be tempted to remove themselves from all society and insulate themselves from the unyielding evils of the world. It seems as though there is a non-stop supply of athletes, movie stars, politicians, television figures, and comedians, who spew obscenities, announce their perverted lifestyle, intentionally lie to the public, or have another child without the benefit of marriage. Commentators, ethicists, medical professionals, and scientists all have opinions that are often contrary, not only toward Scripture, but toward good common sense.

While public figures and entertainers have always been somewhat extreme, private individuals who usually pride themselves on their stability have historically been more conventional. In recent years, however, mothers of cheerleaders plot to kill rivals of their daughters,[3] fathers rush onto the field to attack child athletes of the other team,[4] and parents regularly defend their children's irresponsible behavior.

Our children have become sponges absorbing all the distortions, filth, and perversion the world has to offer. It is here that **parents *must* protect their children from exposure to these models, both public and private.** If not, it is almost guaranteed that he/she will emulate the behavior, embrace the philosophy, and aspire to be like their corrupt model. It is imperative that parents regulate the movies, radio stations, music, television, and internet with the goal of eliminating negative influences. While it may be easy to target Hollywood, let's not forget next door. Competent parents are always watching for adults as well as other children that may be also a negative influence on their child.

When my oldest daughter was about three years old she attended child care at a reputable establishment near our home. One day she came home and innocently began to shout, "f**k it! f**k it!" over and over. She, no doubt, picked up that phrase from another child who most probably heard it from his parents. We may quickly identify Marilyn Manson as a poor role model, but what about the boy your

---

3 http://en.wikipedia.org/wiki/Wanda_Holloway
4 http://www.eadt.co.uk/news/bradfield_st_clare_angry_dad_broke_rival_football_player_s_jaw_in_pitch_attack_1_840607

son spends the night with? That 15 year-old peer who exhibits extreme behaviors and philosophies now has influence on your son. We may identify a well-known comedian as one who makes racially sickening remarks, but what about the well-liked football coach who lead his team to an undefeated season that may make equally as prejudice comments. Your child looks up to that coach as a role model and is likely to imitate his actions.

Can Modeling Be Used Constructively?

Thus far we have focused on the avoidance of negative influences. We have seen how both public and private negative influences have the potential to steer our children in the same wayward direction. But, is it possible to actually *benefit* from this concept? Can observational learning be a good thing? We have acknowledged that a child can learn bad things from role models, but can a child learn beneficial things in the same manner?

Modeling is the single most important aspect of both support and parenting. In behavior, children are rarely discerning toward the particular action or philosophy they observe, they just do what they see and hear. Consequently, this can be a tremendous teaching tool for parents if engineered effectively. Not only is it important to eliminate bad role models, it is equally important to saturate children with *good* role models.

As stated earlier, this begins very early and never stops. It is a constant process of presenting emotionally whole, spiritually grounded, positive, encouraging examples before the child. It should incorporate adults, peers, and children slightly older than your child. Peers that are well-mannered and high functioning can make great role models. If you have a 14 year-old son, a 16 year-old boy who is ambitious, makes good grades, and regularly attends church will have a positive effect on your son. Adults such as coaches, scout leaders, school teachers, band directors, Sunday school teachers, school principals, and youth directors will have a tremendous effect on your child, assuming they are encouraging and stable. But we have omitted the individual with the greatest impact of all. A healthy child also begins with *parents* as their life pattern.

Parents as Models

As a parent you may be squirming in your seat as you hesitate to read on. You may have even come to believe that the school system or government is responsible for your children...not so. Since parents have the greatest impact, they must set the *best* example possible for their children. The law of heredity says that all undesirable traits in your children come from the other parent. Feel free to elbow your partner at this point....death stares should be avoided. Given that, **my regular counsel is for *both* parents to engage in the *exact* behavior they want from their child.** As we think back to the idea of challenge and support, this is the *single best* support tactic that exists. As you apply the ideas of this book, if you apply only one, let it be that of your own positive example. If you want your child to be hard-working, then you as the primary model should be hard-working. If you want your child to be polite to others, then you should be polite to others. If you want your child to be ambitions, then you should be ambitious. Whatever behavior, attitude, philosophy, or approach to life you want to instill in your child, the single most effective parenting tool is to engage in that very same behavior.

If you have a child that is low in self-worth, or seems to be the outcast, this principle is even more important. Bandura found that modeling has an even more pronounced effect on individuals thought of as incompetent, highly dependent individuals, and those lacking in self-esteem.[5] When compared to others, this can result in good modeling having a greater affect, or poor modeling having an even worse affect.

What I will often encounter both in my counseling practice and in the parenting workshops I conduct is a set of parents who want their child to be much higher functioning than they. For example, parents who want a son who to be self-controlled while dad regularly curses out others; a parent who wants her teenage daughter to stop dressing so sexy to impress boys, but who, as a single mother, spends inordinate amounts of time on internet singles chat rooms, dates four nights per week, and spending large amounts of time focusing on her romantic life; a father who insists that his teenage son "get out and make something of himself," but then sits in his lazy-boy night after night watching many hours of television.

---

5 Bandura, A. (1977). *Social Learning Theory*. Englewood Cliffs, NJ: Prentice Hall.

In each of these scenarios the parent expects higher functioning, behavior, and/or character from a child than the mother or father is willing to display. This can be a source of much family conflict and rarely works. **Children rarely rise to a level of character or functioning higher than that of their parents.** This, again, should prompt parents to evaluate themselves and present the utmost model possible for their child to follow.

Jesus as our Model

One of Jesus' prime objectives was to model correct attitudes and behavior. He took this responsibility seriously in everything He did. He knew that His example would be studied and followed for generations. John 13:14-15 says, "If I then, the Lord and teacher, washed your feet, you ought to also wash one another's feet. For I gave you an example that you also should do as I did for you." In this passage Jesus wanted His disciples to serve others in the same way He had served them.

Will our example as parents be studied and followed for generations too? Absolutely! It is common for the impact, good or bad, of individuals to be experienced with grandchildren and even great-grandchildren. Exodus 20:5b states that, "I, the Lord your God am a jealous God, punishing the children for the sin of the father to the third and fourth generations of those that hate me." Exodus 34:7 and other passages also attest to the fact that the sins of the father will be felt long after he is gone. The irresponsible decisions of those in authority are felt by everyone. This is not a reference to a generational curse whereby God automatically and unjustly condemns individuals. This is in reference to the real-world occurrence of parents who are poor role models and who influence their children negatively. Those children then make the same irresponsible decisions and bear children, the pattern of which is perpetuated for several generations. In this case, it is when someone has the courage to make personal changes that result in altering the outcome of the next generation.

Will your children wash feet and serve others as Jesus did? Or will they be self-absorbed and self-indulgent? That depends on their examples. Several years ago my youngest child said to me, "When I grow up I want to be just like you. I want to counsel like you, teach like you, and play the drums like you." The sobering reality is that he truly will be *just like me*, though not in talent, skill, or occupation. He will be like me in character. Why? Because *I am his model.* The popular Christian group Phillips, Craig & Dean express it well in a 2007 song entitled *I Want to Be Just like You:*

> *Lord, I want to be just like You*
> *'Cause he wants to be just like me*
> *I want to be a holy example*
> *For his innocent eyes to see*
> *Help me be a living Bible, Lord*
> *That my little boy can read*
> *I want to be just like You*
> *'Cause he wants to be like me*

Children do some of what we tell them to do, but they *become* what we *are.* Their every standard, every frame of reference, every criteria, and the measure of all things comes from us, the parents. We are the conveyer of all principles and all conditions to which our children internalize. Ideally, we get our standards from God Almighty, which we then pass onto our children. It is therefore up to us to be the absolute best model possible that effectively conveys *God's* standards.

Jesus spent much time while He was on earth healing, teaching, meeting the needs of various people and establishing doctrines on many issues. What He also did was to set an example for us. With His every action Jesus established what a correct life looks like. With his every work He defined reality and created standards. Whether we like it or not, we as parents *are* role models; whether we want the job or not we are already assigned that task automatically. We convey right from wrong, good from bad, and appropriate from inappropriate by the way we conduct ourselves as mothers and fathers.

Paul concurred in First Corinthians 11:1 when he said, "Be imitators of me, just as I am of Christ." Some have argued that this is one more example of Paul's overconfident arrogance. While this may be true, it can also be argued that Paul strived for a standard of conduct so holy and righteous that his life would provide an example for not only those around him, but for all mankind for generations to come. What if we as parents took this same approach and strived for righteousness that likely would have an effect for generations?

MODELING

Parental Perfection?

By now you may be thinking, "I cannot be perfect…everyone makes mistakes. You're being unrealistic in setting a standard that no parent can achieve." **Good parenting is not about being perfect.** Perfection, as mentioned earlier, is not realistic nor is it achievable. The comforting thing is that good parenting is not about getting it all right. No one gets it right all the time. My experience is that children can usually be forgiving toward parents, especially when the infractions are minor or infrequent. The struggle comes when mom or dad makes regular and glaring mistakes, especially when they reflect is a selfish quality. Even when parents do not get it right, a lesson can be learned by parent and child.

As stated previously, parenting is about excellence. It is about doing whatever is necessary to lead, sacrifice, and teach from our lives. Truett Cathy, the founder of Chick Fil-A, has been a family advocate for many years. In his book *It's Better to Build Boys than Mend Men* he says, "Don't be too concerned that your children don't listen to you. Be very concerned that they see everything you do." With our every behavior parents establish a frame of reference. With our every action we define reality. It has been said that far more is caught by our children than taught to our children. The question is not *am* I teaching something…..the question is *what* am I teaching with my example? Titus 2:7a says, "In all things show yourself to be an example of good deeds."

A 2006 country song entitled *Watching You* performed by Rodney Akins says it well:

Driving through town just my boy and me
With a happy meal in his booster seat
Knowing that he couldn't have the toy
Till his nuggets were gone
Green traffic light turned straight to red
I hit my breaks and mumbled under my breath
His fries went a flying and his orange drink covered his lap
Well then my four year old said a four letter word
That started with "s" and I was concerned
So I said son now where did you learn to talk like that

THE TWO SIDES OF PARENTING

He said I've been watching you Dad, ain't that cool
I'm your buckaroo, I wanna be like you
And eat all my food and grow as tall as you are
We got cowboy boots and camo pants
Yeah we're just alike, hey ain't we dad
I wanna do everything you do
So I've been watching you

We got back home and I went to the barn
I bowed my head and I prayed real hard
Said Lord please help me help my stupid self
Then this side of bedtime later that night
Turning on my son's Scooby Doo nightlight
He crawled out of bed and he got down on his knees
He closed his little eyes, folded his little hands
And spoke to God like he was talking to a friend
And I said son now where'd you learn to pray like that

He said I've been watching you Dad, ain't that cool
I'm your buckaroo, I wanna be like you
And eat all my food and grow as tall as you are
We like fixing things and holding mama's hand
Yeah we're just alike, hey ain't we dad
I wanna do everything you do
So I've been watching you

With tears in my eyes I wrapped him in a hug
Said my little bear is growing up

MODELING

He said but when I'm big I'll still know what to do

Cause I've been watching you Dad, ain't that cool
I'm your buckaroo, I wanna be like you
And eat all my food and grow as tall as you are
By then I'll be as strong as Superman
We'll be just alike, hey won't we dad
When I can do everything you do
Cause I've been watching you

(Written by Brian White, Dean Steven, & Rodney Atkins)

The beautiful aspect of this song is that it illustrates a parent's self-evaluation, as well as his willingness to make any necessary changes that would improve his parenting. As moms and dads we must ask ourselves: Would I want my child imitating me? The answer can be sobering if not alarming. But then the question is not intended to be a discouraging one. What parent has no room for improvement? Rather the question should prompt parents to focus in on their own actions and attitudes as a vehicle toward enhancing their own child. While heaping guilt on parents is not the purpose of this book, that emotion *can* be the impetus for a more concentrated effort which will ultimately better develop their children.

Parents must also ask: Do I follow the advice I give my child? Are there inconsistencies in my own life? Am I every bit as ambitious, hard-working, dependable, etc… as I require my child to be? Have I resolved my own emotional issues? The fact is that we parent through the filter of our issues.

During early childhood your son or daughter is not likely to notice any of these discrepancies. But as they enter the teenage years they gain more insight and are exposed to outside references with which to make observations. It is here that a teen will often bring to the attention of the parent that a double-standard exists, and usually in unflattering terms. **This discrepancy will then reduce the child's respect for the parent, reduce the authority of the adult, and provide a model for discrepancies and self-dishonesty in the teen's own life.**

Recommendations

First, **parents must display the *exact* behavior they want from their child.** Parents must consider: Is there any aspect of my life that I would *not* want my child imitating? In a comprehensive and strategic way, Mom and Dad should evaluate the characteristics they want from their child, review various traits of their own, and consider what is necessary to bring their own behavior more in line with their goals for their child.

Second, **parents must not wait for ideal circumstances.** Parents often express a long line of "if-onlys" with personal changes always contingent on perfect external circumstances. For example, if only we had more money, if only we lived in a bigger house, if only I'd had experienced a better childhood, if only we had less children, if only we had more children, if only our car was newer, if only our car was older. The litany of justifications can be endless, and for those without the courage to make personal changes, one excuse is as good as another no matter how valid or invalid. The excuses must all be put aside by parents who take a hard look inward to determine if what they want from their child is what they see in themselves. We must accept our life circumstances as they are and take advantage of teachable moments that come regularly- teachable moments that are often disguised as hardships, disciplinary incidents, or relational opportunities.

Third, **parents should provide both male and female role models for their child.** This does two things. This distinguishes clearly between male and female and well-rounds the child. It also provides numerous relational benefits in same and opposite-sexed relationships when maleness and femaleness are clearly displayed. This is especially important for single parents with limited opportunity to expose their child to the opposite gender. A discussion of gender roles is beyond the scope of this book, but individuals with fairly traditional gender role behavior also report having high satisfaction in life. This is not to say that one should be extreme, or inflexible in their gender role, but that generally accepted and prescribed male and female temperaments seem to work best. A macho husband, for example, who refuses to clean a bathroom because he views this as a job relegated to women will not only have a very unsatisfied wife, but his rigid gender role will lock him into demeaning behaviors that additionally make for an inefficient family system. A well-defined sense of masculinity or femininity is one indicator of an emotionally and spiritually healthy individual.

Fourth, **resolve your own personal issues**. Whether your issues are those of abandonment, neglect, excessive anxiety, shame, grief, or co-dependency, emotional baggage from the past will be displaced onto your children. They will receive small daily doses of your unresolved problems, largely without your notice. As your child's model, these issues will then begin to show up little-by-little over time and embed themselves in your child. Remember, parents establish a frame of reference for everything, and if that frame of reference is skewed the result will be children whose emotional and/or spiritual life will be equally skewed.

Lastly, relax. There is a natural panic from the fourth recommendation above. You may be realizing what a daunting task parenting is, but parents must address one personal issue at a time that over many weeks and months can result in big changes. Parents can also convey to their children that they, too, are working on fully becoming the person God wants them to be, truly taking their modeling to the next level.

Chapter Three Discussion Questions:

1. Who were your role models growing up? Were they rock stars, movie stars, political figures, scientists? Were they worthy of emulating? Were they wholesome role models?
2. Who were the role models in your family? An older sibling? An uncle or aunt? A grandparent?
3. Who was the better role model, your mother or father? Why?
4. Have any of your children picked up a trait from you that you wish he/she had not? What was it?
5. In evaluating yourself, is there any trait, habit, or aspect of your life you would not want your child to follow?
6. Is there any personal issue that, if resolved, would improve your parenting?
7. To what degree do your parenting role and daily routine serve as an opportunity to positively influence your child?
8. How would you define the term teachable moment? How well do you recognize teachable moments in real time?

9. Name several models children typically follow that we as parents must be cautious of, regulate, or eliminate?

10. How does the Bible make use of role models? Are all Biblical characters meant to be followed? Are all parts of a Biblical character's life (Moses for example) to be followed?

CHAPTER 4
Close Relationships

My family and I went to Disney World several years ago and had a fantastic stay. It is no accident, however, that at every turn there are souvenir shops with various themes depending on the section of the park. Tucked away in one corner of Disney World is the 'Pirates of the Caribbean' section complete with a boat ride, sea-roving figures, and yet one more souvenir shop. In that shop hung a pirate-themed t-shirt that I will never forget. The front of the shirt said, "THE BEATINGS WILL CONTINUE UNTIL MORALE IMPROVES." I laughed for twenty minutes after reading that t-shirt. Then I began to think how applicable that is to the way we often deal with our children. They do something wrong and we punish them. They commit a second infraction and we punish them again. Now the child is angry and we do not like their attitude so we again attempt to beat them into submission; and this punitive cycle of bad behavior, negative consequences, declining attitude, and spiraling deterioration of the family continues. Meanwhile, the relationship between parent and child continues to collapse until there is nothing left, and parents wonder why Johnny is rebellious or why he never comes out of his room.

The importance of rules and consequences should not be minimized and will be discussed in another chapter under the challenge section. **Punishment is a legitimate tool to shape a child's behavior. It *must*, however, be accompanied with our second support: a close relationship.** This warm bond is not just something parents like to do, or the equivalent of an extra-curricular activity. It is *mandatory* to insure that your child grows up emotionally and spiritually healthy. **A close relationship with your child is the primary tool used to establish a warm, secure bond that guides, reduces stress, and allows your child to develop normally.** Without it a whole host of security problems, emotional issues, and inadequacies will begin to develop. The absence of a close bond virtually guarantees that the child will enter adulthood with deficits that he will then have to work through to in order to function adequately. Further, some behavior problems that are attention-seeking or passive-aggressive in nature can actually be relationship problems.

Reasons for an Inadequate Parent-Child Bond

Life happens. If, as an adult, you have not had at least one major crisis in your life, you will. Financial problems, loss of work, extended illness, death in the family, housing issues, and legal problems are all examples of crises that happen to us, often through no fault of our own. An individual can be completely responsible and make well-thought-out decisions, and still find himself in disaster status with few answers. Still other times we make a poor decision, or in some cases a series of poor decisions and find ourselves in hardship respectively. These crises can absorb much time and energy, time and energy that should be directed at giving attention to our children.

Other things can also preclude the parent-child relationship. Any number of misplaced priorities can rob our children of their due time. Drug, alcohol, and gambling addictions steal time, energy, and financial resources from families. But, it does not have to be a bad thing for there to be impropriety. Virtually *anything* that replaces the time and energy that our children deserve can *become* a bad thing and result in relational deficits. This can even include good things like exercise, education, work, excessive house cleaning, excessive golf, over focus on romance and dating (single parents), television, computer/internet, volunteer activities, and excessive church attendance. The issue is misaligned priorities.

John Lennon was worth some 50 million dollars at the time of his death. He sang of peace and love, and displayed his musical genius regularly to the world. He is one of the most respected singer/songwriters in history causing many to be grief-stricken when he was gunned down in 1980. But, in the book *John* by Cynthia Lennon (2005), his son, Julian Lennon writes,

"Growing up as John Lennon's son has been a rocky path. All my life I've had people coming up to me saying 'I loved your dad.' I always have very mixed feelings when I hear this. I know that Dad was an idol to millions who grew up loving his music and his ideals. But to me he wasn't a musician or a peace icon, he was the father I loved and who let me down in so many ways. After the age of five, when my parents separated, I saw him only a handful of times, and when I did he was often remote and intimidating. I grew up longing for more contact with him but felt rejected and unimportant in his life. Dad was a great talent, a remarkable man who stood for peace and love in the world. But at the same time he found it very hard to show any peace and love to his first family my mother and me."

The bottom line is that the relationship with your children *must* be the priority. Sometimes beneficial, notable things can become the enemy of great parenting. With a short window of opportunity, we must regularly reach to our children.

What is the Big Deal? What is so Important About Relationships?

As a teenager I went to a Virginia military school. For four years I marched, took orders, and either shined or saluted everything that moved. It was a rigorous environment that emphasized discipline, structure, and submission to authority.

Many groups successfully function in the same manner. Groups of people that must focus on a task or have an important mission function effectively with a strong leader and subordinates who follow, but have little or no input. The followers also have little or no emotional tie to the leader. Places of employment, operating rooms, school boards, courtrooms, a commercial airplane flight, and church property committees are all examples of this kind of group. But, families are *very* different. **If a family is managed in this manner there will be much predictable turmoil and discontent.**

Scripture indicates that we were made for relationships. We are told in Genesis 2 that Adam talked in the garden with God. While there is no evidence that this was dissatisfying to Adam, God also knew that someone who could relate in a similar way but be more like Adam was what he needed. God declared in Genesis 2:18 that "It is not good for man to be alone." One might quickly conclude that this had to do with work- nothing could be further from the truth. It has to do with a deep understanding and appreciation of one another. While most animals can communicate with one another, mankind communicates and relates to one another in a unique and profound way that is a reflection of our maker. Consider these passages that not only demonstrate God's intimate closeness to us, but His unique relationship to man:

- Matt 10:30 *Even the very hairs on your head are numbered.*
- Psalm 34:18 *The Lord is close to the brokenhearted and saves those who are crushed in spirit.*
- Psalm 145:18 *The Lord is near to all those who call on Him, to all those who call on Him in Truth.*
- Jer 1:5 *Before I formed you in the womb I knew you, before you were born I set you apart.*

It is no accident that God is referred to as our Heavenly Father. These verses serve as an excellent model for a level of closeness that we, our children's earthly father, are to have toward our children.

Author Angela Thomas says that males and females early on ask themselves two core internal questions. Boys ask: Do I have what it takes? Girls ask: Am I beautiful? (*Do you think I'm beautiful*, 2003) Children look to a variety of sources, but especially their parents for the answer to these questions. Further, my experience is that the daddy of the family, as God's earthly representative of our Heavenly Father, has far more impact than the mother in answering these questions. The first man in a girl's life is her father; and if that is a distant, rejecting, absent, or neglectful relationship it sets the stage for other relationships with males in the future. It is very common, at that point, for females to then fervently seek out male approval in most any way possible. Once the girl has reached the teen years and develops physically, attention from males comes easier, especially males of low character. Without a warm fatherly bond the female will often be starved for male attention and usually get it through seductive and sexual means. Ironically, however, even these sexual encounters will not be fulfilling and this female will perpetually feel empty and unaffirmed. **Our world is littered with females whose decades of promiscuity and emptiness are rooted in the lack of an affirming male father figure in her childhood.**

The opposite reaction, however, is also common. It is frequently the case that this abandoned female will reject those who rejected her. As a protective mechanism, she now shuns all males since they are "all alike." She may regularly bash males, have anger issues she may not recognize, and even have gender identity issues, all because her femininity has never been acknowledged and the question "Am I beautiful?" never positively answered. Some females begin with the first seductive scenario, including boyfriends and even marriage, but later transition into this rejecting mode of operating since the original issue has not yet been resolved. It is then that marriage problems commence.

Males, too, will have difficulty as an adult without their corresponding "Do I have what it takes?" question answered effectively. While females most commonly respond with promiscuity, males usually counter with anger. This anger is frequently displaced. While he regularly takes his anger out on his little brother, a school teacher, or his bedroom wall, he is actually angry at someone or something else. His toughness is in question in his own mind. His anger is a product of both the rejection he is experiencing and a way to prove to himself he is tough enough.

He may even turn this anger inward in terms of depression. It is through this anger that this family will encounter a whole host of behavioral possibilities including school problems, rebellion, aggression, poor insight, immaturity, sarcasm, hostility, bully behavior, stealing, violence, low motivation, disrespect, isolation, self-punishment or mutilation, suicide, vandalism, lying, or criminal behavior. The teen may not be able to explain his anger and parents will often confirm that it seems non-specific to anything or anyone. The adolescent may also explain it erroneously with a justification that makes little sense since he does not truly understand his anger, or because he is cautious to blame a father in an already strained relationship. Without this "have what it takes" questions answered positively he may become macho or hyper masculine always attempting to prove he is really a man since it is not clear in his own mind. He may even have gender identity issues without a well-defined sense of maleness.

Whether a boy or a girl, these children often engage in oppositional behavior: thoughts and actions that are intentionally contrary to your desires or your position as an expression of anger or rebellion.

There can be positive family factors that can mediate anger and other problems somewhat. The child (and eventual adult) may also do a good job of hiding or masking these emotional issues. Without a clear answer to these questions, however, these behaviors and the accompanying self-doubts will persist. Without an actively-pursued, well-maintained relationship with your son or daughter it will be impossible to adequately answer these questions. With so many absent fathers it is no wonder that children struggle with identity and esteem issues. But how do we as parents address this?

A quality relationship is defined by two individuals getting into one another's worlds. Think back to when you and your spouse first met. You shared information, you asked questions, you smiled at one another, you found common ground, communicated with one another, trusted one another, listened, became honest and vulnerable, you affirmed one another, and you invested in one another. You *got into each another's worlds*. It's the same with your child in that a relationship is built by getting into his world. The difference is their world is immature, a bit selfish, and sometimes more resistant. Nonetheless, attachments are the vehicle that parents prepare children for adulthood, teach/demonstrate aspects of character, and pass on their faith to the next generation. Relationships are the catalyst for imparting everything we want our child to know and become. The difference is that children have little capacity to give back, especially early on. The self-absorbed nature and immaturity of children renders them incapable of reciprocating. However, if a parent will consistently reach out to the child and "get into his world" the child will eventually have both the capacity and desire to give in return to the parent and get into their world.

Rebellion-Relationship Link

Remember the adage that rules without a relationship leads to rebellion? This is one of the most common foundations of rebellion in children of all ages. **Children find it very difficult to receive an instruction or command if they sense the adult is not invested in them or does not care about them.** They can tolerate some level of this for a time, but by the teen years there is a collective quality in which the lack of a relationship has gone on for years. Add this to hormones in both girls and boys, as well as an emerging desire for independence and you have a perfect storm of resentment and family conflict.

If we as parents will initiate the relationship (just as God did?) and invest effort in maintaining the relationship, *children will respond*. If done early in the child's life (and there is not damage otherwise), children will respond immediately. If valuable time has been lost it will take a bit longer. In the case of teenagers with a long history of inadequate parent-child bond, it may take even longer. The innate desire of all humans is to pursue relationships. This desire is especially high in children for the purpose of development and causes youngsters to be highly receptive to our teaching efforts. Children's only hesitation is typically a learned response from hurts or past rejected efforts at relationships. This usually expands to more global trust issues in adulthood.

It comes down to priorities in many cases. As parents we must avoid a preoccupation with work and career, school or training, romantic pursuits in the case of single parents, goals, sports, hobbies, personal interests, or material possessions. Most, if not all of these endeavors are valid. They simply cannot take priority over meeting the needs of our children.

Research on Bonding

There is a beneficial and necessary bond between care-giver and baby that has been termed Attachment Theory. Originally coined by John Bowlby in the 1950's, this concept states that babies have an in-born need to develop an emotional tie to a caregiver from which the child derives security.[1] At its core is a biological drive to survive by longing for an adult who can provide and protect. In other words, newborns need a parent who will form an emotional bond with them that gives them a feeling of safety and protection, and insures their needs will be provided for. We usually think of this parent-child bond as a good thing or something that makes Mom feel good. However, we now know that this bond is *required* for proper child development.

Another key researcher by the name of Harry Harlow performed studies with rhesus monkeys, taking newborns away from their mothers and performing a variety of tests with them as he focused on this parent-child bond. These baby monkeys, though they were given proper sustenance and physical care, were denied their mother's warmth and comfort. As adults these monkeys showed abnormal behavior

---

[1] Bowlby, J. (1958). The Nature of the Childs Tie to His Mother. *International Journal of Psychoanalysis*, 39, 350-371.

in social situations, were fearful of other monkeys and often engaged in unprovoked aggression. The female monkeys raised without a mother displayed difficulty with normal mating and often neglected or abused their offspring. For these primates, the effects of their childhood were felt in lasting ways years later in social and mental abnormalities.[2]

Though similar experimentation on humans is obviously unethical, what has been termed "closet children" are occasionally found by authorities. Discovered chained to beds, starved in clothes closets, and isolated in bedrooms, this abuse evokes disgust and anger in us all. These children have been deprived of human contact, or the normal relational bond violated in extreme ways. These children react and relate to others unpredictably including high levels of fear, social isolation, paranoia, aggression, and lack of trust. While closet children are relatively rare, milder examples walk the streets all around us every day.

Benefits of the Relationship

Inadequate or non-existent parent-child relationships affect individuals in a variety of ways. **In a manner that is often unrecognized, children are often under-developed emotionally, fearful of the world, have a general sense of anger, have difficulty relating to the peers, and possess low quality and minimal friends, due to a marginal or absent bond with their parents.** In some cases an appropriate bond was initially established, but some event or crises has violated that bond, as mentioned before. Consequently, parents must recognize the importance of this close relationship and takes steps to maintain it.

The benefits of a close relationship with your child include:

- A more secure child (extremely important concept covered in chapter 12)
- A happier, more content child
- A more well-adjusted child
- A child/adult who is able establish independence and to solve their own problems
- A child who is not afraid of the world and new challenges
- A child who can establish good boundaries with others.

---

[2] Harlow, H. F. & Zimmermann, R. R. (1958). The development of affective responsiveness in infant monkeys. *Proceedings of the American Philosophical Society, 102,* 501-509.

- A child who does not require the constant support of others in order to perform
- A child who is more compliant, respectful, and appreciative.

How can all of this be achieved in one strategy you ask? *By establishing and maintaining a close relationship with your child.* Like many things, however, this is simple in theory, but hard in practice. It takes *constant* time and attention. It is a relentless pursuit that at times will seem to be fruitless, especially during the teen years when God suddenly fast-tracks internal development. It is the continuous watering of a temperamental plant that often gives you little feedback as to how well you're doing. **It is the largest investment you will ever make, but, it also will pay the largest dividend you will ever receive.** I have never seen a tombstone, or heard a eulogy that expressed regret in the time spent on a child. However, I have heard many people express in their later days that they wish they had spent more time with their children. If only we could project ourselves into the future and live our lives in a manner that would have no regrets, how differently we might then live.

What Does A Relationship With My Child Look Like?

Many parents, especially fathers, are puzzled about what I am talking about. Many adults came from disconnected homes where there was little family bond. The family members went about their tasks, did what they were supposed to, and carried on through the years. These adults may even have no frame of reference for relationships and therefore not recognize that it was absent in their family of origin. These parents usually either resist the notion that relationships are important, or are generally fearful of emotionally connecting with another person since it will mean personal change, increased vulnerability, and relating to others in a completely different way.

Parents who have close relationships with their children intentionally and regularly connect with their child in a whole host of ways.

- They have a high degree of two-way communication.
- They engage in physical contact with their child.

- They enjoy doing things together.
- They are available and make their child the priority.
- They constantly convey warmth and affirmation to their child.

Let's take each of these areas and break them down into specifics.

Communication

Listen! Listen! Listen! **It is *imperative* that parents engage in a high degree of listening with their child.** As a cadet at Frederick Military Academy years ago, no one ever listened to me…they were not supposed to. In that setting it worked! But families, you remember, *must* be different to be effective. Every time you as a father listen to you child you are receiving information, but you are doing something else far more important: sending *value messages*. Every time you look your daughter in the eyes and listen to her concerns, her dreams, her aspirations, you are saying, "You're important to me. I value you. I care about you." Daughters all across America are longing for their dads to convey this to them, but they often come up empty because fathers are focused on the *task*. Dads are concentrating on the logistics, the content, the mission, but completely miss the relational opportunity. **Children need us to say it, but more importantly they need us to *show* it by giving them our undivided attention.** This includes turning off the television, removing ourselves from the computer, and shutting down the cell phone.

    Do not confuse listening with agreeing, however. There is an excellent chance your child or teen is going to spout off some strange ideas. These ideas may even be odd or inaccurate. There is a time for correcting the most bizarre of these ideas *after* you have listened. Listening to your child's thoughts not only conveys love, it also allows the child to hear and re-think their own ideas, as well as give you the parent the eventual right to comment. Without the listening element, that earned right to give your child feedback is eliminated. Listening and talking convey ongoing affirmation- not necessarily affirmation of the child's behavior or ideas, but affirmation of the *child*. Parents must be cautious not to confuse the two. We must affirm the child but address bad behavior when it occurs. More on this in the discipline section.

One question I frequently hear concerning teenagers is 'when should you talk with them?' The answer is whenever you are with them or whenever they want to talk. Teenagers are especially fickle and erratic. Their mood is like a roller coaster at an amusement park, in constant ups and downs. They may talk non-stop one morning and be completely shut-down the next. Parents nonetheless should attempt to engage the child in conversation. Parents must take advantage of spontaneous opportunities and open doors to interact with their child.

Many parents limit their verbal communication toward their child to incidents of correction. These parents miss key relational opportunities. These parents also teach their children that communication is only for correction, or to selfishly get something from someone. The child then absorbs his parents' own approach toward people. It is these children who will develop skills in using communication to manipulate others. These children will come to dad only when they want something: a favor, a privilege, money, new shoes, the car, etc… They are then likely to manipulate their peers, and later other adults in order to get what they want with little regard for the other person.

Parents must also be cautious that it is not always about performance. Asking your child how he did on his history test is a reasonable question that keeps parents aware and holds the child accountable, but it must be about more than *doing*. **It must also be about the *person*.** Remember, communication is primarily for the purpose of building relationships. Anyone who senses he is valuable solely because of what he does will adapt a performance-based self-concept. Children will begin to feel valuable only because of how well they play football, how high they score on the math test, or how well they play the drums. **Children must FEEL valuable simply because they are.** They must feel worthy because God made them…end of sentence. But, do not let this be an excuse for poor performance. (More discussion on this in the chapter on self-development.)

Who should start the conversation? **It is primarily the *parent's* responsibility to initiate conversation.** This does not mean it must always be so; the effort and investment to maintain the relationship must be made by both individuals. Consequently, if you invest in communication first, it will become mutual and your efforts as the parent will eventually pay off, especially by older children. God initiated the relationship with us in that "while we were yet sinners Christ died for us" (Rom 5:8). First John 4:19 tells us that we love Him because He first loved us. God is the "adult" in the relationship and took the responsibility for initiating the relationship, though we are responsible for responding. In that same way, our children should, and usually will respond *if* we initiate it early on and consistently, and if it is done so in a loving manner without a focus on performance. It is often the case that children want to talk at unusual times, late at night for example. While there are human limits to your availability, and it is certainly beneficial to set good boundaries, parents must be willing to talk when children want to talk. While we are not God, we represent and have a God-like role. Since God is *always* available, we must make every effort to be willing to talk even when we are tired, taxed, or at the end of a long day.

What do you talk with child your about? Anything and everything! You mostly talk about what *they* want to talk about. The reader might conclude that this could create a self-centered adult who can only focus on themselves. Actually the opposite is true. It is when there is little or no focus on the child that he becomes starved for attention and seeks to get that need met in extraordinary ways. The result is that he is self-absorbed, fishes for compliments, and is emotionally needy where ever he goes. However, the child who has been given to regularly (supported) by a parent asking about him and listening to him is one who is emotionally secure and is then able to give to his friends, spouse, and children. If we regularly fill our children's cups emotionally, they will eventually have a full cup themselves. They, in turn, can then fill the cup of others. However, when children's emotional needs are not met through a close warm bond and a high degree of communication, they later become adults who have difficulty meeting the emotional needs of *their* children.

Years ago my then 10 year-old son loved dinosaurs. He read books on dinosaurs, he watched TV programs on dinosaurs, and played with his rubber dinosaurs acting out various fighting scenarios. He learned about the plant-eaters, the meat-eaters, and characteristic of each prehistoric animal, as well as the names of scores of different dinosaurs. I, on the other hand, knew little about dinosaurs and was perfectly satisfied in my blissfully ignorant condition. However, when he and I talked, *we talked about dinosaurs!* If you think our discussion was about dinosaurs you miss the point of this story. Our conversation was *not* about dinosaurs, but about my son and my great love for him. It was about my wanting to convey to him that I care for him very much, enough to regularly *get into his world.* Being a good parent is not about the parent...it is about the child! It's about focusing on the child and meeting his emotional and other needs such that he develops properly. When this is done, he then has the capacity to meet the needs of others including friends, a marriage partner, and children of his own.

Physical Contact

In an age where everyone is cautious, if not hyper cautious concerning touching another person we have forgotten that physical touch with family members is important. There is great connecting power in touching our children; and without it much of the muscle of the necessary emotional bond is lost. Physically touching your child will also help them understand appropriate touch. It teaches them how to accurately assess another person's touch, and allows them to respond with healthy sexuality in the future.

Children should be touched often. According to *Touching* by Ashley Montagu, physical contact of infants by mother increases their immune system, encourages physical growth, stimulates brain activity, and encourages liver and heart growth. Touch from a parent gives affirmation, guidance, and reassurance that someone is close by to protect and lead. It also maintains the emotional link between child and parent. This continues to be important even into the teen years.

We would not challenge this idea with toddlers and small children, but we can automatically become cautious as our children get older. By adolescence we often eliminate touch completely, believing it to be either unnecessary or indicating a romantic relationship- neither could be further from the truth. The natural and appropriate sense of independence that emerges during adolescence can prompt teenagers to pull away physically. Parents must allow that independence, but maintain regular touch as a means to preserve connectedness. Below is a list of suggested means of physical touch. Many of the suggestions might be better received by one gender or the other, or one age group over another. Given this caution, the reader might be surprised at what *does* work. Both of my 200+ pound teenage football-playing sons and I regularly hug, and at 15 years-old my daughter use to challenge me at mercy: a game to see who can shove back the others hand and force the person to say "mercy."

Examples of Effective Physical Touch:

- Putting hand on shoulder, back, arm.
- 30 second back rub
- Hugging the child
- Tickling
- Wrestling
- Light physical challenges such as spontaneous pushing matches
- Surprising the other by grabbing them from behind
- Giving the child a playful but mild shove
- Placing a hand on the back of a child's head
- Rubbing a son's bald head

It is especially important that fathers regularly touch both male *and* female children in the above ways. If it is not done regularly, a pattern of manipulation can emerge similar to the way that verbal communication can become manipulation. Girls can become coy operators in cozying up to their dads in order to obtain favors, privileges, etc. Many women today use their sexuality in order to manipulate men. They have learned that standing in close proximity to men, jiggling the right way, or intentionally rubbing against males in a seductive manner that sexually arouses will increase their chances of getting what they want. This manner of operating almost always begins with a poor father-daughter relationship. Rather than sexualizing touch, fathers must use it to establish and maintain an appropriate emotional bond. In this way dads are distinguishing between the touch of a strong relationship and sexual touch, while identifying and eliminating manipulative touch.

Shared Activities

Researchers who study relationships use the term *shared positive experiences*. This simply means that two people enjoy doing something together. It can be simple or elaborate, costly or inexpensive, quick or time consuming. It is important that some or all of these be regularly experienced by parent and child. A family vacation, a spontaneous walk together, a 30-second conversation, repairing the fence together- these are all examples of activities that can be shared positive experiences. **But it is important to remember that the activity is not the end, it is the means to *another* end- maintaining the relationship.**

Several years ago my two sons and I bought an old beat up aluminum john boat. Upon bringing it home we could see how beat up it was, but not how old it was. As we peeled off layers of old license stickers and removed the rotten seats we discovered it to be the long-term home of numerous large and small inhabitants. We scraped, primed and painted the trailer. Then we rewired the trailer including new tail lights and replaced the old dry rotted wench rope. We power-washed the aluminum boat hull, replaced the wooden seats, and installed new screws and hardware. We worked several Saturdays and evenings for a month before it was finished. After much sweat and hard work and some $200 in materials, the boat looked only a little better than when we started. Between my sons goofing off, cutting several boards the wrong length, and distracting me, I could have done the job in half the time by myself, but speed and efficiency was not the point. It was a task, but not *just* a task.

My sons and I will fondly remember working on that boat throughout our lives because we built more than a boat. Yes, we got a newly refurbished boat, but we got much more! Working on the boat gave me an opportunity to teach them patience, how to work with their hands, persistence at a task, and overall character development. The boat provided the stage for man-to-man conversations and bonding. Refurbishing the boat was yet another setting for building the parent-child relationship. And this is how guys think. They like to *do* things, *make* things, *build* things, but if you think this is the only focus, then you are missing the point. Doing things together provided the opportunity to engage in those shared positive experiences by building the relationship. The boat seats will rot again, the trailer will rust again, and the lights will again need replacing one day, but the relational bond we built will stand. This is the caution I issue to fathers: **Do not make the task the sole focal point.** Make the task, the goal, or the activity the *vehicle* by which relationships are formed and maintained.

As mentioned earlier, when parents focus solely on the task, children begin to adapt a performance-based self-worth. Consciously or unconsciously they begin to believe "I am what I achieve", and consequently "I am only important/worthy/valuable if I perform at a high level". Is it bad to perform at a high level? No! Then what is the problem you ask? The problem is linking performance to one's worth.

To be loved by God we never have to *do* anything. We do not have to perform, achieve, or even be productive, and this should be the model for parents. It is imperative that this be crystal clear to moms and dads.

We want our children to achieve because it builds character and allows them to better fulfill God's plan for them. That plan includes becoming eventually independent of parents, providing a model for others, and using their gifts in a way that fulfill God's mission for them. But, it is *never* tied to God's love toward the child. Many adults wrestle with this today in a relentless pursuit of achievement because without it they feel worthless. There is a sense of peace in God's unconditional acceptance of us. It is liberating to realize we do not have to achieve great things, make lots of money, look like a model, or earn a Ph.D. to gain God's approval. This is what we must convey to our children. It is frequently the case that children eventually realize that their parents' emphasis was more about the *doing* than the *being*. This usually results in a child who is angry, disappointed, and hurt because they realize it was about what they *did* and not about them. This insight into their parents combined with hormones (male or female) and an emerging sense of independency can result in much family tension in the adolescent years.

In doing things together parents can get their children interested in Mom or Dad's pastimes. This offered interest can quickly evolve into a shared interest and do an excellent job of building and enhancing the relationship. I have successfully offered my own interest in carpentry, music, and football with my children to soon find them equally as engrossed. But, parents must be careful that this does not become a well-masked focus on themselves, or an attempt to live out their own unfulfilled dreams. It is good to do things you both enjoy; but doing something only the child enjoys says even more. **Love is truly defined in sacrifice, and to give up some of your own time and energy speaks volumes to your child.** This is true especially when it involves something only the child is interested in.

It may also be that your children do not *want* to do things with you. This can be especially true if the relationship is poor, inadequate, or never developed. Other problems (personal and/or behavioral problems) usually surface with this child. **It may be necessary to establish, or re-establish a proper bond with your child to increase security and lower anxiety.** This is done by gently compelling the child to have those shared positive experiences. This can be necessary even if children are bonded well, but have become relationally lazy. I will occasionally *require* my children to become involved in some activity with me. They may protest at first, but I do not accept no. Once we begin our walk, start out traveling in the car, or initiate the task, they soon stop the protests, become engaged, and almost always quickly begin laughing and kidding with other family members. Children want and need an emotional attachment with their parents even if they initially put up a front by acting or stating otherwise.

In the teen years there is a pulling-away that is natural and appropriate. Parents must be cautious that this desire for independence is not excessive or premature. Especially late teens may not *want* parents, but they still *need* them. Moms and dads must also differentiate independence from isolation. A 16 year-old distancing herself to some extent and making responsible decisions is healthy. The same child spending inordinate amounts of time in her room daily with the door closed talking to her friends for hours and disconnected from her family is detrimental.

Relational Credits

There is another byproduct of a close relationship with your children. I mentioned earlier that a close relationship can actually reduce behavior problems. Conversely, a lack of a relationship can *increase* behavior problems because the bad behavior becomes attention-seeking. But, there is another dynamic taking place.

We have established that initiating and maintaining a close relationship is support in that it represents a giving to the child. This daily giving is translated into stored credits, much like bank deposits. In a healthy bank account the individual makes many deposits and few withdrawals. If he does this faithfully the account is solvent and he always has money in the account.

Relationships are similar in that we must make many deposits and few withdrawals. These relational deposits should accumulate throughout the years childhood years in the ways already described. On occasion a withdrawal is necessary in terms of correcting the child in some way. This occurs fairly regularly throughout childhood, but can become especially frequent in the adolescent years when testing limits, increased independence, and challenges to parental authority are more common. If relational deposits have been regularly made then a healthy, adequate account is in place. Withdrawals (corrections) can then be made from this account with little effect on the overall relational account. However, if a withdrawal is necessary (as it inevitably is) and there are no deposits with which to draw from, the relational account becomes overdrawn. **It is here that children rebel, feel used and dominated, and usually believe that the parent does not genuinely care about them.** If it is a teenager with increased intelligence and resources, the rebellion will intensify to such behaviors as cursing at their parents, running away, drug and alcohol usage, sexual experimentation, and isolation. To an adolescent, a lack of a relationship equals rejection: an extremely painful notion that they will not tolerate.

A Natural Desire To Obey? Seriously??

There is an additional way that a strong relationship with your son or daughter can positively affect his/her behavior. As explained earlier, we have been created as relational creatures with a natural desire to build and maintain close relationships. Once that close bond is established in the home between child and parent, the child naturally wants it to continue. It feels warm to the child. It feels secure. It feels pleasant. There is also an unconscious knowledge that if the child disobeys that relationship will be broken. When that relational bond is shattered through disobedience it becomes emotionally painful for the child. The parent is also hurt and disappointed. Now there is a wedge, a barrier between the child and the parent who loves him and has invested in him. Children do not fully comprehend it and could never verbalize it; nonetheless, they still operate within its awareness. This emotional pain both the parent and child feel is caused by the child's own rebellion. **Consequently, the child will *want* to comply since obedience will result in the *avoidance* of the emotional pain.** Because of the warm parent-child relationship, we have created a *desire* to comply with requests and family rules. Children, including teenagers, will actually *want* to be around their parents. TRUE!! Even at the peak potential of an adolescent's rebellious period he will actually *want* to be in the presence of his mother and father *if* they have nurtured this close relationship.

    This is in parallel to God's relationship with us in that when we disobey Him we feel bad because the relationship is severed. Consequently, the close relationship we have with God we want to maintain and therefore obey Him as it avoids emotional pain. This also serves as a natural and ever-present model for children learning the relational truths concerning God and His people.

Therefore, **a close relationship with your child will greatly decrease behavior problems and make EVERY aspect of parenting smoother.** Parents will see decreased behavior problems, decreased attention-seeking, and decreased anxiety simply from specific behaviors meant to enhance the parent-child bond. If, however, there is no relationship between a child and his parents, then there is little or no incentive for the child to obey. In fact, if the child or teenager is angry at their parents, then intentional disobedience is a great way to get revenge. Now there is actually *incentive to hurt* the parents. This intentional hurt can come in the form of mild non-compliance or resistance, or it can be extreme. What better way to get revenge (or attention) on one's parents than to embarrass them by drugs, drinking alcohol, school problems, or run-ins with the law. Then there is the ultimate humiliation to one's parents: sexual activity and becoming pregnant. For a teenage daughter to give away her body to another man, and then display it for the entire world, not only now but for years to come, is the ultimate slap in the face for a father. This is often linked to an absent father-daughter relationship, and sometimes a way to hurt him back for hurting her.

Small Investments are the Best

Weekend trips, vacations, big projects, and long-range goals are all good and necessary. But, the best of relationships are actually made up of small caring behaviors. Smaller doses of consistent relational deposits count for much more than a fewer number of big ones because they represent more thought and consideration. Fathers who barely speak a word to their children all week but then want to compensate by taking their children to a theme park will not be nearly as effective as dads with more consistent communication and involvement. A parent every day or almost every day should:

- Greet their child good morning
- Discuss the day's events ahead
- Hug their child

- Ask the child how their day was, or ask "How's it going?"
- Ask "How was school?" and insist on more than "Fine" as an answer
- Discuss school tests & homework without a performance or task focus
- Inquire about dance team, marching band, football team, school clubs, etc... your child is involved in
- Do something together: make dinner, cut the grass, work on homework, build a model airplane, go fishing, etc...
- Tell your child, "I'm glad you're my son/daughter"
- Compliment or thank the child for something
- Be playful, tease, joke together, laugh together
- Listen to something that happened to your child today
- Tell something that happened to you today
- Make direct eye contact with your child and smile
- Be intentionally pleasant

Yelling

There is a great American pastime you may enjoy as a parent. It is more accepted than hotdogs or apple pie, and older than baseball. It is a custom long-held by families everywhere and on any given evening you can randomly catch many moms and dads engaging in this tradition: yelling. We have a nation of screaming parents!

The parents I talk to have a love-hate relationship with their yelling. Most realize that it is not a good practice and feel guilty when they do it. But, a part of them enjoys the cathartic nature of yelling, as well as the nervous compliance from children yelling can achieve. **For these reasons shouting can be popular and self-reinforcing for parents, as well as give them a false sense of confidence in this practice. Let's face it, most of the time it works.**

Screaming at children is a problem in at least two ways. First, yelling serves as a model for yelling. Parents who yell are almost guaranteed to have children who yell. Both parents and children can easily adapt the habit of ventilating every frustration on each other. Within a short period of time, a family can find itself in regular shouting matches that contribute to household chaos. It becomes a maladaptive part of both handling anger and resolving conflict. This habit for the child is then taken into adulthood and becomes a manner of relating to others, including his family.

Second, yelling causes relational damage. Many parents invest adequate time in establishing the relationship through ways already described. These parents may communicate regularly with their child, engage in various activities, and relate to their children well. They then, however, undo the hard work they have achieved by damaging the relationship with yelling that is degrading and hurtful. This, in turn, becomes the basis for relational and behavior problems in the child. It also becomes the foundation of relational distance between parent and child that prompt him to avoid approaching parents with a problem or admission of a mistake. If anything he will now *hide* his mistake since he knows he will simply be the target of more yelling. Parents must work hard at establishing the relationship, but work equally as hard to *maintain* the relationship through reasonable, respectful communication.

Additionally, yelling can lower motivation in a child, hurt self-esteem, produce anger in the child, and over time provoke the child to rebellion. What can lull parents into a false sense of security is that fact that yelling often gets compliance. A child who the target of yelling will likely jump to attention and do what he is told. However, even the positive effects of yelling wane over time as children realize that dad is just a big blowhard not worthy of the child's respect.

Yelling is often a replacement for consequences. In my counseling office I frequently work with parents who regularly scream at children, but do not use the behavioral tools that change the behavior. This is the worst of both worlds. Here, the child's self-esteem and parental relationship is damaged, but there is nothing to change the unwanted behavior. A much better approach is to curb the yelling, and then implement the behavioral tools that decrease the undesirable behavior. In other words, replace yelling with consequences!

Lastly, yelling sends a mixed message that can follow a child into adult relationships. The message is that love hurts. The message is that I will care for you, but that you will also be the target of my wrath. This twisted, abusive version of love in childhood often sets a precedent that can later become a pattern of romantic relationships in adulthood. **The child is "programed" into linking regular dramatic expressions of anger with romantic love dangerously concluding that this is normal and appropriate. This is often the foundation of abusive relationships.**

Stubborn Cases

What if my child rejects me? That can happen, especially a teenager who has established that pattern of relational distance, been hurt, felt rejected in the past, or believes relationships to be unimportant. The child will have to unlearn what he/she has learned. Be patient. Be consistent. Get professional help if necessary. Continue reaching out to the child in the way this chapter describes. The child may think you have ulterior motives at first and therefore may test you. "You are nice today, but what about tomorrow?" the child will think. Continue to be persistent. Even if it takes months, hang in there. They *will* eventually respond.

Lastly, be intentional. Remember, the high support high challenge parent does nothing by accident. This parent goes by a well-thought-out plan; they never wing-it. They have a goal in place and a deliberate plan on how to get there. What does a Mom or Dad have to do for the parent-child relationship to go sour? Nothing! It will happen automatically! Parents have to *intentionally* pump energy into the relationship for it to have life. They must *intentionally* invest daily in the child by connecting with him one moment at a time.

Chapter Four Discussion Questions:

1. How close was your family as you were growing up? What was it that prevented your family from being closer? Is there any tendency to follow that pattern in your family?
2. To what extent were there "rules without a relationship" in your family of origin?
3. What evidence do we have indicating that God is close to us?
4. Was the question adequately answered when you were a child: do I have what it takes? (male) Am I beautiful? (female). If not, how has this affected you in adulthood?

5. What phrase does the chapter use to describe the process that results in a good parent-child relationship?

6. Did you rebel as a teenager? How was this related to an inadequate parent-child relationship?

7. How would you rate your listening skills toward your children? Do you listen without giving advice? Do you ask follow-up questions to your child's statements? How well do you take advantage of one-on-one moments with your child?

8. To what extend was the attention you received in your family of origin performance-based? As you grew up did you feel loved?

9. To what extent do you engage in regular physical contact and shared activities with your children? How does your level of comfort with physical touch relate to your family of origin?

10. What activities do you and your child share? Are there any unique interests of your child in which you participate despite having little or no personal interest in that activity?

11. Explain the bank account relationship metaphor. Name three relational investments a parent might display.

12. What is the link between a child's behavior and the parent-child relationship? Are small relational investments better or large?

13. Did your parents yell? Name two problems with a parent yelling at their child. What specifically sends you over the edge and prompts you to yell? Do your children yell? How would the overall functioning or mood of your home change if everyone stopped yelling?

CHAPTER 5
Supervision and Feedback

In the early 90's I taught fifth grade at an at-risk Fort Worth elementary school. My students, who were typically 10-11 years old, would commonly recount violent, highly sexual, and mature movies they had seen at home and in the theaters. Parents would pop in a video tape in the VCR player at home as a baby sitter, or have no sitter and be forced to take their children with them to a theater movie. These children were exposed to graphic slasher films, violent action movies, and films that contained explicit nudity and sexuality. When I questioned their viewing of these movies, my students were puzzled. "What's the big deal?" they asked. It was the norm in their household. "It's a good movie," I heard over and over from these children. **These children's natural curiosities, their desire to be sensually titillated, indiscriminant parental approval as their guide, and a measure of adrenaline from watching the movie had all collectively shaped their criteria of what is acceptable.** As I heard these stories I wanted to scream: Where is the discernment. Where is the supervision. Where is the protection. These children were unaware of the poison being dumped into their minds as were their parents. These moms and dads were willing to barter the character of their children in exchange for temporary peace through an entertainment babysitter.

Why Parents Do Not Supervise their Children

Across America children are unaccounted for and unsupervised for a variety of reasons. Parents must work and engage in the normal tasks of life. They run to the dry cleaners, get the dog clipped, attend a dental appointment, and pay an overdue electric bill. This stretching of time and schedules is one of the many demanding aspects of parenting. The myriad of daily obligations and responsibilities all parents

SUPERVISION AND FEEDBACK

face make it very difficult to supervise any child 24/7. It only takes a minute while mom is cooking dinner for her little girl to get into trouble.

Some parents are simply inattentive. Skirmishes and incidents are occurring all around them without notice. Sibling fights break out, a child eats one piece of candy after another, or money goes missing from dad's dresser, all without awareness from parents. Short of an atom bomb going off, these parents are oblivious to any problems.

Other parents are aware of these problems but refuse to address them (low support) since that will take time, energy, and may initiate a battle that Mom or Dad is unwilling to engage in. Others are preoccupied in an out-of-balance manner with their own focus of life. This may include goals, achievements, work, or romantic pursuits.

Still other Moms and Dads are simply overwhelmed. They may be a single parent, their financial resources are low, and/or they have a large number of children that make supervision extremely difficult. With PTA meetings, baseball practice, and Wednesday night youth group, parents often do a day's work after their day's work; and that is without any of the crises that will inevitably occur. Parents may additionally have the responsibility for their own aging parent's well-being. After caring for their own young children, these adults have to manage the grandparent's finances, transport them to doctor's appointments, and run errands for them, further complicating supervision issues.

When I was a child, back when dirt was being formed, a television public service ad used to appear periodically that never made sense to me. A silver-tongued voice would come on and state, "Its eight o'clock, do you know where your children are?" Now as a parent, it makes perfect sense, and, it is a legitimate question. Parents must stay sharp, stay aware, and keep their eyes and ears open. **Parents *must* know *exactly* where their child is, what he is doing, and who he is with at all times.** Too many times we as parents kind of know where our child is, sort of know what he is doing, and (almost know) who he is with. This is a weak link in the supervision chain that not only fails to adequately protect the child, but offers a loop hole in which the child may attempt to deceive parents.

Kate and Gerry McCann were hoping for a quiet, relaxing vacation with their in family in Praia Da Luz Portugal in May of 2007. Their three children were young but certainly able to enjoy the planned family get-away, but on May 3 their vacation turned into a nightmare. Sometime early one evening four year-old Maddie McCann was abducted from the family's hotel room without a trace and never seen again. The startling part of the story is that little Maddie, along with her two-year-old twin siblings, Sean and Amelie, were left in the hotel room alone while their parents went to a restaurant to eat dinner.[1] Sadly this is not an isolated case. **Parents rarely intentionally hurt their children, but they often fail to use good judgment and take the proper precautions that would protect their children and eliminate danger.**

Across America young children are dealt with carelessly, older children are exposed to damaging media stimulation, and teenagers have conned their parents into unlimited freedom with excessive power to boot. The real losers are the children who do not have the insight or maturity to protect themselves from the certain physical and emotional harm that lay ahead.

A Biblical Example

According to genealogical records, King David had numerous sons and daughters by at least eight women, and very likely more that included both wives and concubines. He was extremely gifted and gained much attention for his valor as a teenager as he slew the Goliath: the warrior that caused fear in opposing soldiers that were older and better equipped than David. Scripture confirms that if alive today, David would be the star of the football team, play lead guitar in his own rock band, win first prize in the state poetry contest, be president of his senior class, lead worship in his youth group, and have chiseled good looks that would be the envy of everyone. As an adult everything David touched continued to turn to gold; God truly blessed him in every area of his life, except one. As broadly successful and talented as he was in every area of his life, he is also recorded as one of the worse parents in the entire Bible.

In the first chapter of 1 Kings we are introduced to one of King David's sons: Adonijah. As his fourth son, Adonijah was a child who had made many bad decisions and whose behavior had been a problem. Was this a situation that David was unable to identify? Not likely. David had well proved himself to be a shrewd, astute, intuitive individual. David had recognized his children's defiance and had anguished over it. David had also brought this problem to the God that he loved wanting divine

---

1 http://en.wikipedia.org/wiki/Disappearance_of_Madeleine_McCann

guidance and strength. No doubt God had given him what he asked for, but David never put feet on his leadership with his family. Though he was an incredible success in every area of organization and administration he undertook, David was a failure in his own home. **David took seriously the responsibility for thousands in his kingdom and in his army, but he disregarded the individuals God gave him first priority in supervising.** Speaking of David toward his son Adonijah, 1 Kings 1:6 states, "His father had never interfered with him by asking 'Why do you behave this way'?" In one of the saddest commentaries on parenting in history, a premier military leader and king never once bothered to question his children's behavior. Eventually David was old and sickly, and his children ignored him while greedily fighting one another for his throne.

David loved the Lord, but the insight and leadership skills God gave him were never applied to his children. This leads us to this conclusion: **A failure to implement the *parental power* given by God will manifest itself in problems, character flaws, and family conflict.** Whether through misguided pursuits, a selfish sense of ambition, or passions he failed to control, David did not give priority to his family. He did not guide, manage, or teach them, and apparently for long periods of time. He did not grasp that we as parents have a window of opportunity, a limited amount of time, and an endpoint to the influence over our children. In David's case it was so extreme and his model was so poor that the result was disastrous.

What is Supervision?

According to Wikipedia, supervision means the act of watching over the work or tasks of another who may lack full knowledge of the concept at hand. Supervision does not mean control of another but a careful, supportive, leadership role in a work, professional or personal context. In childcare and general use, the verb "to supervise" means to watch over, and is often used in the context of an adult watching children to ensure they are attended, acceptably behaved, and safe. Parental supervision is a parenting technique that involves looking after, or monitoring a child's activities. Young children are generally incapable of looking after themselves, and incompetent in making informed decisions for their own well-being. For this reason, they require constant supervision by their parents or another adult. Physical supervision, the most basic form of parental supervision, is required to keep children from hurting themselves or others, and to keep them away from dangerous objects and situations.

High levels of appropriate adult supervision have many benefits. First, it insures that children will not behave in a way that harms them now or jeopardizes their future well-being as a result of their natural immaturity or selfishness. Whether child or adolescent, it temporarily regulates their behavior until they have self-control. Second, that external supervision creates security in the child. It lets him know that you will not allow him to inadvertently harm himself, or any outside force to harm him. Supervision indirectly lowers anxiety and fear as a result of an unconscious knowledge that something bigger and wiser is watching over them. Third, it naturally reduces behavior problems by creating an overall sense of "I will know what you are doing." When adults know what children are doing and those children are mindful of it, their behavior dramatically improves. Lastly, it instills values and eventual self-control.

Small children need supervision in terms of safety. They touch *everything*, and what they can touch usually goes in their mouth. This means that anything potentially harmful must be removed or put up. Household floors must be scanned periodically for things like paper clips, marbles, and bits of trash. Toddlers trip and fall on a regular basis such that all sharp edges on coffee tables and fire place hearths should be padded or removed if possible. Toddlers are also very mobile requiring parents to limit their mobility, watch the child constantly, or in a safe environment check on the child every couple of minutes. Mom should come running at either a loud noise or a long period of silence.

Older children are slightly more physically safe, but more energetic but still at high risk. Their dare-devil behavior and trusting nature can cause them to easily fall into danger they are incapable of recognizing. People, situations, and places that can pose much threat go unrecognized by these children. Because of the trusting, inquisitive nature of children and their inability to recognize danger, if combined with the decreased supervision of parents, this age group is at the highest risk for abduction. This is especially true when unsupervised electronics and social media are included. They are also prone to spontaneous risk-taking behavior. If a child says "let's make a ramp" either a cast or stitches are soon to follow.

Adolescents possess a lust for freedom and power that is almost always beyond their maturity and level of responsibility. In addition, teenagers have under-developed brains in which decisions are made that are often based on heightened emotions and distorted thinking. By this time adolescents have often also mastered the art of manipulation that can lead parents to poor decisions. If family issues exist they will usually peak here and will show themselves in teenage overconfidence and rebellion. An underdeveloped brain that is especially typical in male teens often causes him to be unable to foresee danger. This cognitive problem in both males and females causes youth to falsely believe they can escape the consequences of poor choices that they know apply to others. This tends to encourage illegal activity, drug and alcohol usage, and sexual experimentation.

A Case Study

She was 15 years old with a bohemian flare and dyed pink locks. The teen sat in my office, slouched in defiance, and took a generally hostile stance toward her mother and me. This mid 30's mom dressed like a teenager in strong opposition to her daughter's Goth black. In a dramatic manner, this divorced mother recounted to me how the youth had spent eight years with her father in Florida, but had lived with Mom for the last year. Since living with the mother this teenager had started drinking, become sexually active, had been arrested for drugs, often snuck out of the house, and had started skipping school. A question that immediately formed in my head and one that in time I intended to ask was, "How had she been able to get away with this?" Mom had no other children in the home, but had started classes two nights per week at the local community college and regularly dated. Her work schedule required that she leave home in the morning before the daughter. "She has a cell phone, so I check on her a lot", mom told me. This family had many issues, but one that quickly leaped out at me was a lack of supervision. No one was keeping regular and constant tabs on this adolescent. The teen had tremendous freedom and time where no one knew where she was. Mom often thought she was one place when in fact the daughter was at another place. Mom's schedule would also need to be addressed in our sessions. Moreover, without anyone realizing it, the teen's cell phone had facilitated the child's deception.

As is typical there were a number of issues that contributed to this teen's downfall. My handwritten notes contained many bullet points: family conflict that was not resolved, questionable role models, personal unresolved adult issues, inadequate supervision, and a teenager with too much power. Moreover, evidence was that mom's personal goals and romantic life were the priority over her daughter's wellbeing. The question now became: would the parent and child each be teachable? What many moms and dads fail to realize is that for families to improve their functioning, it is often necessary that parents make as many *or more* changes as the children. In order to guide this teen and her mother in the right direction it will be necessary to take back the freedoms given to this child. This will surely be a battle since all her friends have these inappropriate freedoms, not to mention that the youth now believes that she is entitled to them. Convincing mom of these necessary adjustments may be as hard as convincing the child.

Is a High Level of Supervision Unrealistic?

Is it really possible to know 100% of what your child is into? No. That would require that you watch them eyeball-to-eyeball all day and all night; and that simply is not possible, even with one child much less multiple children. But you can know 95% of what they are into with accurate speculation concerning the other 5%. Even this is a challenge, but a manageable one.

I mentioned before that parents need to know EXACTLY where their child is, what he is doing, and who he is with at all times. **Admittedly this takes much time and energy, but is necessary to protect and guide a child.** This includes one-upping the child when necessary. As the child attempts to deceive, parents must think one step ahead of him. As the child continues to increase the deception, parents must persist and continue to successfully out-do him. The final step is that it becomes such a hassle to deceive parents he gives up, or the privilege or freedom he is enjoying is eliminated all together by parents. Junior's strategy is to discourage parents by expending more energy or out-thinking them. If this occurs, however, the child will be the real loser since he will get his way and endanger himself. Parent's lack of supervision creates an open door for problems that parents for which must accept responsibility.

This also begins with an environment of honesty that starts early. **Total honesty in all situations should be the norm in your family.** A family culture of honesty that is modeled by parents will trickle down to the children. But, even small examples of dishonesty such as obtaining a child's ticket price for a 13 year-old will go noticed by children and will give implicit permission for them to be dishonest.

I often think that when Scripture advises us to be as wise as serpents and as harmless as doves (Matt 10:16) it is directed at parents. A snake makes excellent use of his sharp-sighted, cunning, craftiness. He is aware, alert and keen. **Parents must also be sharp-sighted, keen, and aware of what is going on.** Like a mother who is tuned-in to the most subtle of weeps from her baby in another room, we must maintain an attentiveness that keeps our children safe. While we savor the idea of alertness to a baby, as the child becomes older it is easy to become cynical, suspicious, and jaded. This is especially true of teenagers. We can come to think the worse of our children, even to the point of *causing* a negative outcome. I regularly encounter adults who believe that all teenagers are alike: rebellious, flippant, and deceptive. Consequently, Scripture also tells us to maintain the innocence and harmlessness of doves. As parents we must maintain a positive, pleasant demeanor toward our child. We expect the best from our children, but keep our eye heavily peeled for anything less. A healthy skepticism toward even the most honest of children is wise.

While the wayward teenager portrayed previously can be viewed as an exception, most all children at some point will make an attempt at deceiving their parents since it will mean increased privileges, freedoms, or material goods. **A parent's ability to know what their child is into *must* be at a higher level than the child's ability to deceive the parent.** CHILDREN CANNOT HAVE THE ABILITY TO DECEIVE PARENTS. In families where there is successful deception the reverse is present: the child's ability to get over on the parents is at a higher level than the parent's ability to know what their child is into. Parents must do whatever it takes to gain the upper hand including networking with other parents, checking out the exact content of movies, having a working knowledge of the child's friends and their parents, and a strict dropping off and picking up procedure.

In most families where a teenager is repeatedly and successfully deceptive the problem usually started many years ago when the youth was a young child. The deception went unnoticed and/or uncorrected, and when combined with higher order thinking and increased skill through practice, can evolve into extreme behaviors including drug and alcohol usage, major school problems, sexual behavior, and criminal acts. High levels of supervision virtually eliminate these deceptive behaviors, and if combined with other emphases of this book such as parental respect and a close relationship, the odds of deception are even further reduced.

What many parents fail to recognize is that it requires certain prescribed circumstances to get away with stealing candy from a store. It takes a certain set of predictable conditions for a teenager to be sexually active. Repeatedly using a cell phone after hours necessitates certain circumstances. For a child to successfully have incomplete homework night after night requires certain factors in his environment. **It is these conditions and circumstances that *must* be eliminated for appropriate supervision to exist in a family.** If parents can be preemptive, they can usually eliminate problems even before they happen.

This mean that parents must adjust schedules accordingly, make child the necessary priority, and refuse to deal with junior in a naïve manner. It also means making whatever sacrifice necessary to reach the level of supervision necessary. Children are likely to resist, if not dramatically protest this level of accountability. This must not deter parents or effectively push them away.

Let's Get Specific

I recommend supervision in six specific areas:

1. Friends

Even before adolescence, your child's group of friends will have a very powerful influence on him/her. In fact, your child will likely *become* his/her friends. These friends will also introduce your child to ideas, pictures, language, music, television, movies, and lifestyles, as well as other friends that may all have harmful consequences to your child. Parents may also have a false confidence in numbers concerning children. By conspiring together, the wrong friends can team up with your child to more effectively deceive you. Somehow parents tend to believe two teens more than one in such things as where they are going, what movie they plan to see, and what they have been doing for the last four hours. Statistically the opposite is true: unsupervised, children tend to engage in more inappropriate behavior when there is more than one because they believe that the responsibility for the action is divided among them. It is only through increased supervision and a proven track record of honesty that parents should trust their children's friends. **Your child's friends should be everything you want your child to be,** *especially trustworthy.*

2. *Media and Electronics*

Recently I walked into our living room to hear Sponge Bob declaring, "I'm gonna kick your butt even harder." This example, albeit small, is not innocent. The images your child is exposed to can have a lasting effect on him/her. Consequently, these images must be positive, wholesome, and beneficial. The media has an enormous effect on the culture…a culture in which children and teenagers want very much to be a part. Children simply want to conform to the behavior, standards, and knowledge of their peers. Unfortunately much of what kids want to conform to is detrimental. The media regularly glorifies evil, gives extreme emphasis to physical appearance, downplays positive character traits, excuses irresponsible behavior by Hollywood, and portrays parents as outmoded, ineffectual losers. Increasingly the media has been focused on destroying the innocence of children for their financial gain, and parents *must* be privy to their ways. Areas to be mindful of include movies, television, music, concerts, Internet, and magazines.

3. *Activities*

Anything that your child *does* will affect him in some way. As a youngster my cousin and I spent the night with one another, stayed up late, and put together model airplanes. In decades past family entertainment including things like playing the guitar, reading, playing board games, or quilting. Today there is an incredible recreation and entertainment focus that is often shallow and objectionable, and leaves children over-stimulated but under-satisfied. While once a small part of our lives, entertainment has now taken on a life of its own, consumes most Americans, and has evolved into something done to us rather than something we invest in and profit from. This new approach is not all bad, but it can represent a lack of wholesome simplicity in which the intensity must be ever increasing to be satisfying. Activity can also become something that comes *between* family members rather than something that *unifies* them. For example, a child isolating himself for hours playing a video game is far inferior to a family game of cards.

Anything a child does or might do must be known by his parents. By the preteen years this becomes even more important since now the child can make a decision that can potentially affect the rest of his life. It is here that a child can take drugs, become pregnant, run away, and consume alcohol, all of which can have permanent consequences. **Parents must have *full knowledge* of any activity, interest, or pursuit engaged in by their children.**

4. Privacy

A boundary is an invisible line between you and everyone else. It establishes the extent to which you will get into another person's world and they will get into yours. Privacy is an appropriate way to keep others out of your world verbally, visually, electronically, or in terms of physical touch. However, when children are alone and enjoying appropriate privacy they then have the ability to deceive adults including the areas of stealing from family members, outside communication, inappropriate or illegal behavior, self-harm, running away, drug or alcohol usage, or sexual behavior. It becomes a tight rope for parents to walk and one in which teens can effectively hold parents hostage. My approach is one of privacy *with* verification. A teen who consistently demonstrates himself forthright and trustworthy should be granted privacy. If, however, that privacy is taken advantage of in the smallest way it should be decreased for some amount of time. I also advise parents to allow children to close their bedroom door when changing clothes, but to otherwise keep their door open. **Our obligation to keep our children safe supersedes our child's right to privacy.** Regardless of your son or daughter's age, full information about your child is not nosey, interfering, snooping, or prying. *It is good parenting.*

5. Appearance

An intricate part of the culture in both adults and children, is in the way one looks, including hair, makeup, and clothing. Additionally, teenagers are developmentally immature such that they are egocentric believing that everyone is focused solely on them. This, in turn, causes them to be hyper-sensitive concerning their appearance. Moms and teenage daughters regularly go toe-to-toe whenever it becomes time to shop for clothing, and with good reason. It is not just a battle of wills; it is a legitimate search for clothing that is affordable, appropriate, and fashionable. Finding the unique combination of all three criteria can be a bona fide scavenger hunt.

The marketing of vanity has been very successful in America, and children are leading the way. Manufacturers of hair care products, clothing, and cosmetics would like nothing more than to foster pride and conceit in your child and compromise your son or daughter's character development since doing so will increase the company sales. Clothing manufacturers have become increasingly and intentionally seductive in their designs. Some clothing chains promoted directly toward teenagers even shamefully focus on and promote a sensual and entitled lifestyle. These stores and manufacturers are somehow at peace with trading the sexualizing of our children for their hefty bank account, a deal parents must refuse to make. It is not necessary, however, for children to wear potato sacks in order to be appropriately covered. However, many parents are not sure what constitutes appropriate.

What I have discovered is that females find it difficult to see their clothing and appearance the way that males do. Consequently, what females believe to be fashionable males often find sexy. Go to any high school or college campus and the observer will quickly see that sexy is the norm. Without realizing it, young adult females can objective themselves by their clothing or lack of it. What these females are not cognizant of is that in relationships, how a girl markets herself determines the kind of boy she will attract.

This sexy norm should frighten all mothers into soliciting Dad's or older brother's opinion when selecting clothing. Secondly, it is helpful to better understand and to stay clear of what is sensual. **Two useful criteria are: 1) the more skin the more sensual, and 2) the tighter the outfit the more sensual.** Consequently, moms and daughters should strive for modesty and be mindful of these two criteria, lest their child be a stumbling block to male peers or even grown men.

High status is also important as evidenced by ordinary jeans commanding outrageous prices. Makeup usage can be excessive and should also be monitored. I recommend makeup be an earned rite of passage that begins very slowly at about 12 years of age. It should be moderate, enhancing existing beauty rather than depending on it to *be* the beauty.

6. *Whereabouts*

As a child, Halloween was surpassed only by Christmas. The thought of playing my favorite character, getting legitimate permission to act foolish, and run from block to block by myself at night gathering enough candy to make me sick many times over was a dream come true. I have heard others adults state that their standard family rule when they were a child was "be home before dark" or "be home by the time the street lights come on." Whether these practices *ever* represented satisfactory supervision is debatable. What is clear is that in today's world parents could not allow a child to be adequately supervised with that much freedom. The world is simply a more threatening place today than in the past. This requires that parents know where their child or teenager is at all times.

Supervision Stratagies

1) *Maintain a Strong Relationship with Your Child.* This one strategy will decrease problems because it will increase honesty in the child, as well as a desire to associate with parents. A strong relationship eliminates a child's reasons to be deceptive or avoid home.

2) *Look at and make direct eye contact with your child many times each day.* By looking at the child you know what he is doing. You also are letting him know *you are aware* of what he is doing. It has been said that the eyes are the window to the soul. Unless the child is extremely deceptive, direct eye contact gives the parent opportunity to detect dishonesty. When a child makes no eye contact, limited eye contact, or very brief eye contact, something is probably going on.

3) *Connect with and monitor the emotional state of your child.* Many children and teenagers are depressed, overwhelmed, angry, grieving, or sad for many months without their parent's awareness. Consequently, parents cannot address the problems being experienced by the child. Parents must daily monitor their child's range of emotions since this is a good barometer of the internal state of the child. This includes facial expressions, energy level, body posture, hygiene, and mood that combine to give an overall picture of the child's emotional state.

4) *Keep your child fairly close to home and limit the number of outings by the child.* Children often seek a constant emotional high due to either immaturity, expectations from the past, or in order to cover up emotional difficulties. Children, and especially teenagers, can actually become

addicted though conditioning to the adrenaline high they receive from constant activity. Teens also often have an entertainment obsession or expectations of a lifestyle of non-stop partying. Limiting outings promotes a bond with parents and other family members, exposes problematic issues in children, helps monitor adrenaline dependence, and serves to limit and control the bond with friends. Parents should allow the child to have friends and social interactions both at home and away from home along with increased freedoms as the child gets older. Teenagers, however, can begin to form emotional dependencies on friends that are inappropriate and detrimental to the child. Limiting the number of outings also instills a proper balance in their entertainment and activity level. Even wholesome outings can strain a proper balance on a teenager's life or prevent needed relaxation.

5) *Carefully screen your child's peers and their parents.* It is not enough to know your child. Parents must also know the friends with whom your child associates, as well as those in charge of the friend. While you may have firm limits, others may not. Children can be put in dangerous situations, be exposed to provocative images, and be minimally supervised while in the care of another parent. You child's friend can be into many harmful practices that can then put your child at risk. Do not apologize to other parents for being cautious. Say "no" until you get to know both the parents and the friend thoroughly.

It is surprising how many parents will take their child to a friend's house, meet the parents for the first time, and drop off their child. The parent then leaves with almost no knowledge of the character of the other parent, entrusting the safety and supervision of their child to that unfamiliar parent. When parents put their faith other parents who are untrustworthy, bad things happen to children. We *must* make an accurate assessment of other parent's integrity and stability. **I recommend knowing another child's parent for at least one year before allowing your child to go to their house.** During that year, a competent parent sees the other parent many times, in numerous settings, and has an abundance of conversations of varying lengths. This establishes an overall picture of the character and stability of the family.

6) *Limit your child's power.* Monitor and limit your child's ability to deceive you. This includes any device with which your child can communicate with others or allow information to enter your home, such as phone, cell phone, Internet, and iPod. I regularly treat teenagers in my office who talk on their cell phone many hours per day, make calls at 3 a.m. to unknown friends, chat on the internet with total strangers, or download the most violent, sexual, and contemptible music imaginable without their parent's knowledge. One sixteen year-old once told me she text-messaged over a thousand times per day. All of these examples represent a waste of time, potential danger, and excessive levels of power.

Small amounts of influence and control can be given to children, but increased levels must be earned upon successful use of low levels of power. **To give higher levels of power to a child who has thus far demonstrated irresponsibility is foolish.** Moreover, it will likely increase the danger to the child. Children at all ages should be required to be responsible *first*, and then receive the desired freedom, privilege, or material possession. Parents who give the privilege first with the promise from their child of responsible behavior will find themselves betrayed. Giving an irresponsible child privileges only gives him better tools with which to be irresponsible. Chapter eleven contains a more thorough discussion of children and power, as well as the accompanying tools.

7) *Control heavily the child's use and exposure to media.* Parents must control both the amount and type of media in the home. Television and video games, for example, must be monitored in terms of both the number of hours of played/viewed and the specific game/program viewed. With a lax, amoral society, everything must be under suspicion. Several different web sites give good guidance and commentary, as well as specific content of every movie and DVD that is available. Internet usage must be accompanied with parental controls and/or filters. Magazines should also be monitored as objectionable pictures and philosophies can enter your home and your child's mind. A television in a child's bedroom offers convenience for parents and an electronic nanny, but is a bad idea since it gives Junior great access to inappropriate images and indoctrinates the child to a television addiction.

8) *Keep your eyes and ears open for any sign of a problem or potential problem.* Ineffectual parents see bad signs and believe it to be a phase, or they believe it will go away on its own. Anything that does not smell right probably is not and needs to be checked out. When things do not seem quite right, investigate regardless of the age of the child. When a child knows that his parents are will to investigate incidents and go to whatever length necessary, incidents decrease. Address issues sooner rather than later as later guarantees that the problem will bigger in magnitude and become a more deeply engrained behavior pattern.

Years ago when our second child was about 4 years old we began to notice she was sneaking cheese from the refrigerator. We heard the crinkling of the plastic covering as she unwrapped the slice of cheese. We heard the refrigerator door opening and closing. We noticed cheese missing from the refrigerator. These were all signs that something was going on. We could ignore these signs or pursued the signs. The reader would probably agree that a young child snitching cheese is a small event…..almost comical, but the deception it represents, as well as the lack of accountability if we had not addressed it, is significant. Moreover, these problems would surely have grown if she had not been held accountable. The important issue is that we were alert and aware, and were willing to pursue any inconsistencies or anything unusual in the home.

As mentioned earlier, some parents believe firmly in their teenager's "right to privacy." They therefore, close their eyes to notes, e-mails, and phone calls of a suspicious nature. Unscrupulous teenagers then use that against their parents to shield themselves from parents knowing too much and limiting the teen's behavior. These parents falsely believe that the supreme principle is their child's privacy and in effect naively jeopardize their children's safety and well-being. I have read many teen journals that declared suicidal intentions and suicidal pacts, not to mention drug usage and sexual activities: all information that would keep the child safe, and in some cases alive if the parents knew. Privacy is an important principle of respect, but this principle is superseded by the parent's duty to protect their child, even from themselves. This does not mean sneaking around or entrapping a child, but being open to knowledge and information that may prevent a child from being harmed. Know early and address promptly. Preventing problems is always preferable to correcting problems, and knowing early is better than knowing late.

Not Oppression

It is important to bear in mind that we are not talking about oppression. Nor does supervision imply hovering over a child or a lack of freedom. To the permissive parent this chapter may sound like a bearing down on a child that is tyrannical. To keep a close eye on and limit the freedom of a child may seem like a domineering approach to parenting. Cages are meant for animals, not children, and children should experience all the freedom they can handle.

We often use the word "strict" to mean oppressive. Oppression is characterized by keeping a child from flourishing, growing, or improving in some way. Oppression is keeping a child from something good. **Proper supervision, however, is the opposite. It seeks to *promote* good things, but also *protect* the child from harmful things.** Supervision is not oppression, but a high degree of monitoring and safety that ensures the child fully enjoys life.

Good supervision also involves the removing or keeping of various influences from the child. Censorship has become not only a buzz word in recent years, but a term that evokes one's rights to do and see what they want and to expose others to the same. While censorship can apply to the public's right to information that concern or affect them, the word also has an "anything goes" connotation. Those who have children must realize that kids go through developmental periods in which exposure to a harmful stimulus can have a permanent and detrimental effect. There is such a thing as too much too soon. While parents must be careful not to insulate the child such that their boy or girl to becomes ill-prepared for the world, less is generally better than more. **The best approach is one of slow exposure to the evils of the world that are age-appropriate, with parents always close by as a safety net to protect, explain, and interpret.**

Feedback

We have videos of numerous birthday parties of our five children with many different themes over the years that bring back fond memories. During the time frame that the movie *Beauty and The Beast* was in the theaters, our middle child had a birthday complete with that theme. On her cake was a plastic Belle figurine that stood about five inches high and tested the limits of my daughter's self-control. We have her on video tape clandestinely reaching over to remove the figurine, gazing at the camera to see if it was OK to do so, and then slowly retracting her hand without the figurine. Over the course of about ten minutes the video captures her going through this routine four times!

Children *must* have feedback. They want it and they need it in order to develop a realistic perspective on the world. Children normally and habitually engage in some behavior and then seek out their care-giver for feedback concerning the behavior much like my daughter on her birthday. At times they will also explore their environment for a moment, and then return to the care-giver for feedback in what is termed a home-base approach. Comforted and gaining new insight, they will then set out to explore again, and the ritual continues. Though most easily thought of in terms of toddlers, children and even teenagers behave similarly. It is often the case that our teens will go to the mall in an afternoon, or to a school dance, and upon returning home will want to discuss it and get an adult's perspective. This desire for feedback by teens and preteens is a good sign typically indicative of accountability and trust in parents.

Feedback is defined as information relayed to the child concerning the truth of a behavior, thought, idea, or feeling. As mentioned in a previous chapter, parents define reality. If we define it correctly we will likely have a happy, well-adjusted child. If not we will have one who will be perplexed, under-developed, and eventually have to figure out the world on his own.

Feedback gives approval or disapproval of a behavior, thought, idea, or feeling. Feedback confirms or disconfirms it. When a child looks to his parents for this feedback, he is asking, "Is this OK?" "Am I on track?" "Am I thinking about this correctly?" "Is this feeling valid?" "Is this action going to hurt me?" "Is this idea a good one?" With clear answers the child will feel secure and function in the world effectively. It is imperative that children be given accurate and almost constant feedback concerning every aspect of the child. But how is this done?

The most common form of feedback is verbal. Simply stating your assessment of their behavior, attitude, idea, or feeling works very well. For some parents this will mean an increase in communication. For small children especially, this will mean almost minute-by-minute verbal communication. This is only part of what is exasperating about having a young child. As the child becomes older, somewhat less communication is required, but remains very important as you continue to instill a frame of reference into the child. Beyond the problem of inadequate perspective on reality because of little feedback, another problem exists. Inadequate feedback toward children can instill an eschewed perspective in the child, but there is another problem.

Is Feedback the Same as Criticism?

Parents must realize there is a difference between feedback and criticism. Children will often feel hurt, angry, or just blow off the feedback from parents if it is not dispensed wisely. Teenagers are especially sensitive to feedback, often interpreting it as criticism and reacting sharply. The goal is to give the necessary parental perspective that prompts changes in the child's actions, but leaves the self-worth of the child intact. **Successful feedback will result in the child understanding a correction of him while maintaining a love for him.**

Teens must not feel disapproved of, condemned, or judged for them to accept parental feedback. It is the parent's job to carefully evaluate and assess, but moms and dads must target the behavior, not the child. When this loving appraisal is combined with the strong relationship described in chapter four the feedback becomes even more palatable. If, however, feedback is given angrily, aimed at the child personally, or is harsh and void of any relationship, the child is likely to react dramatically. This is especially true concerning the culturally important elements to a teen such as music, dress, movies, etc. If clearly given in love, parental points of view will be listened to and heeded. After the feedback, always offer a gesture of encouragement such as a smile or pat on the back to further clarify that the comment was not an indictment on the child, but on a particular behavior of the child. Lastly, it is helpful to give negative feedback in private, but positive feedback by way of compliments in public.

Tacet Approval

We attended a large church in Fort Worth when we lived in Texas. I had been a musician in high school, enjoyed it, and joined the orchestra at our church. As we were handed music each week, there was one word I hated to see on the sheet: TACET. That word meant that I would not being playing for this entire piece of music: I would be silent. As parents, our silence can instill confusion in children, but our silence can also give implied approval for a behavior, especially if the behavior has its own rewards built in.

As a teenager I lived in rural Suffolk, Virginia. We had a set of neighbors that were a young couple with two girls that were about six and eight years old. I was interested in cars and so was the father of this family. Consequently, I went to his house once or twice a week to visit, talk cars, and affirm one another's testosterone. These were very nice people but in hindsight very permissive. Their two children would turn their living room into a gymnastics competition that would rival the Olympic Games. The girls would jump from the sofa to the love seat to the matching chair and back to the sofa. All they needed was judges holding up score cards to complete the scene. Mom and Dad would pause briefly and then go about their business with nothing to say concerning the living room Olympics. Even as an immature teenager I can remember thinking: what is wrong with these kids?

What was wrong was that these parents inaccurately defined reality. Since no one had given these children the feedback that jumping on furniture is wrong, the children assumed it was acceptable. The feedback that should have begun early in the lives of the children was non-existent. This was enhanced by the fact that to the kids, jumping on the furniture was great fun, and consequently self-rewarding. **Not addressing a behavior that is inappropriate, but desirable to a child, guarantees the behavior will not only continue but probably increase in frequency.** By giving *tacet approval* these parents conveyed that jumping on furniture is acceptable behavior. This behavior was then likely to affect these children's safety, overall self-control, and sense of assumptions. Ultimately the children would need to re-learn acceptable behavior in this area. But, too little feedback is not the only potential problem.

Feedback from Children

This book has emphasized good listening and communication skills with children. But, how much credibility should parents give to the preferences and opinions of children? Years ago I worked with a single mother with a very disturbed 8 year-old son. The boy was developmentally delayed and presented with a blank stare and sad expression much of the time. The perpetually troubled look on his face was testimony to what he had been exposed. I observed the child several times but worked mostly with the mother. Over the course of many months I learned about the functioning of the family. The mother lived with several brothers in their 20's that had typical young adult male tastes in entertainment. Among other questionable choices in movies was *Friday the Thirteenth*. In their audience as these young males watched this horror movie was the child, who was four at the time. The boy then began requesting the movie, to which mom regularly obliged trusting his judgment and wanting to avoid conflict. "He liked it," mom explained to me in one counseling session as I questioned the movie choice. The child eventually became obsessed with the movie, watching Freddie Kruger multiple times daily. Over and over through the years the child was traumatized by the blood and gore of disturbing images of killing and dismembered human bodies.

In a similar manner, I will often suggest a parent use timeout or a similar discipline measure. More than once the parent will respond to me, "But my child doesn't like it."

This begs the question: do we as parents accept the preferences and feedback of children. If a child reports enjoying something, is this the "go-ahead" to provide more of it. Is a child's personal enjoyment the criteria for acceptance or approval? If a child *does not* like something does this mean we eliminate it. Can we trust the evaluation skills of our sons and daughters?

Feedback from children is a positive thing. It represents communication, as well as an opportunity to affirm the thoughts of our kids. But, **children often report that they like things that are unmistakably bad for them.** Movies that push boundaries, television that is too mature, songs that are inappropriate, friends with authority problems, and clothing that is too revealing are often judged as acceptable by kids. Children also often report they do not like things that are good for them such as hard work, getting up early for school, and punishment for bad behavior. The internal compass for most children is: 1) their misguided perspective based on selfishness, 2) what pleases and impresses peers, and 3) the cultural standards of the time period. All of these standards are extremely unreliable and likely to expose the child to too much too soon.

Then there is another aspect of the thinking of children that I call the *titillation factor*. This refers to the fact that children tend to pursue anything that excites or stimulates them at a high level. This is the fascination of teenagers with roller coasters; except roller coasters do no harm. **Most any provocative, adrenaline producing, sensual or fear-based stimulus will arouse curiosity and grab a child's**

senses. This is part of what makes pornography so damaging. Once a teenage boy sees an erotic image, for example, it is so visually and mentally pleasurable that it borders on an instant addiction. It is this kind of titillating, erotic, or shock images that send the brain into orbit, damage the character, and create an immediate hunger for more. It is the exposure to this kind of stimulus that parents must guard heavily against.

Parents must be cautious in relying on the evaluations of their child. **Children are not equipped for issues of evaluation of most any kind where there is *potential* danger.** This includes people, the media, freedoms, electronics, and character evaluation of others. This, in a nut shell, is what parents are for: to make decisions for children that they are incapable of making. However, harmless preferences that are safe can give a child decision-making practice and build confidence, while maturity, self-control, and character are being cultivated. For example, given the choice of two suitable movies or two appropriate outfits of clothing, a child gets practice making decisions, gains confidence, and learns acceptable standards. The standards children instinctively use must be replaced with a criterion that supports character. Therefore, moms and dads should listen, but must always maintain veto power with firm guidance in the home.

Overparenting

I lived in Virginia Beach in the late 1980's. On the north end of Virginia Beach was a hard 90-degree turn that came abruptly and caught many drivers by surprise. In fact, this one short stretch of road caused concern for the city as the number of car accidents here was unusually high. Signs were erected in both directions warning drivers of the upcoming dangerous curve, but the problem became worse. A careful study of the road immediately before the curve revealed that there were no less than thirty-six road signs coming from one direction alone. Drivers were supposed to watch the road and concentrate on driving while reading, comprehending, and complying with each of these 36 signs. Because of sensory overload, drivers simply ignored *all* of the signs but quickly entered perilous conditions as they approached the curve too fast.

Children can feel this way too. Feedback is important and necessary, but a balance must be achieved. While some parents constrict their communication and provide too little feedback, others overdo a good thing. Parents must guard against verbal reactions that are irritatingly continuous. It is possible, especially in young children, to comment, criticize, and respond non-stop all day long, and if you are an especially talkative adult this may be tempting.

This overparenting is tempting because the nature of small children is that their limit-testing, immaturity, or selfishness rears its ugly head almost constantly and cries for attention. But, if every one of the smallest episodes of immaturity were constantly addressed it would create a very unpleasant atmosphere. Moreover, as with the drivers in Virginia Beach, the child would simply begin ignoring all adult comments including the especially important ones. This is especially true if combined with a lack of enforcement. I am not suggesting parents ignore bad behavior. I am suggesting that feedback be reasonably moderated by addressing your main concerns, as well as balancing your commentary with positive comments.

Chapter Five Discussion Questions:

1. As a child or teenager could you get over on your parents? How? How easy was it?
2. What three W's define supervision? Is this realistic? What is the link between supervision and safety in regard to children?
3. What would your parents have to have done in order to supervise you better as a child and keep you safe?
4. Describe why it is necessary for parents to be "wise as a serpent and harmless as a dove?" What are some dangerous possibilities when a child has the ability to deceive his parents?
5. Name the six areas of supervision? How might each of these be detrimental to your child if not monitored? Which of these six areas would be the most challenging for you as a parent?

SUPERVISION AND FEEDBACK

6. Why would a close relationship with your child aide in supervision? Why is controlling media an important aspect of supervision?

7. How does the chapter define oppression? Did you have strict parents?

8. How would you define feedback? Why is feedback toward children important?

9. Define tacit approval. Have you witnessed tacit approval in another parent recently? As you observed that parent, what was the result in the child? How does tacit approval as a parenting style affect the child's behavior?

10. How does the nature of children affect the false feedback they often give parents? What is a recent example of feedback from your child that you chose not to trust?

CHAPTER 6
Guidance

Children are puzzling creatures of paradox. They often want one way but need another. They state one position, but send out messages to the contrary. Your child may say, "I hate you" but actually hates something entirely different. Your teenager daughter may say, "I don't want to talk about it" but desperately desires a conversation that clears up her restless confusion.

One of the contradictions during this time is that children and teenagers are constantly sending messages that they do not want parental intrusion. Whether it is a toddler slurring out "I do it" or a youth who is focused on excluding his parents from his life, children reject the help of adults. At the same time, **children seem to have an unconscious knowledge that they are naïve, over-confident, and immature, and regularly want parents to intervene and love them enough to teach them and prevent them from self-destruction.** Sadly, many parents respond to the rejection by withdrawing the very support through guidance that children must have to survive. Their children become effective at pushing Mom and Dad away through a variety of means that ultimately harm the child.

Truett Cathy, the founder of Chick-fil-A, says "Children all around us are growing up without strong positive guidance from their parents, who are busy, absent, or who choose to be buddies instead of parents to their children."[1] Anyone would be hard-pressed to find someone who would disagree with this statement. Absent or preoccupied parents are extremely common; and yet, we all find inadequacies easier to recognize in others than in ourselves. Having described the supervision of children and the importance of supporting your children with feedback in the previous chapter, we now turn our attention to more direct intervention.

---

1 Cathy, Truett, *It is Easier to Build Boys than Mend Men*. Decatur, Georgia. Looking Glass Books, 2004.

Elements of Child Guidance

Former Arkansas Governor Mike Huckabee says, "My father disciplined me patriotically. He laid stripes, I saw stars."[2] Obviously I am not advocating abuse. What I am promoting is firm, leadership in the home. Consequently, **it is important to *actively correct behavior*.** This means addressing an issue as soon as it appears and continuing to deal with the problem area until it subsides. It also may mean being persistent with a child who may be stubborn, tenacious, and may have learned that if he outlasts his parent he will get his way. Strong leadership in the home that instills confidence and clearly conveys who is in charge will produce children who are personally secure. They know that their parents will do what is necessary to establish proper boundaries and protect all family members. On the other hand, parents who institute weak leadership, allow themselves to be manipulated at every whim, or who give their children more power and freedom than their maturity and responsibility dictate create insecure children who are likely to put themselves in dangerous situations.

Parents must provide firm, decisive, leadership! Children can smell a crack in your lack of confidence a mile away. Children will play on your emotions, your guilt, or your sympathy. Children can be manipulative, dramatic, quibble, demand, negotiate, resist, and compare your family to others. This requires that parents set firm limits.

One thing I have observed over the years is that the nicest people can have the most difficulty in leadership and parenting. This was true of a fifth-grade teacher I once had. She loved children and was a good teacher, but a very nice person who let the class run over her. I remember the class daily taking advantage of her kindness with endless chattering and throwing spit balls. Despite the chaos, she rarely called us down and never enforced it. The frustration on her face indicated she recognized the pandemonium, but she did little to address it. She lasted several months and then resigned. My classmates and I never saw her again.

Nice parents have a hard time setting a firm limit and following through with enforcement. When they do enforce a rule appropriately, they are prone to renege on the punishment. Hence, a week of grounding becomes two days' worth and a 10 minute timeout becomes 5 minutes. **Nice people often feel guilty when they enforce rules.** They feel like they are being mean to the child, when they are actually providing good leadership. These parents may need to see their discipline more objectively, and rely

---

2   Mike Huckabee speech, West Des Moines Hotel, Des Moines Iowa, 27 December 2007.

less on their own subjective feelings as a guide to their parenting. Sometimes we forget that God has unconditional love and acceptance of us, but not unconditional approval or favor.

A firm limit means that a well-thought-out standard with the individual or family's best interest in mind is clearly established with sure consequences if violated. Consequences will be more fully discussed in the chapter on obedience, but let's address the other aspects of firm limits.

First, **guidance should be normal part of the family functioning**. Deuteronomy 6:7 tells us, "Impress them on your child. Talk about them when you sit at home and when you walk along the road, when you lie down and when you get up." When should you provide guidance to your child? The answer is: all day, every day, in every situation, with every conversation. Child guidance is not a special emphasis, nor is it only to be used when there are problems. Guidance should be the default, the norm, the typical mode of operation of the family. There should scarcely ever be a time when you are *not* guiding in some direct or indirect way.

Second, **avoid basing decisions on emotions.** Many parents base their parenting judgment on whatever they are experiencing at that moment. The emotional highs and lows felt by some parents dictate whether permission is given for a myriad of privileges. Equally as bad, many parents deliver a habitual and mechanical "NO" barked out as if generated by an involuntary reflex. This reaction is likely to lead children to their own emotion-based decisions. These reactions will also result in children who simply stop communicating with their parents. How can we expect our children to rationally think through their decisions if we as parents do not model it for them? A pause should follow a child's verbal petition while the parent gains more details of the request, weighs the pros and cons, and considers the maturity and responsibility level of the child. Then a firm decision should be made with no opportunity for negotiating.

A third issue is that of what is truly good for the child. **What a child wants and what is good for him are often two different considerations.** Parents should strive to say "yes" while being on guard to manipulation and the selfish nature of children. While parents cannot completely prevent bad things from happening or protect a child from all the evils of the world, many problems are predictable. It is the parent's job to foresee danger of all kinds and eliminate it from their child's future. Ask yourself questions such as, what is in the long-term best interest of my child? What will grow and mature him into making good decisions as well as protect him, but not hold him back from beneficial events? Will exposure to this truly help or hurt my child?

Fourth, what about conflicting goals? At times one family member's goals will conflict with another family member's. The greater good must always be sought here. In some cases the importance of one individual's goal outweighs the other's. Again, parents must carefully consider all aspects of the decision and then stick to that decision. Rarely is it prudent to reverse a decision because it implies instability, mounting emotions, or weak guidance. Typically, only with new information should a parents change their minds, a rare scenario that may otherwise suggest inadequate initial processing or information gathering.

Structure

Children also need the consistency of structure. This is achieved through a set schedule that is followed throughout the day. Children should have a predictable schedule each day with which they can count on. This includes wake-up time, getting dressed, meals, school, church, bath time, and other age-determined events. This regimen will also serve to shore-up family emotional security.

Consistent rules are another important part of structure. In some homes:

a) A rule one day does not apply the next day
b) Mom's rules do not correspond with Dad's rules
c) Or rules are situational.

For example, we obey this rule now, but when Mom is on the phone we do not have to obey it. Children will not only be confused, but are likely to exploit the situation to their own advantage. Rules must be consistent across situation, days, and between parents. This usually requires practice and a commitment to apply a standard every time.

It also requires that Mom and Dad be on the same page in their household rules. Businesses, whether large or small, must focus in a single direction if they are to be successful even though various managers or board members differ in points of view. It may be a surprise to the reader to hear that it is *not* necessary that Mom and Dad think alike or agree on every parenting approach. However, **they *must* present a united front with their children having agreed to a particular rule or decision they will both adhere to.** It is imperative that parents support one another publicly in a single decision even if they disagree privately. Parents who bicker with one another and engage in power struggles over their discipline direction will find their family chaotic, the children inappropriately offering their own opinions, and with divided loyalties toward Mom or Dad.

With a regular schedule and firm rules in place, it is important to remember that your goal is consistency, not rigidity. The purpose of the regulation is to serve your family, not the family serving the regulation. There is a time for all schedules to be altered. There is a place for all rules to be flexible, but this should be the exception. The normal course of events on any given day is that of appropriate structure. Strict, stern, and unyielding approaches to parenting will likely result in rebellion, but, a lack of firm rules will produce a loose, weak family system that flounders in attempts to find direction. Firm rules, structure, and clear communication are necessary parts of guidance and should be put in place in every family.

Sibling Rivalry

It's been said that one child makes you a parent, two make you a referee. With multiple children, a family is guaranteed to struggle with senseless competition. **Sibling rivalry usually involves two children making enough noise to triangle a parent into the conflict with each child having the goal of winning.** That noise typically includes complaining or tattling about a brother or sister. Mom or dad must then decide if the tattling is legitimate. Parents must also decide the extent that they want to reward the snitching behavior. Some tattling is necessary in that a child may be in danger or is hurting someone. Parents need to know about these situations and must take action. The line of demarcation is if the information from the child is for the sole purpose of being malicious. This can include general unkindness, revenge, mean-spiritedness, or inciting conflict.

The Bible is full of families with problems not unlike those of today, including sibling rivalry. Cain became jealous when he believed God was favoring his brother Able. The hostility became so intense that Cain eventually murdered his brother. In one of the more dysfunctional families in Scripture, Jacob and Esau were each favored by different parents such that they competed intensely. On one occasion, Jacob tricked his brother out of his inheritance. Leah and Rachel competed for the affections of the same man: Jacob. And Joseph's brothers became so jealous of him that they sold him into slavery.

Unnecessary competition between brothers and sisters is based on the selfish desire to win that is not likely to wane soon. Many adults continue to engage in hostile competition with their siblings that began decades earlier as a pattern in childhood. However, several principles can work to lessen sibling rivalry, both short and long term. First, parents must create an overall atmosphere of teamwork and unity within the family that includes praise for cooperation. By exclusion, teamwork cancels out at least some competition. Siblings can even work on a project or task together where they must join forces, accommodate one another, and generally unite in order to accomplish the task. Parents may even assign specific tasks among two children who are especially high in rivalry.

Second, work hard to ensure equity among children. The selfish perspective of children promises that they believe parents are favoring the other children over them. Trying to convince them otherwise may have mixed results. This is likely to be a maturity and perception issue within the child, not reality. In some families, however, favoritism *does* occur and causes animosity among siblings. This hostility and bitterness typically increases adolescence and can continue into adulthood. Attention, discipline, and parental responsiveness should be the same among all children.

Third, let children handle their own conflict as much as possible. Quickly stepping in and resolving sibling conflict is tempting since it stops the fighting parents despise, but it teaches little other than how to triangle parents into their battles. Also, much of conflict and rivalry is about one child winning while the other child loses. The immaturity of children virtually guarantees competition. **Parents should refrain from the role of referee in this competition as much as possible since this role determines a "winner" and offers no incentive for the children to manage their own conflict.** If the children are not successful at resolving a specific conflict, step in and give them a reasonable time limit for resolution. Explain that when the specified time is up your decision will ensure that neither will win. This gives them a time table and an incentive to resolve it peacefully, while removing any motivation to argue or compete. When children catch on that attention-seeking conflict will result in a lose-lose situation, they are more likely to regulate the problem and solve the conflict themselves.

Arguing

Once a good parental decision has been made and the decision is communicated clearly, your children will gratefully and fully meet the terms of your request. Not likely! There *are* compliant children who are quick to obey without opposition, but they are rare. Moreover, it will be the very same tenacity that defies you that will also stand up to opposition and temptation when he is older. Consequently, over-compliance is not necessarily a good thing. Some resistance and independent thinking can be good and is often the foundation of great leadership or achievement in adulthood. In the midst of bantering with a pint sized defense attorney, however, it is hard to remember this.

When I poll parents in a group as to how many of them have a child who like to argue, I typically observe a sea of hands. Most children argue as yet one more extension of their selfishness. **Despite being an enormous problem, parent-child arguing is an almost totally controllable problem.** In some areas of parenting, moms and dads bring on problems without realizing it. Arguing is one of those areas.

Arguing is the unproductive communication between adult and child in which each attempts to coerce or manipulate the other into an action or point of view. It is perhaps the most common form of resistance. Further, much of the benefit of a close parent-child relationship is nullified by arguing. The first rule for parents concerning arguing is: *no arguing!* Your first thought was likely that the last statement applies to children, but it applies to moms and dads also- in fact, even more so. Parents must *not* argue with children, ever, in any situation!

If the intensity begins to increase within a conversation between any two random individuals, to which either person makes a conscious decision not to argue there *cannot* be an argument. The same can be said between parent and child. In other words, for a parent and child to argue they must both cooperate and implicitly *agree* to argue. Parents do not verbally decide to squabble. No parent says to their child, "I insist that we argue intently twice a day." But, by their *actions* they agree to argue. **Without a parent's behavioral agreement to argue there can be no argument.** Since children are selfish and immature, however, and arguing might just be the process that gets them what they want, it will need to be the *parent* that makes the decision not to argue. This clearly illustrates that 1) we should expect children to argue since it coincides with a child's nature, and 2) we as parents have the power to control our children's arguing.

Look back at the definition in the first sentence in this paragraph. Do you see something wrong with the adult aspect of that definition? The words *coerce* and *manipulate* should have caught your eye. In arguing, the adult is striving to convince or persuade the child into something when it is often the child's advantage *not* to be persuaded. From the child perspective, being convinced means I have to comply, and I do not want to comply. Hence the battle begins!

Arguing is about a competition of opposing forces. Good parenting is about the child's compliance to his parent's instructions with consequences matching his response. **It is only when there is an assumption on the part of both parent and child that negotiation is possible that arguing can ensue.** It is the false assumption that there is equal authority between parent and child that initiates arguing, when their authority is *not* equal. It is only when there is an unspoken understanding between parent and child that communication is a competition that one actually ensues. It is these assumptions that we as parents must change.

Arguing also validates and reinforces the child's quarreling. It sends the message that the child has something to argue about. It confirms the child's statements, no matter how selfish, erroneous, flawed, or illogical. It substantiates childish nonsense, and the attention it receives acts as a reward.

Romans 14:19 states, "Let us therefore make every effort to do what leads to peace and to mutual edification." Many passages in Scripture admonish us to live in peace. Families are not excluded from this goal. Mom and Dads must take specific steps to promote harmony in the home. Refrain from rolling your eyes at this point. This can be done; not that you can easily overcome the immaturity of your children. But, parents can model and teach peaceful coexistence that will produce results long-tern.

Assumptions in Arguing

There are number of foundational assumptions by mom and dad when a parent and child argue:

1. *My decisions are negotiable.* If so, they are not decisions. A firm, decisive parent makes decisions.

2. *Parenting is a battle of the child's will against the parent's will with the loudest or more intense person the winner.* In many homes there is a strong competitive quality to the parenting. Parents and children are on opposite sides in a continual quest to "win" rather than a sense of team in which all family members are going in the same direction. Should a competition of volume determine family decisions?
3. *Mom and/or dad can be manipulated out of a decision.* Should children have the capacity to manipulate parents out of decisions?
4. *Every point or comment from a child needs a response.* As we will soon see, not every question or comment from a child deserves a response, especially if it is manipulative in nature.
5. *If I do not argue my child will win.* Not necessarily. In fact, at a deeper level if a child "wins" he actually loses.
6. *My child and I are equal in authority.* Arguing is about two equal counterparts hashing out issues much like a debate match. This dynamic should never be present in the parent-child relationship. The way the parent relates to the children, speaks authoritatively, enforces decisions, and generally carries himself/herself, should convey the unspoken assumption should be that the parent is clearly in charge.

Avoid the Prime Causes of Arguments

First, differentiate discussions from arguing. Discussions are calm, respectful, dialogues that take place before the decision. Discussions are rational conversations relatively void of emotions in which each person considers the other person's thoughts. Discussions are progressive in that there is positive, productive movement within the conversation. Arguments, on the other hand, are competitive, intense, and disrespectful to one or both individuals. Arguments often get stuck or cycle through the same points, and continue past the point of a decision. In arguments individuals listen with the goal of refuting the other person's thoughts. Also, in parent-child arguments the child refuses to accept the decision of the adult. If the discussion begins to take on the characteristics of an argument, the parent must end it.

Once the rule or decision has been made there should be no more discussion. **The discussion takes place *before* the decision is made, not afterward.** Parents then *calmly* state the decision with an *optional* explanation of the rule. (God is not obligated to explain everything to us. We must obey regardless).

Second, do not take the hook. Children are like skilled fishermen with effective and specialized bait aimed at you, the parent. They are surprisingly good at reading mom or dad and using bait unique to the situation and parent. Regardless of the particular bait, it is a statement or accusation made by the child that pushes your buttons, puts you on the defensive, and often starts an argument. Consider the statements below levied by a child:

"The divorce is all your fault!"

"You don't love me!"

"You're mean!"

"So you're saying I'm stupid?"

"You let HIM watch TV why can't I?"

How would the reader respond to these accusing, somewhat disrespectful statements? Most parents would launch into a defensive rant that would last twenty minutes. Or they would spend inordinate amounts of time trying to convince the child that he, the parent is correct, or that he (the parent) loves the child. In all of these situations the child has thrown out the bait and the parent has bitten into the hook and been caught, and an argument is the results. **Parents must *not* take the bait!** The most effective response the above statements is either no response or a brief response such as "That is not true."

Third, many arguments begin out of an attempt to talk a child into compliance. Parents often beg, plead, whine, and grovel for their child to do everything from homework to chores. Not only does this undermine a parent's authority, it is a poor, ineffective practice. In fact, I believe most parents talk excessively in discipline. **Promoting and fostering the relationship requires a high degree of verbal communication, but discipline or correction does not.** When correcting, make fewer words count rather than a lecture you child will likely ignore anyway. To avoid an argument, a more effective strategy is to state the rule, decision, or command in a manner that conveys authority. Many parents make the mistake of giving their child instructions in a weak-willed, unconvincing manner suggestive of the child doing the parent a favor. This is contrary to the firm authority promoted throughout this book. If the child does not comply then consequences should be implemented. More on consequences in chapter nine.

Specific Stratagies to Stop Childish Arguing

1. *Refuse to argue.* Reject the idea of bantering back and forth in a competitive manner that implies you and the child are equal, or that your instructions are negotiable. A child baiting you into an argument does not necessitate that you take the bait.

2. *Keep communication calm.* Be aware of your own volume, tone, body language, and eye contact that convey unnecessary intensity. Do not match or compete with the child's intensity. Allow your calmness and composure to inspire your child to lower his intensity. Harshness or yelling will only give the child permission to be equally out of control.

3. *Carefully think through decisions.* Clearly state the rule or decision and possibly the explanation. You are not obligated to explain, and it may be counterproductive to do so.

4. *Continue the discussion as long as it is productive and progressive.* Stop the discussion if any disrespect, intensity, or lack of benefit or productivity occurs. Parents must not continue to make the same point repeatedly or attempt to convince the child of the decision.

5. *Redirect the child if he becomes disrespectful.* Parents cannot tolerate disrespect. The child is now becoming frustrated and upping the ante making it even more important the parent holds his ground. The child may be acting disrespectful because arguing has been successful in the past but is unsuccessful this time.

6. *Restate the rule or decision if necessary, demonstrating consistency.* This is an opportunity to display stability and maturity, and fortify the child's inner security. Nothing should change simply because the child is arguing or badgering the parent. Be firm, calm, and in control.

7. *State calmly but firmly and authoritatively, "Stop arguing!"* Restate it if necessary. Do NOT respond to his statements, questions, or demands. Take charge of the conversation and focus only on the arguing! Lead the child verbally rather than him leading or controlling you.

8. *Disengage from the discussion.* Eliminate eye contact, walk away, turn your attention or move to another room. Eliminate all responses. This will halt arguing immediately since it is impossible for one person to argue by himself. During this strategy parents *can* state something like "The discussion is over" or "I am not arguing any more". I generally encourage parents to do it rather than say it. The problem with saying it is that it constitutes attention which tends to reinforce the child actions. Moreover, saying it simply contributes additionally to the argument. Should he persist by disrupting you, becoming loud, disturbing you, or impairing your functioning, you should consider this disrespect and punish appropriately. Later restore communication by conveying that you will not tolerate arguing. It is important in disengaging that adequate attention and affirmation exist in non-arguing, non-disciplinary situation. Otherwise, disengaging can be interpreted as neglect. But, with plenty of attention toward the child as a part of ordinary family functioning, the distinction is clearly made between neglect and intentionally refusing to argue through disengaging.

This is a showdown that you, the parent, must win. If the child wins, he ultimately loses since he will believe that getting his own way is important in every arena of his future adult life. He will then likely become aggressive and self-absorbed, and find it difficult to focus on others around him including his friends, and eventual spouse and children. If childhood arguing has persisted for some time, it will take strong efforts and patience to eliminate. It may also require many successful trials and one or more confrontations until this behavior is corrected. Eventually, however, if Mom and Dad are persistent little Johnny will learn that no amount of his arguing will achieve his goal. While his understanding and insight may remain immature, compliance will be learned. It is then that parents will feel a sense of accomplishment and begin to grasp that they have gained the necessary control over their child that will then guide him.

As mentioned previously, parents can become cynical or hyper-suspicious, losing the appreciation and wonder of children. This can especially be true if behavior problems have been allowed to flourish. **Moms and dads must maintain a personal sense of awe and marvel at being a parent,**

appreciate the role, and consider it a privilege. If that is lost children will become no different from a new puppy in the house to be trained. While maintaining that sense of awe about our children, we must acknowledge the immaturity and self-centered nature in children that can lead to self-destruction if not guided. Parents in their active guidance must be one step ahead of their child. Children can smell a defect in parent's confidence and then exploit with expert precision. That exploitation is known as manipulation.

Manipulation

In homes all across America there is a game being played out between parent and child. It's not Candy Land, Scrabble, or Chutes and Ladders. It is a game of cunning strategy, calculated efforts, military-like tactics, and deliberate timing. It is a game that sparks excitement, challenge, and a striving toward victory. The surprising thing is that this game is being played out sometimes by children who can barely talk. The game is known as manipulation, and although all parents would say they despise it, most are willingly engage in it.

Manipulation is identified as the use of shrewd and deceptive means to achieve one's self-centered goal. Like the innate ability to suck, grasp, and swallow, children seem to have the natural ability to manipulate. In fact, there is good evidence that it is a biologically-based survival instinct gone awry. Even as toddlers, children have wants that they realize may not be achieved unless they can out-smart Mom or Dad. One of the purposes of manipulative behavior is to gain a feeling of safety, security, or a basic human need. However, selfishness is clearly an additional motive. As stated before, it is emphatically up to adults to give children a *realistic* perspective of the world, convey the difference between needs and wants, and emphasize that we all must operate within our given resources. But, how does manipulation begin in children?

Virtually all children manipulate. Typically the child's normal selfishness prompts them to explore manipulative strategies early on, and then pursue the ones that give a hint of success. Consequently, we as parents should expect it and prepare for it. While normal selfishness *sparks* manipulation, it is success that *fuels* it and therefore perpetuates it. It is easy to understand that a particular behavior by a child that achieved a pleasurable end would be repeated. After being repeated many times, the action becomes a habit that can evolve into a regular pattern of relating not only to adults or parents, but to all individuals. Consequently, while the manipulation habits usually start in early childhood they blossom in adolescence through practice and higher cognitive skills. A child can use one manipulative act, or several, or one manipulative practice can transition into another. If manipulation is unchecked it will lead to major character flaws and relational issues. In fact, when combined with parental neglect or other relationship inadequacies it can result in clinical personality disorders.

More commonly, however, manipulation is often left unaddressed and produces numerous negative effects upon the child as he moves into adulthood. Shades of these negative effects can often be seen in young children long before adulthood. These include:

a) Losing friends because they wise up to the cons
b) A blurring of lines in the child's own mind between reality and fantasy
c) A continued use of manipulation since it is the only way known to relate to others
d) The disintegration of a healthy conscience
e) Difficulty in accepting responsibility
f) An increase in depression and self-esteem issues

General Strategies to Decrease Manipulation

Since manipulation is fueled by success, it is only when the child experiences a *lack* of success that the fuel source is cut off and parents will observe the manipulation decreasing. Consequently, **the key strategy in manipulation is that it *not work*.** If it does not work for the child it will disappear, or at least stay at a low level. If it is successful it is guaranteed to continue.

This means that parents must be at least as cunning as the child and able to identify incidents of parental exploitation. Parents must recognize and even label in their own minds manipulation techniques that children themselves cannot identify but may use regularly. Once identified, the particular manipulation practice should be brought to the attention of the child to help him in his understanding.

Parents should not be lulled into believing that this new insight on their child's part will translate into changed behavior, however. Understanding is good, but it is not the ultimate goal of parents and not enough on the part of the child. It almost always requires that parents take specific *action* as well to squelch manipulation. Generally speaking, parents must curtail the child's success in achieving his goal. For example, a child manipulates in order to get a second ice cream. If he does *not* get the second ice cream, his manipulation will decrease. If a child manipulates with the goal of getting out of cutting the grass, manipulation will decrease if he still must cut the grass. When a teenage girl manipulates in order to stay up late, manipulation will decrease if she still must go to bed on time.

Having generally outlined how to decrease manipulation, it is important to emphasize persistence. Manipulation by a child that is deeply engrained and recurring develops over a period of weeks, months, or even years. It will now take time to reverse these behaviors. It may also be the case that efforts have been made in the past to change the behavior but the child has been able to prevail. This may now add an additional feature to the degree of difficulty in modifying the behavior since both his persistence and his knowledge of circumventing your efforts have been profitable. **It is *imperative* that parents surpass the determination and shrewdness of their child.** Without the fortitude, awareness, and skill concerning manipulation, the parent will be out-gunned and the child will be victorious. With a general knowledge of manipulation, let's now look at some of the specific techniques children and teenagers use, some examples, and how the handle them.

Thirty Most Popular Manipulation Practices by Children

Read the description of the manipulation practices below. In some cases it may be necessary to read the description more than once to fully comprehend it. Examples are included for clarity. For further understanding of manipulation problems in your family, the reader may want to place a check beside any items that you have observed in your home.

1. *Believing your own fantasies/lies.* This child assumes that if I think it, it must be true. Or, if I said it, it must be true. This type of self-deception is usually brought on through ruminating

on the particular thought until the self-deception is complete. This is dangerous because it blurs the line between fantasy and reality in the child's mind such that even *he* is eventually confused.

EXAMPLE: Ten year-old Matthew was playing with a ball in the house when it knocked over and broke a lamp. His mother ask Matthew if he did it, but the son lied and said no. Since all evidence was that the boy broke the lamp mom continued to press him. But Matthew continued to hold his ground such that he now actually believed he did not break the lamp. Without accountability or consequences, this became the foundation of a pattern of Matthew believing his own lies from this incident forward.

2. *The "Huh?" technique.* Either "huh" or "what" said immediately after a question or statement by an adult meant to buy time in order to think up the best answer rather than the honest answer. It is intentional and calculating at first, but becomes automatic over time as deception increases. The automatic nature of this manipulation technique can be recognized by the "huh" eventually being said even before the parent's statement is finished.

3. *Pushing adults away.* Several techniques used to discourage, intimidate, and drive away adults. These techniques can include talking in a loud volume, sarcasm, threatening stares, threats of aggression, condescension, or an intimidating posture. This can also include the child being flippant and dismissive (as in "whatever") and the use of the hand in the adult's face.

4. *Manufactured dramatics.* This practice is meant to add impact and emotionalism to a statement made by the child such that it is more convincing. Numerous dramatic displays including anger, crying, overreacting, yelling, cursing, pouting, general reactionism, temper tantrums, physical complaints, frantic demands, playing sick, storming off in a huff, a crisis perspective, acting bored or uninterested, a catastrophic point of view, flamboyant, colorful facial expressions, and arm-waving and other body language are used to generate tension. Children can become highly skilled, Oscar-winning performers if their end goal is achieved.

EXAMPLE: Sixteen-year-old Cheryl became upset and cried when told she could not go to the football game Friday night. She spent the next two hours yelling, pacing, and pouting. Not wanting his daughter to be disappointed, and feeling bad over his original decision, her father recanted and told Cheryl she could go. This new pronouncement eliminated Cheryl's dramatic behavior.

5. *Martyrdom.* Used to convey the great extent to which the individual has sacrificed for the other in order to elicit sympathy. One of the potentially lesser used practices, it will usually focus on the many chores done by the child or the many nights the child has stayed home for the sake of the family.

6. *Parent splitting.* Otherwise known as divide and conquer. After attempts at a request are turned down by one parent, this child approaches the other parent in hopes of a better answer. The child's success depends on parents *not* being united and checking with one another. Children will usually begin this tactic with the more lenient parent. This can include other adults such as grandparents and teachers.

7. *Withdrawing.* A child self-distracts in any number of ways including looking away, playing with fingers, or fiddling with anything handy when communicated with in order to sidetrack his own thoughts, and reduce attention and compliance. A higher level of self-distracting involves the child removing himself emotionally or physically from the conversation.

8. *Making false promises.* This child "swears to do better" in anything from grades to chores with no concrete plan to do so in hopes that the parents will later forget the promise. The child's empty assurance of "I'll try" depends on the crisis-based thinking of the parent. Success of the child in this technique is also dependent on mom or dad forgetting about the issue once the parent's emotionalism is wanes (i.e. once Mom calms down the problem magically becomes a non-issue and is no longer discussed).

9. *Covert non-compliance.* Also known as under-the-radar disobedience. Rather than outward defiance, refusal, or rebellion, this child does not put up a fight. Rather this child simply avoids, delays, procrastinates and does what he wants in a sneaky, inconspicuous manner. There is the unspoken assumption in many homes that obeying a parental command is

optional. The child may even cunningly schedule an activity or engineer circumstances that support his non-compliance.

EXAMPLE: Though his mother was sure he did not want to, Joey gave no response to being told to take out the trash. He just intentionally never did it, so Mom took out the trash.

10. *Passive-Aggressive.* Getting back at a parent or adult through a lack of cooperation, pleasant resisting, or deliberately inconveniencing the other person in some way.

EXAMPLE 1: Sixteen-year-old Jane was furious at her mother for taking her cell phone away. In order to get revenge, Jane made her Mom wait thirty minutes in the car while she talked to her boyfriend after school even though the pickup time was prearranged.

EXAMPLE 2: In order to inconvenience his father, eight-year-old Joseph took twice as long to pick up his blocks as he usually does.

11. *Dumbing Down.* Acting mentally dull, unintelligent, or incapable in some way to reduce personal responsibility or get out of a duty or task.

EXAMPLE 1: Though he had done it before, ten-year-old John acted as if he did not know how to make his bed in order to get out of making it.

12. *Perseverance.* Asking the same question over and over, or using 'please' repeatedly until the desired answer is achieved from the parent. Sheer volume of talking is this child's best weapon. Child success here depends on tired, weary parents who can be worn down easily by the child's superior energy. Impulsive, quick, negative responses by adults also increase the likelihood of manipulation as the parent will often feel guilty over saying "no" even though it was the best decision. This also plays on parent's excessive guilt, over indulgence, soft-heartedness, and lenient tendencies.

EXAMPLE:

Daughter: Can I spend the night with my friend?

Mother: (quickly barks out) No!!

Daughter: (with hands clasp together) Please, please. I won't ask you for anything else.   Please, please, please.

Mother: (feeling guilty) OK, go ahead.

13. *False Regression.* A child acting younger or immature than her/her age in a cute and endearing manner. Different from true regression that is a reaction to excessive stressors or trauma in the child's life.

    EXAMPLE: Six-year-old Emma was otherwise mature and articulate. But, when she wanted ice cream she turned her head in an adorable, juvenile way and stated, "pweeese can I hab some ice kweem?"

14. *Quibbling.* A distraction from a point by arguing on a minor, irrelevant but related point, while emphasizing on the stupidity of the adult.

    EXAMPLE:

    Father: Last Wednesday I told you to get the large garbage bags from the garage, take the new rake, and begin raking the leaves on south side because that's where the leaves collect the worst.

    Son: No, it was Tuesday.

    Notice the child's focus on the irrelevant point while correcting the inaccuracy of the adult. This throws off the thinking of the adult and usually creates anger and defensiveness in the parent that, if displayed, can make the parent appear even more incompetent.

15. *Comparisons.* A focus on what other children have, places they are allowed to go, and things they are allowed to do, falsely emphasizing the overprotection or oppression of the parent.

    EXAMPLE: Fifteen-year-old boy: "Why can't I have an ipod? My friend has one…and he gets to go to the mall by himself too."

16. *Partial compliance, temporary compliance.* Intentionally carrying out part of the request of the parent, or carrying out the request for a limited time. This creates thinking in the adult that "I can't fully punish him because he did some of what I asked." Note the deliberate aspect of this practice, that the child knew how to do the task, and the fact that the child understood the expectations. Parents must also be careful that one occasion of lack of accountability or lack of consequences sets a precedent. It is at this point that children will often state, "I did it before and you did not say anything."

17. *Overstating/Exaggeration.* Overplaying, embellishing, or magnifying a point beyond reality in order to achieve a goal. This often includes using the terms "always" and "never" to overstate a position.

18. *Being charming or seductive.* Acting especially polite, flattering, sensual, pleasing, affectionate, complimentary, cooperative, or alluring in order to create false impressions or achieve leniency.

EXAMPLE 1: A home has a rule that the children may have no caffeinated drinks after five o'clock. At 7p.m. twelve-year-old Billy thoughtfully brings his mother a Coke along with one for himself. Mom is impressed with Billy's kindness and says nothing.

EXAMPLE 2: Some teenage girls physically cozy up to Dad and tell him how nice he is to achieve their goals.

19. *Playing the victim.* A child falsely emphasizing how the parents have persecuted, picked on, or generally mistreated him in order to gain sympathy. Victims can muster great power against their (false) perpetrator using this manipulative technique.

20. *Blaming.* Refusing to take responsibility for your own actions, decisions, or attitudes with the goal of releasing you of responsibility. This can also include accusations by the child with phrases like, "You don't love me." "You hate me." "You don't trust me." The purpose is to lay blame anywhere but where it belongs- with the child. A variation of blaming is deflecting. When confronted with an irresponsible behavior, this child quickly brings to your attention that someone else did the same thing, seemingly to absolve this child of the responsibility.

EXAMPLE:

Dad to twelve-year-old son: You forgot to pick up your clothes in the bathroom after your shower.

Son: (with intensity pointing to his sister) Well so did Cindy!

21. *The "Why" technique.* Asking the question "why" intended to challenge the authority or competence of the adult. Disguised as a seeking of understanding, it initiates arguments in which the teen will refute every point made. Parents often feel obligated to answer 'why'

and get baited into this manipulative practice. Typically children do not care why but use the word to push back and resist compliance.

22. *Disagreeing with rule or request.* Argumentatively opposing a rule under the false assumption that a child must agree in order to comply. Children must comply regardless of agreement, or understanding of rationale.

    EXAMPLE: A teenage boy to his father: "I'm not cutting the grass, it doesn't need it! It doesn't make sense to cut it every week!" Dad, feeling dejected feels he must agree with the son and the grass does not get cut.

23. *Red herring technique.* Distracting the adult from a point by focusing on an unrelated point.

    EXAMPLE:

    Mother to son: "I need you to take the trash out."

    Son: "Can we go to Wal-Mart; I want to look at iPods."

    Notice the child cleverly did not respond to what the adult said. Instead he ignored the mother's point, brought up an entirely different point, and was able to shift her attention away from the trash.

    Another form of this manipulation practice is that of doing something good in order to achieve something bad or disobedient.

    EXAMPLE 1: Dad told his teenage daughter not to go out of the house all afternoon. When dad came home at five o'clock he found that the daughter had helped their elderly neighbor plant flowers. Nothing was even said to the girl. The "kind" act of the daughter became a distraction from her willful, intentional, and probably strategic disobedience.

    EXAMPLE 2: Eight-year-old Billy was procrastinating and working slowly as he performed his homework when his mother walked into the room. He got up and went to hug her legs affectionately. This pleased the Mom who embraced him not recognizing the hug was a manipulative one that further allowed the boy to delay doing his homework.

24. *Self-serving interpretations.* Interpreting or inventing understanding of a rule or instruction that benefits the child. This is a twisting of words and ideas such that assumptions are made that are suspiciously in line with the desires of the child. This also includes not asking

permission to do something, but simply assuming it is acceptable. The child then acts on those false assumptions. Children then often become very convincing such that parents begin to question themselves and what they *did* say.

EXAMPLE 1:

Child: "Can I go to the movies tonight."

Mother: "Maybe, let me talk to your father about it."

Child: (later) "I'm ready to go; the movie starts in twenty minutes!"

A version of this technique is the child's use of the statement, "It's not fair." Success using this manipulation practice depends on the adult allowing the self-centered child to define what is and what is not fair, as opposed to a more mature and objective standard of fairness established by the adult.

EXAMPLE 2:

Child: "Can I go with you to the store."

Father: "No, I'm in huge hurry this time."

Child: (accusing) "That's not fair!"

Father: (disgruntled & controlled by the child) "Alright, come on."

25. *Misrepresent with half-truths.* Different from a full-blown lie, this technique mixes honesty with dishonesty in order to achieve the goal and avoid the full penalty of a falsehood. The child often leaves out the more objectionable aspects of a story, and hence avoids being forthright. This leaves only the more positive aspects of the event to be considered.

EXAMPLE: Brittney told her parents she was going to the library to study. While Brittney did briefly study at the library, she also met her friends at the park and went to Starbuck's afterward. When she got home four hours later, her father asked her where she had been. Brittney's response was, "the library."

26. *Holding parents hostage.* The child making strong demands or refusing to comply. This is accompanied with stated consequence to mom or dad that the child will carry out if the demands are not met or if the child is made to comply.

EXAMPLE:

THE TWO SIDES OF PARENTING

A child says, "If you make me do "A" I'm going to do "B."

A= do a chore, go to school, go to bed, come out of my room, go to church, etc…

B= run away, have sex, kill myself, hold my breathe, cut myself, etc…

-OR-

A child states, "If you don't let me do "C" I'm gonna do "D."

C= use the cell phone, use the internet, stay up late, see my boyfriend, go to the mall, etc…

D= run away, have sex, kill myself, hold my breath, cut myself, etc…

27. *Bogus Bargaining.* A child making a deal that lowers the penalty for their irresponsibility. A variation on bargaining involves a child promising to perform some chore if allowed a certain inappropriate privilege. In either case the chore/task may or may not get done.

EXAMPLE #1: Eight year-old Marci received two F's in math recently. Her mother grounded her from entertainment activities until the math grades improved. Since she liked several Disney television programs, Marci pleaded with her mother successfully to let her watch TV by promising to fold laundry.

EXAMPLE #2: Fifteen year-old Rachel wanted to download R-rated "Cannibal Holocaust" to watch during her sleep-over that weekend. Knowing that it was a violent horror film, her mother emphatically stated no. But, Rachel bargained that she would clean the entire house if her mother allowed the movie. Finding the benefits of a clean house too tempting, mom reversed her decision and allowed Rachel to download the movie.

28. *False Remorse/False Guilt/False Apologies.* Acting in a regretful way without being sincere. This is usually done by the child without the composed peace of mind that true repentance brings.

EXAMPLE #1: A flippant teenager says "sorry!" in an obviously insincere manner then quickly asks for money.

29. *Junior Attorney.* A child who pleads his case fervently, persistently and endlessly attempting to negotiate, make excuses, and debate to achieve his goal. This is usually displayed by intelligent or well-practiced children.

30. *Shame-inducing, guilt trips.* Making statements that lead a parent to potentially feel guilty for real or imagined mistakes in order to achieve a goal.

    EXAMPLE: Twelve-year-old girl to her mother: "It's your fault I can't have new jeans! You got a divorce and you got new shoes last week too!"

Parent Responses that Make Manipulation Worse

Parents are often unsure what has happened when their child has manipulated them. They feel disrespected. They sense that the child got the best of them. They feel violated in some way, or they feel their authority has been undermined. But, how it came to pass is unclear. The interaction may have happened so fast and they felt so backed into a corner that it was difficult to think clearly. This lack of understanding then leads them to respond in a way that is at least unproductive, and may even exacerbate the problem.

1. *Over-Reaction.* This involves escalating the conversation quickly in tone, volume, and intensity. It usually results from a parent's frustration or panic in not controlling the manipulation of the child. It is usually fueled by easily heightened emotionalism in the adult.

2. *Under-reaction.* This does not refer to ignoring the behavior or extinction (to be discussed in chapter nine). This involves a lack of taking the necessary and reasonable actions that hold a child accountable. Failing to do so allows the child to be deceptive and get his way. Ultimately this child will be exposed to a host of harmful elements that repeatedly spell danger.

3. *Over-responding.* This involves a constant barrage of verbal responses that overwhelm the child while eliminating behavior-altering consequences toward the child. This also removes much of the choice from the child through over control, that if allowed to would shift the child away from manipulation.

4. *Unrealistic expectations.* Bad behaviors rarely go away quickly, they die a slow death. Consequently, a parent's expectations should be that changing a particular manipulation

practice will take a while. Even if caught early, children will often attempt the same technique again to give it a second try.

Parent Stratagies to End Manipulation

As stated earlier, the best overall strategy is to prevent manipulation from being successful. By insuring it fails there will be no incentive for it to continue.

1. *Confront the manipulation.* Armed with the knowledge of the thirty manipulative practices mentioned, you should be on your way to identifying them in your children. An excellent way to take the power out of a manipulation habit is to name and expose it to the child. Deceit of all kind detests being exposed to the light of day, but it is exposure that reveals the motives and truth of manipulation. Moreover, there is an excellent chance that the child himself has not labeled or defined it though he may practice it regularly. Providing the words and language to the child will give him the feedback and tools he needs to develop an understanding himself and life.

    EXAMPLES:

    "You're acting dramatic"

    "Don't apologize if you don't mean it"

    "What other children have is irrelevant"

    "Stop parent splitting"

2. *Refuse to respond.* Having identified the manipulation as the parent (badgering, the drama, or other technique), do not respond to the request. Allow the child to waste whatever time he chooses using whatever technique he chooses *without success*. The child *must not* receive the payoff of successfully manipulating the adult. Reinforcement and punishment techniques will be discussed in another chapter; suffice to say here that any attention or other reward given by the manipulation will cause it to be used more by the child. As a parent, be hyper-attentive to *any* payoff or reward to the manipulation that will perpetuate it.

3. *Hold the child accountable.* In clear imperative terms look the child straight in the eye and state, "Stop manipulating." This should not be yelled, the child should not be cursed at, and no fingers should be waved in the child's face. Should the behavior continue it may be necessary to include a punishment when the child manipulates. A lack of success for a child, however, is typically enough to squelch it. Include with "stop manipulating" a second statement, "Tell me what you want without manipulating or trying to deceive me." This promotes a more direct communication of requests. It will also be necessary for parents to have the ability to detect any rule violations or behavior that is not permitted.

A Final Word

The recommendations outlined in this chapter are very challenging, as is all of parenting. These ideas take an almost constant focus even by the most well-practiced parents, and even higher levels of concentration by parents who have difficulty with discipline. This must not shame or discourage mothers and fathers. Parenting is a skill like throwing a football, carpentry, or playing the violin. Parenting skills come from a variety of sources such as what was modeled when the adult was a child, formal education or instruction, inborn ability, and intentional practice. **The difference between parenting and other skills is that a child's future stability in life is at stake.** This makes playing the violin a fun hobby, but learning good parenting skills *mandatory.*

Deuteronomy 21:18-19 says, "If a man has a stubborn and rebellious son who does not obey his father and mother and will not listen to them when they discipline him, his father and mother shall take hold of him and bring him to the elders at the gate of his town." Who are "the elders at the gate" in this 21st century? It is anyone who is willing and able to help. This could include a next-door neighbor, a grandfather, an uncle, a Sunday School teacher, a church deacon or elder, a pastor, a professional counselor or family therapist, a psychiatrist, or a social worker. In some cases family members can be extremely helpful. An understanding grandfather, for example, can be the quiet stability or firm leadership that a young boy needs. As a boy with a neglectful father, my uncle stepped in to encourage and provide the masculine example I needed. In other cases, however, family members can be critical, overconfident, know-it-all, and intrusive individuals who offer far more advice that is wanted. Sometimes extended family members are astonishingly confident and verbal in their advice, but do a poor job of their own parenting. Depending on the severity of the dilemma a professional may be necessary to accurately assess the problem, make recommendations specific to the issues, and teach the parents more effective ways to deal with the child.

Since not all counselors are equal and not all counselors understand child management issues, it is best to seek out an individual who specializes in parenting. The best way to discover this person is by asking several people who have had a similar problem, talking to a pastor for a referral, or calling a mental health facility. This should give you several names you can call to gather more information and narrow your decision to one counselor. Even then it may not be a good fit. There should be a therapeutic alliance (a bond of confidence between you and the therapist) that develops within a few sessions in which change can be observed. There should also be a sense of competence from the therapist indicated by confident, concrete recommendations that have an air of predictable effectiveness. The child should display some reasonable "warming-up" to the therapist, though this can take a while given the child's level of defiance.

Parents must be ready to change in many potential ways. It is also important that parents and therapist evaluate the marital relationship since that is frequently intertwined with children's behavior issues. At the risk of overwhelming the reader, in some cases it is also necessary to deal with past unresolved conflict of Mom or Dad from their family of origin.

Chapter Six Discussion Questions:

1. In your own words, how would you describe firm leadership in the home?
2. Do people think of you as a nice person? Has this caused challenges in your parenting? How?
3. Are you or your spouse more prone to emotion-based discipline? What is typical outcome in your family? What helpful tip would you offer an emotion-based parent?
4. How would you define structure in a family? What are the benefits of structure to children?

5. What specific strategies does this chapter suggest to parents in decreasing sibling rivalry? To what extent do you promote your children resolving their own sibling rivalry relative to their age? Do you think the problem of sibling rivalry be completely eliminated? Why or why not?

6. With ten being the worst, how would your rate the arguing in your home 1-10. Read Matt 5:9, 2 Cor 13:11, Ps 34:14, Col 3:15, & Rom 12:18. What would peace realistically look like in a home with children?

7. What arguing assumptions from this chapter have you bought into in the past? Which strategy for stopping arguing would be the most difficult for you?

8. Do your children ever bait you by pushing your buttons and putting you on the defensive? How does the chapter suggest a parent handle this? Do you ever attempt to talk your child into compliance? How does the chapter suggest a parent handle this?

9. What two ideas in this section did you find most helpful in decreasing arguing in your family?

10. Explain the link between manipulation and the nature of children. What is the single most effective strategy in eliminating manipulation in children? Of the thirty manipulation practices listed, which two or three are most common in your home?

11. Do you have one or several individuals whom you could go to for practical advice or mentorship with a family problem?

CHAPTER 7
Limit Cultural Influences

I recently saw an amazing YouTube video of a large group of birds flying as one. Tens of thousands of birds would swoop in one direction and then another in a choreographed wave that was mesmerizing. The birds were highly in sync, cooperating and reading each other's every move as if they were one entity. There seemed to be great pressure on each individual bird to follow the group. Never did I see one bird stray from the enormous cluster. As I watched the mass of birds I wondered if this served a purpose. Protection perhaps? What if the group of birds flew into danger? What would happen if the birds were flying in the direction of a jet airplane? What if they flew into a mass of predator birds? Would many birds get eaten at that point?

With alarming accuracy this presents us with a picture of the environment in which children have inescapably been placed. They are part of a large number of their own kind. This group flows in one direction and then another for a specific purpose. **Like the birds that are all headed on the same precise path, there is great influence on each individual child to follow the masses.** If that direction is positive and constructive, our child benefits. But, what if the group goes in a bad direction? Will your child and mine stray from the group, or will they get eaten?

The definition of culture is a set of shared attitudes, values, goals, and practices that characterize a group of people. This group can be of any size. The United States, the Midwest, California, a city, a community, and your family, are all groups that possess different attitudes, values, goals, and practices. For the purpose of this book, we will consider the national culture and its effect on children.

LIMIT CULTURAL INFLUENCES

Parents tend to think that all culture is good if it is approved by an authority or has some educational value. A closer look tells us that there are good and bad parts of the culture. The worse parts of our culture are shallow, materialistic, egocentric, ungodly, narcissistic, superficial, unrestrained, sensual-focused, desire immediate gratification, and possesses a warped sense of values. Over several decades increasingly bad behavior and attitudes have been glorified and emulated. This is true especially in the media and especially with the rise several years ago of reality television. High levels of conflict and even physical altercations are great sport and viewed as desirable and even good. **The important thing to remember is that our culture has great potential to have a negative effect on our children.** In this last area of support (what parents give to their child) we will look at the positive and negative aspects of the culture and how they affect our children.

What are the limits?

First, as already suggested, not all culture is bad. Many areas of American cultural are important anchors by which we pride ourselves and form an identity. Aspects of food, entertainment, music, fashion, sports, and language are important parts of who we are. Some aspects of each of these areas, however, will require wise discernment to filter out the harmful features. Your children will need cultural knowledge to function. But, that knowledge should be age appropriate. **Too much too soon will destroy the innocence of your child.** The media in general and Hollywood specifically are constantly pushing the boundaries and exposing our children to more and sooner. Promotional ads for movies have gotten more risqué and traumatizing, especially romantic movies and horror movies. Commercials for various medications, treatments, and feminine and sexually-related products have become increasingly bold and uncomfortable. Ads for menstrual period hygiene, erectile dysfunction, sexual enhancement, and birth control prompt me to squirm in my seat when my children are present. Although these products legitimately improve life. They also have the potential to destroy a small part of my child's innocence depending on his age, as well as lower personal modesty standards that serve as natural barriers between girls and boys.

Second, **we must emphasize character over culture.** A prevailing school of thought is that all culture is good since it enriches the lives of individuals. This notion omits the reality that all aspects of the culture have a component of morality. The bad can enter our children's lives along with the good. Consequently, cultural information, practices, and involvement must be filtered through the standard of character.

Given the chance that you think this is a prudish position or exaggerated problem, consider the following examples:

- Most pop songs encourage early and inappropriate sexual activity. Without even knowing what is currently on the music charts, I assure you that nine out of the top ten songs (and maybe all ten) heavily promote casual and early sexual behavior, present it as normal and good, and equate it with feelings of love and romance.
- Reality shows glorify lying, cheating, gossip, laziness, spoiled and bratty behavior, and portray conflict as good. Abusive verbal confrontation and live physical assaults on television have become normal family entertainment.
- Most video games contain excessive violence. Video game creators have discovered that provocative, violent, fantasy-based, and high energy video games give young adult males an identity and consume their time. Many parents have discovered that video games make a great baby sitter. Consequently, this form of entertainment is a large and dysfunctional part of many households.
- Most movie stars live immoral lifestyles. Emotionally whole, mature, addiction-free movie and television stars that display stable committed relationships and would be good role models for children are extremely rare.
- Most women's clothing for sale is shear, low-cut, or extremely tight to promote sexuality in females. Few men or women even recognize this as inappropriate any longer because it so permeates our society and has become the norm. Sexy is the look that most teens and young adult females portray with no awareness of a problem or its harmful effects.

A Different Direction

If you lead your family in a direction away from the prevailing trends you will likely find yourself in the minority. On various issues, behavior, and modes of thinking you will frequently find yourself the lone fish swimming with a school of fish going the other direction. If the reader rejects parts of the prevailing culture, his parenting and his family will be different from most others. **This is a reality that our children must also embrace as they mature, that different can be good, especially if the outcome promotes high character.** Third John 1:4 states, "I have no greater joy than to hear that my children are walking in the truth." It is this "walking in the Truth" that will the difference between you family and others.

Another issue is that, based on the immaturity of children, there is a natural desire to fit in. Popularity is extremely important as teens and preteens begin to form an identity, seek to define themselves, and look for value and approval. It is often the case that children of this age will go to great lengths to fit in or be popular. This can include modes of dress, hair styles, ways of talking and materials possessions, and expensive items indicating high status. This accounts for the trend in expensive clothing in recent decades. It is not uncommon for a family living in poverty to buy their teenage son tennis shoes that are endorsed by a basketball pro and exorbitantly expensive. And $200 jeans are now common place in high school. Virtually any expensive item promotes high status and is desirable because it refutes personal insecurities in children and proclaims "I am better than you". It is not hard to see that this superior attitude, as well as an inordinate desire to fit in is contrary to character. Moms and dads must regulate these attitudes rather than feed into them. **Parents must de-emphasize to their child the importance of popularity and fitting in, and convey that there is a price that is too high to fit in.**

As competent parents we must:

- Recognize there are character-damaging parts of the culture.
- Prefer what is right over what is popular.
- Prefer character over culture.
- Lovingly protect, but not insulate.
- Maintain their innocence, not their naïveté.

Remember, **the goal is not to *eliminate* culture, but to regulate it and its influence.** In some cases the particular cultural aspect is so harmful is *must* be eliminated, but prudent regulation is usually the better option. Knowing when and how much to expose a child is a matter of much wisdom. It does no good for our children to enter adulthood naïve. They will be ill-equipped to function in the world if they do not have cultural knowledge. There is a difference between knowledge of the culture and participating in the culture. We should introduce various parts of the culture slowly when their age and maturity have prepared them, and while we as parents are there as a safety net for them.

A Word About Movie Ratings

In 2003 well-known film critic Roger Ebert stated, "Movies that ought to be R are being squeezed down into PG-13 in a cynical attempt to increase the potential audience."[1] Would it surprise you to learn that Hollywood cares nothing about protecting the innocence of your child? As long as your money is in their pocket Hollywood is happy. If luring your child in and exposing him to inappropriate material is what it takes to get your money, they will gladly oblige. There is no rating more worthy of caution by parents than PG-13. The lower ratings are fairly cut and dry, and relatively harmless. And few parents would take their child to an R-rated movie. **The PG-13 rating, however, contains the widest variance of material of any rating.** It spans the gamut today from an inoffensive movie which seems more like PG, to a movie that contains graphic violence and language, as well as full frontal nudity.

Further complicating the issue is that many parents falsely believe that PG-13 automatically means that the movie is appropriate for thirteen-year-olds. The movie *Spiderman*, for example, contains what is known as stylized violence, a cartoon-like exaggeration of action meant to convey a certain atmosphere. While rated PG-13, I would consider this movie light PG-13, but most movies of this rating are not so harmless.

It is hard to believe that movie ratings did not exist at one point in time. They were not necessary as those in the movie industry did a good job of regulating objectionable material. Today ratings are necessary, but can be easily misleading. While a movie rating is a good place to start it

---

[1] http://usatoday30.usatoday.com/life/movies/news/2003-07-01-pg-rating_x.htm

is a horrible place to finish. The rating gives only the basic information about a movie, as well as Hollywood's permissive, self-serving recommendation. Parents must search further for more detailed information about the contents of any movie their child wants to see. This can be done through any number of public web sites. Parents must be careful to distinguish between commentary and content. A movie reviewer's opinion can be valuable, but the question then becomes whether the writer shares the same cautious perspective and goal of high character as the parent. Specific content can be of greater value since it tells you minute aspects of a movie such as violence, sexuality, or cursing, and then lets you decide if it is appropriate for your child. There are sites that actually record the number of curse words, the number of camera shots of a woman's behind, and the number of crude bodily references. This is an advantage since it reveals the *amount* of objectionable material.

Parents must play this conservatively. Referring back to the influence of modeling- what your child sees, hears, and experiences they are likely to imitate, especially if it is done so repeatedly. Movies incorporate various philosophies of life of which our children are exposed. These movies have the potential to negatively affect children, especially if the harmful perspective of the movie is presented in a positive light as is the typical practice of Hollywood. The 2007 movie *Juno* is about quirky sixteen-year-old who discovers she is pregnant after casual sex with her best friend. The main character is fast-taking, energetic, sassy, and adventurous.[2] Juno MacGuff is presented to the audience as positive and likable. She is void of the character problems, relational problems, and enormous responsibilities related to teenage motherhood. This is typical of the movie industry to the detriment of our children. **Hollywood often takes low-character individuals, immoral situations, and poor choices and puts a humorous spin on them such that the person or situation becomes entertaining and enviable.** The movie-making industry generally promotes objectionable content at an earlier age than is prudent because they believe in art for art's sake. In other words, all (movie) culture is good. From a protective, character-building perspective it is easy to expose our children to too much too soon, while it is hard to make a mistake by limiting exposure to certain movies, especially in the PG-13 category.

---

2 *Juno*. Dir. Jason Reitman, Perf. Ellen Page, Michael Cera, Jennifer Garner. 2007. 20th Century Fox, DVD.

Frantic Romantic

We are obsessed with romance in our culture. Disney television shows depict 7-year-old girls pursuing a boyfriend, pop songs portray a preoccupation with romantic love as normal and good, and many unhappy singles are regularly on the hunt eager to bag their prey. **Warm, fuzzy tingles that are highly unreliable are the guiding force behind many relationship decisions.** A partner is presented as a need, not just a want. Short-term passion and impulsive feelings are a welcome substitute for measured investment and long-term stability. Even dedicated Christians delight in a movie displaying premarital sex if it is shrouded in a romantic setting, manufactured longings, and unfulfilled desires.

It has become the pinnacle in life for many teenagers (and adults?) to have a boyfriend, girlfriend, husband, or wife. A primary purpose of marriage is to mirror and help us understand the close, exclusive, and permanent relationship we are to have with God. Rather than *reflect* this relationship with God as He intended, it has *become* the ultimate relationship to many people. Romance has gone beyond a normal and appropriate interest to an obsession and something we now worship. And all forms of the media are the prime transmitter of this philosophy. Where did we lose our way?

An individual's romantic obsession can stem from compensation of feelings of ineptness, relational emptiness from childhood, emotional and/or financial dependence, or acceptance of romantic cultural norms. Some parents, especially mothers, gain vicarious fulfillment through their child's romantic endeavors, and may unconsciously promote romance. Whatever the case, **a neurotic pursuit of love in our children can be the foundation of poor romantic choices, sexual promiscuity, a crisis pregnancy, inadequate personal development, and short-term cycles of relationships that promote emotional damage and cynicism.** Moreover, rather than fulfillment, it is this very approach to opposite sex relationships that increase the likelihood of perpetual emptiness, even in marriage. This romantic obsession that become an ideology can begin early, consume the child, divert focus, and distract from proper self-development that would actually help prepare the child for a romantic relationship and better ensure marital success.

LIMIT CULTURAL INFLUENCES

We might argue that romantic interest in teenagers is a result of hormones. But, it is often the case that a romantic obsession begins long before hormones become apparent. Moreover, even a hormone-filled youth must control his focus and behavior. It is often the environment that cultivates an over-focus on romance beginning in childhood. This early indoctrination, in combination with negative and false expectations that "this is the way children are going to act" can have a disastrous outcome. Consequently, it is once again the environment of which we parents are in control, that teach and prepare a child, in this case for a stable, healthy romantic relationship. With that in mind, here are my recommendations:

1. *Demonstrate a healthy marital relationship to your children.* Even if not married, model appropriate relationships with both same and opposite sex individuals. Be on the best terms as possible if you are not married to your child's other parent.
2. *Connect with your children.* Fathers are especially important in affirming daughters, defining an appropriate relationship, and setting relational and physical boundaries.
3. *Be aware of and regulate sources of unrealistic romantic obsession in the media.* This includes movies, television shows, music, and books. Allow more wholesome, beneficial portrayals of romantic love.
4. *Affirm in your child a healthy level of interest in the opposite gender.* Use this as a teaching opportunity and especially focus on evaluating the character of the other person. Minimize physical attributes, material possessions, or family money since these items have no bearing on a successful relationship. Disallow any romantic obsession.
5. *Do not promote romance with children.* Parents should strongly reconsider allowing your child a boyfriend or girlfriend since this arrangement is rarely beneficial to a child, has no practical purpose, wastes time, serves as a distraction to self-development, opens the child up to greater potential for sexual activity, and is an imitation of adult behavior. The early and fanatical focus on romance that is common in children must be reevaluated in light of its detrimental effect on character and practical functioning.
6. *When appropriate allow occasional group dates with trusted others.* This can be increased slowly beginning at about 16 years old, especially as the teen grows more independent.

But, with this overall balanced strategy, a child entering adulthood is likely to take a healthy approach by taking relationships slow, being patient, emphasizing preparation and self-development, keeping romantic emotions in check, and emphasizing character in a partner.

Other Aspects of the Culture to Regulate

Aspects of the culture parents must limit or eliminate are almost endless, and that list seems to grow daily. In addition to movies, video games, clothing, and television, parents should consider magazines, books, music, clubs and organizations, philosophies and religions, toys, teen idols, stage plays, museum displays, and artwork. Several years ago Andres Serrano displayed his photographic artwork of a crucifix in a jar of urine.[3] And before his death in 1989, Robert Mapplethorpe was famous for producing taxpayer funded artwork with graphic homoerotic and sadomasochistic themes.[4] These are the more blatant displays…these are the no-brainers. It is the covert, well-concealed, or grey area that is more difficult to discern. **The wise parent takes an objective, critical look of every aspect of the child's life, what the world offers, and the effect that it has on their child.** It is the effective parent that keeps his head out of the sand, refuses to look the other way, and takes the time to evaluate aspects of the culture that affect his/her child. Good parents make it their business to invest time in knowing, and to do whatever it takes to find out. This requires that we be culturally informed and maintain our knowledge base of all aspects of the culture.

Chapter Seven Discussion Questions:

1. The analogy has been used that your child is one bird in a large flock of influential birds. What similar analogy would you use for the influence the culture has on your child?
2. Compare and contrast innocent with naïve.

---

3 http://en.wikipedia.org/wiki/Andres_Serrano
4 http://en.wikipedia.org/wiki/Robert_Mapplethorpe

3. Some feel that the evening news is traumatizing for children. Where do you stand on this issue?
4. What does it mean to regulate the cultural effects on children? Is this different from eliminating aspect of the culture?
5. Give several examples of character-damaging aspects of our culture.
6. Would you take your child to a pop music concert? Why or why not?
7. What steps do you take to control the harmful effects of movie, television, and video games?
8. Summarize this chapter's ideas on PG-13 movies.
9. Is it hard for you to be objective concerning romantic comedies, raunchy comedies, or romantic movies in general? What about action or suspense movies? Does your enjoyment toward part of a movie or television show encourage acceptance of objectionable parts?
10. The chapter makes the case that our culture is romance obsessed. What evidence cited suggests this is true? Whether from the book or your own ideas, how will you prevent this obsession in your children?
11. Is innocence something that can truly be maintained in our corrupt world? Having now read this chapter, what is your strategy in achieving this?

CHAPTER 8
Independence

English novelist Alan Garner said that possessive parents rarely live long enough to see the fruits of their selfishness.[1] The reality is that efforts to hold on to our parenting job, and hence our children, are futile. They will one day leave us. Or we will leave them through some circumstance. **The only question is how well we will have prepared them for that exodus.** How well will we prepare them for self-sufficient functioning that does not depend financially or emotionally on extended family, the government, or a romantic partner?

For some parents the idea of their child becoming independent is threatening. The notion of the son or daughter being required to think, act and operate without the parent is a scary idea! As a young child Junior can make mistakes that may inconvenience us, or cost us time or money. These mistakes are typically fixable. By the teenage years, however, the stakes change. It is at this point in the child's life that he has the potential to make mistakes that are life altering. Habits or even one wrong decision related to drugs, alcohol, sexual behavior, and/or a suicide attempt can drastically change the rest of a child's life. Most individuals who smoke begin in the teenage years with no thought that it will become a life-long habit that drains their finances and ruins their health. Again, this underscores the importance of our parenting assignment.

Ultimately good parenting consists of two jobs:

1. Instilling the highest of character in the child.
2. Parents working themselves out of a job.

---

1 http://www.sayingsnquotes.com/quotations-by-subject/family-quotes-proverbs-and-sayings-3/

INDEPENDENCE

1 Corinthians 13:11 says "When I was a child I spoke as a child, I understood as a child, I thought as a child; but when I became a man, I put away childish things." It is up to parents to help their child put away childish things and think, act, and operate as an adult. It is God's plan that our children become adults and function successfully without us. The reader may never have thought of their enormous task this way. **There needs to be a point in time that we no longer have a job.** We must plan ahead of time to support the point in time when we will no longer have the job known as parenting. We must prepare both us as parents, as well as our children for that point in time. At that point we transition from parent to mentor.

Too many parents knowingly or unknowingly, hold on to their parenting job too long, encourage dependence from the child, and effectively sabotage their child's adult functioning. We must strategize, even as our children are young, to give up the control, the life funding, and the authority that parents have. In many different ways we convey to our children the expectation of becoming independent from us, and the confidence in them that they will succeed. As a part of this, we accurately anticipate that our children will be successful at the thing called adulthood because we have prepared them well.

Admittedly there is a sadness surrounding this independence. The emotional, material, and financial investment seems anticlimactic, if not unfair, for our children to ultimately leave us, but we must grasp the profound Truth that this was the plan all along.

Wayne Watson says it well in his 1987 song *Water Color Ponies*:

There are watercolour ponies
On my refrigerator door
And the shape of something
I don't really recognize
Drawn by careful little fingers
And put proudly on display
A reminder to us all
Of how time flies

Seems an endless mound of laundry

And a stairway laced with toys

Gives a blow by blow

Reminder of the war

That we fight for their well-being

For their greater understanding

To impart a holy reverence

For the Lord

But, baby, what will we do

When it comes back to me an you?

They look a little less

Like little boys every day

Oh, the pleasure of watching

The children growing

Is mixed with a bitter cup

Of knowing the watercolour ponies

Will one day ride away

And the vision can get so narrow

As you view through your tiny world

And little victories can go by

With no applause

But in the greater evaluation

As they fly from your nest of love

May they mount up with wings

As eagles for His cause

INDEPENDENCE

While sad, there is also a liberating aspect to becoming unencumbered parents of an empty nest. This can free the parents to travel, move, establish new goals, take up a new hobby, and invest in new challenges. Those who prepare their children and themselves well can bask in the fulfillment of a job well done and enjoy the secondary fulfillment of their children's independence and successes. However, **parents that hold on to the job, that ill-prepare the children for adulthood, or that fail to anticipate working themselves out of a job will be plagued with dependent children.** This dependence will likely be financial, emotional, and/or material. This child will need many things including borrowing money, a place to stay, transportation, regular advice, and/or motivation. Because the parents did not transition the child well throughout the years effectively moving from heavy amounts of support to high levels of challenge, they must now continue to sustain the child in one or more ways. Now that the child is an adult the windows of opportunity are gone. The teachable childhood years have passed. Now the adult child must initiate and follow through with changes on his own- a task that will be very difficult.

Enmeshment

Joey and his mother were always close. In fact, when he was younger she referred to him as her little prince. The two shared a bond much stronger than this mother with the other siblings, especially after she divorced Joey's father. Even before the divorce mom would share information with this son that she would not reveal to anyone else. After the divorce mom was scared to sleep alone, so Joey slept in the same bed until his feet extended beyond the mattress. Mom was often sad and hopeless, until Joey would sit with her and cheer her up. Mom never did much disciplining of Joey, but fortunately he did not need it. As a teenager, Joey began to have ambitions of college and owning his own business. But, the mother discouraged it since it would mean turning his back on her and the family. Now eighteen-year-old Joey has no direction or interest in leaving home. He figures he and his mother will simply take care of one another.

One of the primary threats to a parent working himself out of a job is through the concept of enmeshment. Enmeshment can occur between any two individuals: boyfriend and girlfriend, husband/wife, two friends, neighbors, two co-workers, parent/adult child, etc... Enmeshment in any form is undesirable because individuals lose their unique identity and their growth is stifled. As it relates to the scope of this book we will consider enmeshment between parent and minor child. As it relates to parenting, enmeshment is a relationship between parent and child in which the two are excessively close. You may be thinking, "I thought a parent *should* be close to their child as has been emphasized in this book." Enmeshment is different.

Think of the idea of incest. As I write this, a grimace has already appeared on my face and probably on the reader's face as well. Incest is taboo in virtually every culture, and there is nothing more revolting than the notion of sex between a parent and child, but this presents an accurate picture of enmeshment. **While incest is an excessive and inappropriate *physical* relationship between parent and child, enmeshment is an excessive and inappropriate *emotional* relationship between parent and child.** It is a fusion of parent and child, an over-bonding.

An enmeshed relationship leads to many negative outcomes for the child. The root of enmeshment usually stems from the parent's reasonable needs not being met in *his* or *her* childhood. That child grows up to become an unfulfilled and empty adult, and in a host of ways expects his/her child to compensate, step in, and meet those needs.

How does a parent know if he or she is enmeshed? Read the statements below. They could easily be said by any devoted parent, but they could be taken literally and indicate enmeshment. Have you ever said:

"My daughter is my whole life"

"I would do anything for my kids"

"My children are my everything"

"I couldn't live without my children"

"My children are my whole world"

At the onset these seem like loving things any parent would say, but look closer. Should a child be my whole world? Should a child be a parent's everything? Should a child be my whole life? A well-balanced person is self-developed and has relationships, hobbies, work, goals, aspirations, interests, a spouse, a faith in God, self-improvement, and/or ambitions. Should a parent do *everything* for their children, or does it actually do harm to do anything for the child that they could do for themselves. If the child can tie his own shoe, do his own math homework, clean his own room, or fill out his own job application, he must be required to do so. A parent who does excessive things for the child keeps him dependent and immature regardless of his age. Though we would not want to live without our children whether minor or adult, should we not be able to? Despite whatever tragedy might occur, it would be God's plan that we complete His calling in *our* lives with or without our children.

This poses a whole different way of thinking and relating to our children, with an accompanying different goal and way of parenting. Now we can grasp the idea of working ourselves out of a job rather than holding on to our job. Now we can focus on the best interest of the child rather than what meets *our* needs.

Below is a more specific list of characteristics of parent/child enmeshment. No parent possesses all of the characteristics, but the reader may see himself or herself in many of the items. Bear in mind that the more items that apply, the more enmeshed a parent may be, and therefore the more that changes are necessary. The reader may want to check off any items that apply, and then re-check after reading the expounding information in the paragraphs that follows.

- Blurred boundaries, too emotionally close
- Reversed roles in decision-making
- Soft, permissive, or indulgent parenting
- Parent has difficulty setting limits, defends bad behavior
- Parent easily manipulated by the child's unhappiness
- Emotional dependence from parent
- A secret alliance with one parent
- Parents strong "need" for their children, cannot live without them
- Over-involved in child's life
- A misdirected expression of love
- Relationships are driven by parent's fear of abandonment
- Parent has unmet emotional needs

- Child sleeps with parents
- Parent receives excessive emotional support from child
- Parent rescues the child practically and from negative emotions
- Parent turns to the child for comfort
- Parent thinks of the child as a friend
- Parent experiences separation anxiety when apart from child
- Parent has inadequate individual identity
- Child not allowed individual identity
- Parent has difficulty seeing the faults of the child
- Parent believes/treats the child as superior, dotes
- Parent often 'fixes' things for the child
- Parent feels what the child feels
- Marital or partner discontent or extreme conflict
- Parent avoids rejection by the child
- Parent uses physical interaction from child for emotional comfort
- Parent is under developed emotionally and sometimes comprehensively
- Children's achievements define the parent's worth
- Separate thoughts/opinions/goals of the child are viewed as disloyal to the family

The Problem with Enmeshment

Enmeshed parents have conflicted boundaries. They are not sure of the accurate identity and description of their role. If their parenting was part of their employment, its job description would be vague and poorly defined, and this would greatly affect their job performance. Because of this poorly defined role, both decision-making and emotional support is confusing. Who makes the decisions and when? Who takes charge? And, very importantly, who emotionally supports who? **A key question in every family is whether parents are here to emotionally support their child, or is the child here to emotionally support the parents.** How this question is answered will have huge ramifications on the functioning of the family.

INDEPENDENCE

In healthy families parents emotionally support their children. The distinction is clear and apparent. While some incidental and unintentional support flows the opposite way, it is never the goal or intention. As we watch our children reach various milestones such as taking their first steps, learning to read, or making a shot on the basketball team, we feel a sense of pride, but that pride is *never* the goal. A sense of personal fulfillment is never the objective in our parenting decisions. If it is, then our children's existence becomes for *our* gratification. A parent may not even be aware of this. Whether conscious or unconscious, in enmeshed families this dynamic becomes a springboard for a host of flawed parenting decisions.

Enmeshed parents want their children to be happy. This goes beyond a simple desire to a goal. In fact, achieving and maintaining happiness in their child is a major emphasis in the family. Why is that a big deal you ask? Do not we WANT our children to be happy? Is this not the desire of all parents, you say? Of course we want our children to be happy, but at what cost? And should this be a parental *goal*?

First of all, happiness is a personal decision. This is a message our children need to hear- that ultimately no material thing, no person, no privilege, and no amount of money truly make us happy. They can *contribute* to our happiness, or make life easier or more enjoyable, but they will not make us happy. We must all make the decision to be happy by finding and following our unique mission, and maintaining a right relationship with God and others, as well as develop ourselves in ways that are fulfilling and contribute to others. Second, if we as parents establish the goal of our children's happiness, they will quickly catch on to the notion that *they* will determine the standards and conditions under which they are happy. Those conditions are likely to be selfish and detrimental to their character. As a six-year-old girl staying up late will make me happy. As a ten-year-old boy a $300 pair of tennis shoes will make me happy. As a thirteen-year-old girl staying out all night makes me happy. As a sixteen-year-old boy having an endless series of girlfriends and being sexually active will make me happy. In order to ensure happiness parents must oblige with few, if any limits. In all of these examples, soft, permissive, and indulgent discipline standards become the rule. These parents are easily manipulated by their child's whining, pleading, and power plays. The parent starts out well-intentioned in the child's life, but by the teenage years this dynamic takes on a life of its own and becomes difficult to reverse. A parent may even rescue the child from unpleasant emotions, difficult tasks, the consequences of his irresponsible behavior or the other parent's firmness, all with the goal of ensuring the child's happiness.

In my home I never focus on happiness. I would not necessarily want my children to be unhappy; it is just not my goal. What I *do* focus on is character! Traits like respect for others, honesty, working hard, and treating others with dignity are non-negotiable ways I insist that all family members will act. **The interesting thing I find is that, whether child or adult, the individuals who possess these traits tend to be the happiest.** Those with the highest character tend to be happy. It is the lack of character that ultimately backfires and makes one unhappy.

This also relates to the strong desire for enmeshed parents to "fix" things for the child. Since problems are unpleasant the parent must rush in and solve all of Junior's problems. In fact, this parent often adapts a pre-emptive strategy in which he is over-involved and over-manages the child's life in order that problems never have a chance to occur. A much better approach which teaches and gives practice to the child is to allow him to manage his own life and solve his own problems relative to his age.

There is also much emotional dependence from enmeshed parents toward the child. This dependence is a significant holdover from childhood when the parent's reasonable childhood emotional needs were not met. This parent goes beyond *wanting* their child, to *needing* their child, as well as the child's approval, emotional support, and affirmation. Because this mom or dad has little ego strength, he or she needs someone to be their cheerleader- someone to tell them they can do it! And they will typically depend on the child for this encouragement, rather than the other way around. As in other aspects of enmeshment, early on the child will sense this dependence and usually begin to use it against the parent by withdrawing their support and affirmation as a way to manipulate the parent to get what he wants. There is a "hostage" quality in the parent-child relationship since the child will re-affirm the parent once his demands are met.

Enmeshed parents often see their children a victim. They believe that others, including adults, frequently mistreat their child whom they view as special. Consequently, schools must often deal with various complaints and allegations. A strong protective or over-protective quality permeates the relationship since the parent's emotional well-being is at stake.

Another interesting aspect of enmeshment that I have observed is that enmeshed parents are prone to have their children sleep in the bed with them. This issue is addressed fully in chapter eleven. The question is: Why would parents want or encourage their child to sleep with them? Is it for the comfort and security of the child or the parent? Is it to meet the emotional needs of the child or the parent? In many cases it is the latter.

Secret relationships between one parent and child are also a part of enmeshed families. Known as an alliance, the child and parent are so emotionally close and dependent upon one another that they hold secrets against the other parent. Information concerning special treatment, favors, privileges, and indulgencies are closely held between the child and the enmeshed parent. **As a result, the close bond between husband and wife has been shifted to parent and child.** In some extreme cases, the parent and child are so close that the child actually becomes a surrogate spouse minus the sexual relationship. The "leave and cleave" unity that God demands of marriage has now been destroyed, or at least threatened, by or as a result of this secret relationship.

The enmeshed parent often sees his child as a friend. Friends do not have power or authority over another person. In order to guide, teach, and protect children, however, we *must* have this power and authority over them. Consequently, these parents often give up their parental role and take on more of a peer role. The relationship takes on more of a fun quality rather than a guiding/teaching quality. In some cases, especially when the child enters adolescence, the parent may even dress or act like the child. At this point the teenager may recognize the "borrowed life" on the parent's part and be embarrassed or resent the parent's appearance or behavior. Either parent or child may consider the other as competition at this point, and resentment can emerge. Or in some cases the teenager welcomes the young, hip approach of the mother and how she fits in with her friends. In either case, however, this relationship is extremely detrimental to the child.

Within this friend relationship, enmeshed parents want to be liked rather than respected. Consequently, these moms and dads hate rejection. Rejection is an emotional dagger in the heart of an enmeshed parent. These parents will often go to great lengths in order to avoid rejection. As with other similar unhealthy parent practices, the child will quickly recognizes the parent's Achilles heel. Because of the child's innate selfishness, he will begin to use it against the parent. The child will sulk, storm off, yell "I hate you," reject the parent's comfort, and give mom or dad the silent treatment meant to manipulate the parent into one thing or another.

Marital conflict, marital disconnectedness, and even divorce are common in enmeshed families because unhealthy tends to marry unhealthy. There is a tendency for individuals who are emotionally immature or ill-prepared for marriage to marry one another, which greatly increases the likelihood of heavy conflict or divorce. Secondly, the non-enmeshed parent will often not faithfully meet the emotional needs of the enmeshed spouse. The enmeshed spouse then turns to the child to get those needs met. This enmeshed parent will often be under-developed and with inadequate identity. Those traits and the enmeshed parent's neediness may be overlooked during dating but become very unattractive once married.

Enmeshed parents believe their children are superior to other children. This mom or dad has a psychological need to believe that their child is better than other children, and is the basis for special treatment, a preoccupation with, indulgence, and doting on them. They may boast about their children to an unrealistic extent. These parents often make statements of how smart, talented, or athletic their child is, whereas by objective measure the child may be average. The parent's strong, but unbalanced feelings for the child affect his objective assessment of the child.

Enmeshed parents often operate out of a fear of abandonment. As stated, a large part of enmeshment between parent and child is that the child is expected to meet the emotional needs of the adult. This is never stated, but is understood based on the relational dynamic and unspoken relational communication between parent and child. This message emerges in conversations, body language, facial expressions, and every other form of verbal and non-verbal communication.

It has been said that ships are safe in the harbor, but that is not what ships are for. Children are safe and cared for at home, but it is contrary to their purpose to keep them there. At some point it dawns on the enmeshed parent that their child will grow up, become an adult, and eventually leave the home. The notion of their source of emotional support abandoning them is a threatening idea. "What am I going to do? Who will meet my needs?" the parent ponders. There is a solution to this dilemma- make sure the child does not or cannot leave! Consciously or unconsciously, intentional or unintentional, enmeshed parents either guilt their children into staying with them, or ill-prepare them for adulthood to the extent that they cannot leave. These parents keep their child immature and dependent, either emotionally or practically, so that by eighteen years of age the child lacks the desire or wherewithal to function in society and is usually very fearful of the world. Home is a warm, safe, place where the child is loved and cared for. Moreover, the child may not want to leave since he/she has been assigned the role of emotional caregiver to a parent.

Three Problems That Summarize Enmeshment in Families

1. *Parent's needs are the focus.* If parent's needs are the focus, this means that the child's needs are *not* the focus. It means that the legitimate needs of children that mature them and prepare them do not occur. Because children follow our lead and respond to our version of reality, they begin to feel obligated to meet the needs of their parents. This becomes the family's twisted version of "normal".
2. *Maturity and independence are discouraged.* The child is kept immature and dependent so that the needs of the parents can continue to be met…indefinitely if possible. This is so extreme in some cases that the child will not or *cannot* function as a self-sufficient adult.
3. *Discipline and character are compromised.* Flawed discipline decisions are made since the goal is that the child be happy and that they like the parent. This is in opposition to decisions made that are in the best interest of the child regardless of his reaction or happiness.

How To Fix Enmeshment:

1. *Separate yourself from your child relative to his age.* Early on the child need much support. In fact, the challenge/support is 100% support at birth. But, as previously stated, gradually it shifts until by about 18 years old it is close to or at 100% challenge and the child is able to make all his own decisions. Throughout childhood that balance is constantly shifting: less support and more challenge. This approach truly prepares the child for adulthood.
2. *Work on neediness.* If you find yourself an emotionally needy individual, explore its roots. Work toward a more emotionally self-sufficient you. Get your legitimate emotional needs

met through friendships, spouse, and extended family, and take great care not to get these needs met through your children.

3. *Pursue outside interests, goals, and relationships.* This can include hobbies, travel, volunteerism, recreation, and community and church sports teams. It can (and should) include new interests and things you've never done before. These pursuits contribute to a parent being well-rounded and engaged in life. They provide the parent with a mental break. These are things that are valid since they will bring you happiness and contribute to your well-being. With these pursuits it also makes it less likely that a parent will seek excessive fulfillment from their child. Consequently, with regard to your family obligations, these pursuits actually make you a *better* parent if practiced in balance.

4. *Deal with personal guilt.* Guilt is a poor and unreliable motivator. Guilt can cause us to make a whole host of flawed parenting decisions. We must separate true guilt from false guilt by determining if there has been parental irresponsible, intentional hurt, or neglectful behavior. In many cases the adult has been fully responsible, yet still *feels* guilty. And because they *feel* guilty, their parenting is compromised accordingly and usually in a soft, permissive manner. Striking down false guilt will provide much more confidence in your parenting decisions. Even in a situation where the parent has made mistakes and true guilt is experienced, the mom or dad must forgive themselves and grow from the mistake. Another situation I frequently encounter is that a parent feels a peculiar combination of guilt, regret, discomfort, and sadness due to a hardship their child has endured. This hardship can be a family divorce, extended illness of the child, poverty, handicap, incapacitation, or any adversity the child has experienced. The parent in this situation may attempt to compensate for the adversity with the idea that "my child has suffered enough....I cannot make them suffer more with rules or high standards". This can then prompt the parent to implement soft or indulgent discipline.

5. *Promote firm discipline despite the child's reaction.* Competent parenting is not defined by a child's positive, receptive response. A child will rarely welcome discipline because it thwarts

their selfish desires. Various child reactions can also be used to manipulate the adult. Firm discipline is fairly clear-cut as outline in this book. It is not some lofty, undefined notion that would forever cause you, the parent, to second-guess your every decision.

6. *Eliminate spoiling or over-focusing on the child.* Parents must take note of the freedoms, privileges, and material possessions that are excessive, undeserved, or have not been earned. Gifts for special occasions are acceptable: birthday, Christmas, graduation, for example. Otherwise gifts should be rare. Beyond that, the parent may be unconsciously attempting to gain acceptance from the child, or be liked by the child through spoiling. By not over-focusing on the child you get to have a life and he manages his own life and solves his own problems, relative to his age of course.

7. *Accept the child's unhappiness.* Again, it is not my desire for children to be unhappy, but unhappiness can have benefits. It can prepare a child for the difficult aspects of adult life. Discontentment can teach valuable lessons in which the child makes better decisions in the future that avoid the despair. It also empowers a child to make changes and improvements that produce a more pleasant life. Additionally, it sends a clear message that ultimately he (the child) alone is in charge of his happiness.

8. *Encourage your child's decision-making abilities.* As stated earlier, the goal is to slowly decrease and eventually eliminate your job as parent. One way this is done is by preparing the child and giving him practice at guiding his own life relative to his age. This can start very early in areas of his life that seem unimportant, and then move slowly over the years to more significant decisions. A child who does not get practice at making decisions will depend on his parents for those decisions and ultimately stifle his growth and self-sufficiency.

9. *Set appropriate boundaries with your child.* This includes boundaries in your roles as parent and child. There should be a clear distinction, especially in power and authority. This also includes boundaries in physical space, responsibilities, and in self-soothing (more on self-soothing in chapter eleven).

10. *If married, maintain a high quality marriage.* In a good marital relationship each person works to meet (some of) the needs of their partner and contribute to their happiness. When this occurs

enmeshment becomes less likely. This also serves as a healthy role model for children to follow in *their* future marriage. Maintain strong marital unity that is the foundation of your family.

Encouraging Unhealthy Dependence

By now the reader should have a good idea of what healthy independence looks like, as well as its positive results as a child enters adulthood. Encouraging unhealthy dependence typically has one of two results:

1. *Rebellion.* We have established that a system of rules without a relationship equals rebellion. A strict, oppressive family environment without strong relationships and expressed love make rebellion highly likely. At some point during the teenage years the child recognizes accurately that they are not allowed the reasonable and appropriate increased freedoms and privileges that their peers are allowed. The child recognizes that they are not allowed to grow up and are kept from good, beneficial things, despite having proven their trustworthiness. This unfairness of this typically angers the child, often promoting rebellion. If the child is nearing the legal age, he will likely express this rebellion in poor decisions and experimentation simply because he can. This may also be an indirect way to get revenge on the parents since they will disapprove and may even be embarrassed.

2. *An extended over-dependence.* In over-dependence the child also has some recognition of the family oppression with some negative internal reaction, but his fear exceeds his anger. Though equally as unprepared as his rebellious counterpart, this child cowers in excessive dependence. He recognizes his inadequacy in dealing with the many aspects of adult life such as employment, relationships, college, or moving out. He may participate in some of these areas with half-hearted commitment, but he will likely fail because of his ill-preparation or self-sabotage. Hormones and/or emotional neediness may drive this child toward a premature opposite-sex relationship, but he or she will not have the relational tools, maturity, or emotional strength to sustain it.

Many years ago I had as counseling clients a set of 15 year-old twin girls in Texas. They were a part of a loving family with adequate financial resources, but there was a fierce sense of strictness between parent and child that was oppressive. Though neither of the twins had violated their parent's trust, mom and dad rarely allowed them out of their sight, including taking part in church or school functions. This prevented the children from the benefits of many different experiences which would have helped prepare them for adult functioning. It also angered the teenagers, a situation that continued to fester throughout our therapeutic relationship. As we dealt with various behavior and attitude problems, this parental suppression emerged as a major foundation of this family's problems. These parents simply needed to begin letting go, but mom and dad would not hear of it. With a lack of preparation for adulthood, and anger as a motive, these children were destined for hard times, if not failure, as they turned eighteen.

I saw the family in counseling for five or six months before discontinuing counseling. As I kept track of the twins I learned that each had followed one of the two paths mentioned earlier. One twin began sneaking out at night to meet with her boyfriend. She eventually ran away, dropped out of school, was arrested for theft, and became pregnant. The other twin went the path of an extended over-dependency. That child graduated for high school, but found adult life overwhelming. She had a boyfriend briefly, but that turned abusive. She was employed for a while but found it too defeating. She did manage to complete one year of college, but never finished a degree and never used that education. By the age of 23 she had settled into a life characterized by lack of challenge, minimal social life, unemployment, and almost complete emotional and financial dependence upon her parents.

Independence Versus Rebellion

By now the reader may be thinking "OK, I should encourage independence but discourage rebellion… so what's the difference?" In some ways they are the same. Both are expressed as a moving away from parental authority with increased decision-making by the child, but that is where the similarities end.

Independence is the age-appropriate ability to be self-governing and self-sufficient. It is the child successfully making his own decisions and managing his own life relative to his age. This manifests itself in various ways depending on the child's age. In younger children it includes things like dressing, tying your own shoe, menial chores, and basic cleaning. Middle children can manage their school work, do the dishes and cut the grass, and do short-term babysitting. Teenagers can and should manage most aspects of their lives and solve their own problems. They still need supervision and guidance, and decisions concerning outside people and events still need approval, but older adolescents should be managing most of their lives since they will soon be a legal adult.

Regardless of the age, allowing (or insisting, depending on the willingness of the child) Junior to accept various responsibilities and stretch himself prepares him for adulthood. It is a long, steady, gradual acceptance of the tasks and responsibilities that instill confidence and teach practical skills he will one day need.

Rebellion, on the other hand, is a defying of proper and necessary authority. It is an aggressive seizing of power before the child is ready or has earned it. It has nothing to do with confidence, but overconfidence. Rebellion is a self-assurance that is beyond reality or preparation that virtually guarantees disaster.

Rebellion in teens rarely starts in the teenage years, it just culminates then. Defying parental authority almost always begins years earlier; it is just more noticeable as it peaks during this adolescence when the child has increased where-with-all, increased physical size, and increased false confidence. It is imperative that parents' power always exceed the child's. Again, parents must win these battles early on so that challenges to authority remain small or non-existent. Years of lost battles are difficult to reverse. In addition, other elements are usually present in rebellious children beyond mismanaging the power hierarchy in the family. The most common additional elements I have observed include the absence of a close parent-child relationship, poor role modeling by parents, and/or excessive cultural exposure.

Rescuing

In working with parents in both educational and counseling settings, I have yet to encounter a mom or dad that does not love their child. Almost universally parents convincingly report they love their children fondly; however, parents sometimes do things that work against their child's best interest. Some moms and dads make decisions and relate to their child in a way that promotes irresponsibility, encourages bad behavior, and stifles growth. They mean well but often do not think decisions through, making small mistakes at first that crescendo into huge issues with big consequences years later. One of those issues is rescuing.

Rescuing is defined as removing the natural and appropriate, but painful consequences of a child's irresponsible behavior. Often in life a poor choice has a poor outcome. This outcome is inconvenient, emotionally painful, causes opportunities to be lost, generally hinders our life, or costs us time, energy, or money. These are the natural cause and effect workings of the world under which we all must operate. When children learn this they become well prepared for adult life (remember this is the goal). The way they learn is for the family to operate in exactly the same manner: cause-and-effect.

The problem arises when the family system violates this cause-and-effect principle. This happens most often when mom or dad assume the responsibility or try to undo the inappropriate actions of the child. The lesson that is learned is that I can make mistakes, act irresponsibly, shirk my duties, or be lazy, and someone else will pay the price. This plays itself out in small, seemingly unimportant ways when the child is young, but grows to enormous potential years later. Like many issues in parenting, a small mistake that is never corrected increases in such insignificant increments over time that it goes unnoticed until the problem is difficult or impossible to correct. The primary message parents must convey is that we are all responsible for our own actions- good or bad. This is one of the hallmarks of mature functioning.

Rescuing a child sends the opposite message. Rescuing says "I will be responsible for your behavior", "I will bail you out in life." Whether you leave your toys in the floor, skip doing your chores, miss a homework assignment, or run up a cell phone bill, I (your parents) will take care of it. **Over the long run it establishes a dangerous norm that will be the foundation for many mistakes in adulthood.**

Whether natural or engineered by parents, consequences are a great shaper of behavior. Allowing unpleasant outcomes are a very effective way to discourage irresponsible behavior *if* the outcomes are consistent and age-appropriate. These outcomes send a clear message and are the thing the child would like to avoid in the future. It is this avoidance of a painful outcome that will prompt the child to make a better decision. This notion taps into the immature brain of a child that focuses on maximizing pleasure. In later years, and if other parenting elements are in place, the child will gain godly insight, emotional maturity, self-motivation, a sense of moral obligation, and develop a more mature foundation for responsible actions. Until that point in time various forms of consequences must be put in place. If we as parents remove that inconvenient, unpleasant outcome, we do our child a tremendous disservice since a valuable life lesson is being omitted.

Why would parents do such a disservice to their child and rescue them? There are several possibilities:

1. *Codependency.* Remember back to the section on enmeshment? One of the characteristics discussed is that a parent *needs* his child. In codependency that same need is very strong and is for the purpose of taking care of self. The parent *needs to be needed!* As long as junior remains irresponsible there is a *need* for the parent to compensate and be the counterbalance with actions that keep the irresponsible lifestyle of the child unhindered. The codependent parent has a purpose, a role. The rescuing fosters emotional and behavior problems in the child that then require parental involvement. The parent never works himself out of a job, but rather disrupts the child's growth in order to remain needed.

2. *A need to be liked.* That fact is that children enjoy it when others take up the slack for them. Their natural sense of immaturity and selfishness will rarely prompt them to stop a parent from rescuing them. Children enjoy both the rescuing behavior and the parents when they cover for the child's irresponsible behavior. Conversely, a child can have anger toward a parent who does not rescue them- something many parents find intolerable. While the child may like the rescuing parent, the far more important trait of respect from child to parent is lost.

3. *A misdirected expression of love.* Families have various symbols of love. For some families love is expressed in terms of demonstrative physical affection such as oversized bear hugs and kisses on the cheek. In other families large home cooked meals represents love. Still others families express love by doing for one another, often too much and to the extent that they encourage irresponsible behavior in one another. What a parent might call "love" through rescuing might be one of the most unloving things a parent can do toward their child in the long run.

4. *A guarantee of success.* When we as parents rescue our children (and manage their life excessively) we sometimes want to insure their success- success that we cannot place in their hands since it might jeopardize achievement. This requires excessive control, unwarranted management, crossing appropriate boundaries, and over-involvement in the child's life beyond what is healthy or beneficial to the child.

The danger of rescuing a child is that he grows to expect it, decreasing his own sense of obligation and responsibility. Over time this false norm causes him to blame others for events and problems which he caused. This lack of ownership then causes him to fail to address his own sphere of responsibility or correct areas in which he is responsible. These areas can be personal, legal, relational, or financial. It can affect his family and his career. **Parental rescuing, in short, can set in motion a dangerous pattern, teach irresponsibility, hurt self-esteem, and cause many long term issues to a child, which in adulthood will likely cause him much pain and a struggle to correct.**

Chapter Eight Discussion Questions:

1. From your perspective, what is the scariest aspect of your children growing up? What would lessen this threat for you as a parent?
2. According to this chapter, what are a parent's two jobs? Elaborate further- what specifically is meant by these two jobs?
3. What emotions are evoked as you think about your child becoming an adult?
4. Almost all parents display some traits of enmeshment. Having read this section, how enmeshed are you? What issues in your family have emerged as a result of this enmeshment? What three summary problems exist with enmeshment? What are two adjustments that would help you lower your enmeshed family relationship? Have you recognized excessive emotional closeness and dependency in other areas of your life?
5. To what extent did your parents encourage a healthy independence in your family of origin? Did you engage in either rebellion or an extended dependency?

6. What is the difference between independence and rebellion?

7. Define rescuing in your own words. Name two payoffs to a parent in rescuing their child. What is the difference between helping and child a rescuing?

CHAPTER 9
Obedience

The word obedience has been given a bad rap in recent years. It conjures up notions of iron rule, domination, excessive control, or dictatorial authority. The word obedience invokes ideas of hyper traditionalism where the father is the master of the home and the wife and children are his invisible, subservient subjects. You may envision a sixteenth century puritan community where children are submissive followers forced into long, hard labor, and being punished harshly for non-compliance, while using the Bible as justification.

Obedience is also a politically incorrect word in our culture. The media in recent years has reinforced the cultural notion that parents should suggest, ask, or propose to children that they should do certain things. To require the high standard of obedience is cruel and excessive. Yet, we would not apply this standard to any other group that must perform a task or function. Whether a company, a church, or a basketball team, someone must be in charge and direct others in order to reach the goal. Someone must, in a selfless but uncompromising manner, convey the behavioral standards that are acceptable in order for the organization to thrive. And in a family- that is mom and dad.

The definition of obedience as it relates to children is following the modeling, feedback, and guidance a parent has already provided. Parents take a leadership role and initiate what children must follow. In a healthy family, role modeling, feedback, direct control and regulation of all aspects of the family are provided by mom and dad, and children abide by it. This not only ensures a well-functioning family in which children internalize appropriate behavior, but it creates emotionally stable children. What many parents fail to realize is that a byproduct of a structured family with high standards is children with low anxiety and a felt security in their world. Children to not fully understand it and cannot express it, but they want someone outside themselves who is big and strong, and has knowledge to guide and protect them. This again parallels the relationship we have with God in that we desire the same thing from Him.

Permissive Parenting

In a 1963 Andy Griffith TV episode entitled 'The Spoiled Kid' the town's patience is tested by a boy's poor choices. The child largely runs his own life and chooses to ride his bicycle on the sidewalk. After several warnings by the sheriff, the bike is impounded. The boy then persuades his father to storm the courthouse and demand the bicycle be returned. After several minutes of bantering between the dad and Sheriff Taylor, the son's bratty, spoiled behavior is intensified as the 10 year-old pounds on the desk and screams "I want my bike back!" In an epiphany that highlights the episode, the father gazes at the son with new found insight and comes to realize that children do a poor job of managing their own lives.

In a permissive parenting style the child guides himself, making most or all of his own decisions. Regardless of the age of the child, he decides when to take a bath, when to go to bed, what to eat, where to go, and what activity to engage in. In a May 5, 2014 interview on Fox and Friends, actor Sean Astin said of his parenting, "The one thing is that kids are pretty self-regulating. If there's something scary…they do not want to watch it. That said, my feeling is….I'm very liberal about what they watch (on TV or movies) as long as they know that I'm going to talk to them and we have to communicate." In other words, anything goes as long I talk with a child afterwards. Children can see, hear, be exposed to, or experience whatever they choose as long as it is discussed later. This is the essence of permissive parenting.

Permissive parenting assumes that your child and mine will make the right decisions that are in their best interest. Given the self-centeredness and immaturity we have already established, this is a huge and unrealistic assumption. **Children rarely make good decisions on their own; they almost always make decisions that will please them in that moment.** They have neither the foresight nor the impulse control to see beyond right now. After several years of modeling and guidance, young children can *begin* to make small decisions. When combined with maturity, those small decisions can expand slowly throughout the years with the eventual goal of full relinquishing of control. Remember, one of the goals of parenting is to work yourself out of a job. Consequently, throughout the childhood and teenage years parents must appropriately regulate and control the freedoms, privileges, and the decision-making power children have.

Permissive parenting lacks the firm guidance children need. Children universally want to make their own decisions, but at a deeper level they know they are not good at it. They do not have the knowledge, understanding of the world, and life experience to make decisions that keep them from danger and provide for their needs. Children cannot articulate it, and do not have any acute understanding of the topic, but there is an unconscious awareness of their own limitations in decision-making and abilities. The danger is that the child's meager understanding of his limitations can easily be over-powered by his selfish impulses. This self-awareness of his limitations can be tapped into, nurtured, and developed, but only minimally relied upon for years. If parents rely on this innate awareness too much or too soon, the child will operate with excessive power and put himself in danger. **This is how permissive parenting becomes detrimental to children- it does not *regulate* power and guide children at the level they require.** The selfishness, immaturity, and age of the child must dictate the level of management we as parents provide. In permissive parenting this management is too low relative to the maturity level such that the child is not taught. Moreover, the decisions of the child not regulated by parents put the child in dangerous situations as he guides himself.

This principle is so important that it could be said that permissive parenting is a betrayal of children since permissiveness lacks the firm guidance and insistence of obedience that children need for leadership and protection.

Clear Instructions

A large part of competent parenting is communication. We must accurately communicate standards and expectations to the child, or we cannot expect him to follow them. Decisions should be stated in a manner that leaves no room for self-interpretation or confusion. It is often the case that parents have a decision, rule, or idea in their head that is not conveyed accurately in what they say. This can be further complicated by self-serving biases on the child's part. It may be necessary for the parent to ask "do you understand?" or "do you have any questions?" Another technique to ensure good communication is to get the child to repeat back to you what you said. It may also be necessary to get the child to look directly at you, eyeball to eyeball. The goal here is to eliminate any misunderstandings, intentional or unintentional. In any case parents must:

- Give clear instructions
- Close all loop holes
- Establish iron-clad rules

Consider the dialogue below...

Child: "Dad, can I go outside and play?"
Dad: "Well, it looks like it's going to rain."

In this example the communication from parent to child is unclear? Without realizing it, the father's vague response opens up opportunity for intentional or unintentional miscommunication. Dad probably believed he was being clear. But any clarity is based on an assumption that if it rains children cannot play outside. With this answer from dad, the child can either misunderstand what he said, or act on his own self-serving interpretation and desire to go outside. Even if the dad's decision is clear to the child, junior may act on what he wants to do. Some possible examples of clearer communication from the father might include:

Dad: It looks like it may rain any minute so stay inside.
Dad: You can go outside, but if it starts raining come in immediately.
Dad: Let's wait a while and see what the weather is going to do....stay inside for now.
Clearer? Definitely! Now there is no room for miscommunication.

Another example of unclear parent-child communication:

Teenage daughter to mother: "I want to go to see *Bridesmaids* at the Malco with my friends Friday night."

Mother: "Oh that looks like a cute movie."

It is again unclear whether the child can go to the movies Friday with her friends. Then there is the additional issue of the specific movie they will be seeing. Neither point is addressed accurately in mom's communication. With such vague parental communication, this mother leaves herself wide open to intentional manipulation by the teen girl. If this daughter is like many, she will get dressed on Friday night and approach her mother at 6:30 declaring "OK, I'm ready to go to the movies." Mom cannot remember the specifics of the movie conversation three days earlier, is confused, and thus relies on the truthfulness of the child. This mother ponders in her head…."I guess I said it was OK" and takes the child to the movie. This is contrary to every notion of intentional parenting. Moreover, mom has given little thought in the appropriateness of the movie in which the child's world view will be shaped.

Below are examples of clear, concise communication toward children:

- Please be home by five o'clock sharp so that we won't be late for your soccer game.
- Sometime before dinner I need the clothes folded and put away.
- You may cut the grass either today or tomorrow.
- Take your bath immediately.
- I checked on the movie you wanted to see and it's too violent for me to approve it.
- You may talk to your friend on the phone for 15 minutes, but no more.
- Since its Friday night, you may stay up until ten o'clock.

Never Bluff

Remember the old adage, "mean what you say and say what you mean?" Often parents give their children a command without truly meaning it. How does a parent convey they mean it? Through enforcement! With every rule, policy, decision, or command, a parent must hold the child accountable to it by:

a) knowledge or proof that it has been carried out
b) a willingness to implement consequences for a lack of obedience

If a parent is not willing to enforce a decision, the parent should not verbalize it, but if it is stated, the parent *must* follow through with enforcement. Decisions or commands without enforcement or follow-through water down a parent's authority. This sends the message "Even though I said it, I do not really expect this of you." I assure you, your child will fully oblige! Whether you want your child to unload the dishwasher, do his homework, comb his hair, or cut the grass, it will be little more than a suggestion if not enforced.

Too Much Explaining!

A view that some parents hold is that a child must have adult levels of willingness and understanding to obey. A dad may spend a large amount of time explaining in great detail why Junior must do chores. Or mom lectures brilliantly for hours explaining the details of wearing minimal makeup to her thirteen-year-old daughter. In either of these examples, the child may be too immature to understand the reason for the obedience, or cultural influences and peer pressure supersede the child's ability or willingness to grasp the concept. It amounts to unrealistic expectations of understanding from a child. Moreover, if the assumption on the parent's part is that the child must understand in order to comply, there is great incentive *not* to understand. With this as a foundation, the child can effectively hold the parent hostage indefinitely with non-compliance because of his/her lack of understanding.

In adult life we operate similarly. It is often that we do not understand a decision by someone in authority over us. We may not understand or even agree with a ruling by a judge, a decision by a professor, or an instruction by our boss. Does this mean we are not obligated to comply? No!

At certain points in our life biblical principles may be puzzling to us. A new spiritual epiphany may not fit with what we have believed thus far in our life. Or maybe it does not conform to our existing theological or relational framework. What do we do in the mean time? Are we still obligated to obey God because we disagree or do not understand? The rich, potent combination of compliance toward God and maturity usually brings about understanding down the road. It is the very idea that God loves us and makes decisions in our best interest that brings about a close, reliable relationship with Him. It is the same dynamic in the parent-child relationship, as understanding may not be present initially.

It is here that we as parents must be loving but firm. We also must be careful that this is not the impetus for an argument. A brief discussion- yes, an argument- no. Consequently, obedience is not contingent upon:

- The child agreeing with the instructions
- The child liking the instructions
- The child understanding the rationale of the instructions

In a perfect world children would like, agree, and understand all instructions, and as a result be able to foresee the benefit of various actions years down the road, but they cannot. Children simply do not have the maturity or insight to achieve this. They will, however, if modeling, a close relationship, and other parental elements are in place.

Consequences

There are three ways to change a child's behavior: consequences, consequences, consequences! Without consequences there is little incentive for children to act in ways that are beneficial for them, both in the short-term and long-term. In some cases children will naturally behave appropriately or may want to please their parents with good behavior. Even at best they still need firm guidance and consequences that form strong character and positive conduct.

OBEDIENCE

Throughout Scripture the principle of sowing and reaping is conveyed.[1] The idea is that actions have immediate, long-term, and eternal results. Our decisions, choices, and the way in which we live our lives determine the outcome and our degree of success in life. **If this sowing and reaping principle is duplicated in the home the result will be increase obedience.** This principle also produces a child who is better prepared for adulthood since this reaping and sowing spiritual law is how the world works.

At its simplest level, a consequence is a response by a parent immediately after any action by the child. The parent's response predictably makes the action by the child either more likely or less likely in the future. The child either likes the response or does not like the response. If he likes the response he will want to repeat it by engaging in the same behavior as before. If he does not like the response, he will want to avoid it by stopping the behavior that brought about the unpleasant response. This easy, straightforward principle is very powerful in shaping the actions of children beginning at about 18-24 months of age. It can be repeated and varied in many different ways to successfully guide our sons and daughters.

Most parents have some idea of this principle but do not use it effectively or unknowingly provide enjoyable consequences to unwanted behavior. Consider this scenario that starts out well but ends in disaster: A mother goes into Wal-Mart with her four-year-old little girl to do some grocery shopping. Mom gets a basket, puts little Gracie in the seat section, and begins walking the isles periodically inserting grocery items. Almost immediately the little girl makes a request of a candy bar. Mom tells Gracie "no" and continues shopping mission. But, the child has been through this before and knows she just needs to be persistent. She continues to make the candy bar request, but more intently as time goes on. Mom tells her no again and offers her wisdom that it will ruin her teeth and spoil her dinner. Firmly convinced that the condition of her teeth will not matter in 20 years, Gracie transitions from a request to a demand. "I said I want a candy bar!" she insists. Gracie's mother denies the candy again and continues her mission, but the child is relentless as they saunter up one isle and down another. Ten minutes, fifteen minutes, twenty minutes,....they have danced this dance before. This sweet, angelic little girl knows just what she has to do. Wanting to up the ante (and hence her

---

[1] Galatians 6:7, 2 Corinthians 9:6-8, Luke 6: 38.

chances at the candy bar) the child now becomes disrespectful and loud. Other parents are taking notice. Mom is embarrassed. Gracie has honed her acting chops in other similar encounters. She now musters a scowl to convey passion. The child senses mom is nearing the breaking point. It is fourth and inches to the goal line! In a final push Gracie yells out, "If you loved me you'd give me a candy bar!" To which mom says. "Alright, shut up! Here's your candy bar!"

This scenario, with subtle variations plays itself out every day in homes all across America. Once Gracie got what she wanted, she quieted down and Mom got the peace she wanted, but at what price? In this scenario who is training who? What is clear is that Gracie is in charge, and what she is learning from this is how to manipulate others. With a battle of this magnitude at four years old, what does the future of Gracie's behavior and the mother-daughter relationship look like?

The behavior of little Gracie is not unusual. Even her persistence is not unusual. The problem that is fueling the bad behavior is that it worked for her. Remember, children do what works. A pleasant consequence was the response of the bad behavior. **As long as bad behavior is met with something enjoyable, the bad behavior will continue in the future, if not intensify.** Moreover, there is confusion over just who is calling the shots in the family.

As stated before, a consequence is the outcome or response by the parent after a behavior of the child. By providing certain responses parents can increase or decrease the likelihood of the behavior. Put another way, by our response parents can get more of a behavior or less of a behavior. The basic strategy to be adapted is that good behavior gets good consequences, and bad behavior gets bad consequences. The closer in time the consequence is to the behavior the more effective will be. Therefore, a consequence immediately after a behavior is most effective. A tight, sure system that follows this idea of consequences is very effective in directing a child's behavior and instilling responsibility and character. This is especially true if combined with the other principles already covered. The pages to follow explain how to correct the 'Gracie' problem and more effectively use consequences to shape a child's behavior. Now that you have an example and basic understanding of consequences, I will present three consequence tools: positive reinforcement, extinction, and punishment, explaining each and giving examples and cautions where applicable.

Consequence Tool #1: Positive Reinforcement

Decades ago Edward Thorndike theorized that, whether human or animal, we do things that lead to outcomes that we like. Thorndike did experiments in which kittens, with almost no worldly experience, were able to lift a latch on a cage and escape. It was this escape which brought the kitten pleasure, and effectively "taught" the kitten to escape more often and more efficiently.[2] This is the idea behind consequences in a broad sense, and positive reinforcement specifically.

Positive reinforcement is defined as a pleasant consequence that follows good choices and behaviors. It is a payoff, a reward. The old managerial philosophy goes: catch them doing something right and compliment them on it. Anything the child finds enjoyable presented just after the desired behavior constitutes positive reinforcement. If done consistently it will increase the likelihood of the desired behavior. What kind of things act as reinforcers? Positive reinforcers include anything your child would like to do or like to have if given the option. It includes anything he/she would automatically gravitate to if allowed, especially in the areas of privileges, freedoms, and material possessions. This gives us as moms and dads almost unlimited options!

Some parents are uncomfortable with the "bribe" nature of reinforcement. Bribe is not entirely inaccurate, nor is it a dirty word. How many of us would work our jobs if we were not "bribed" with a salary? Without a paycheck as an incentive, most of us, no matter how much we enjoy the work, would willingly write our own pink slip and never show up again. What are some examples of reinforcers that can be used with children?

Examples of Reinforcement:

- A trip to Disney World
- $5.00
- A smile
- Going to the movies
- A new Matchbox car
- Staying up late
- A note of encouragement

---

[2] Thorndike, E. L. (1898). Animal intelligence: An experimental study of the associative processes in animals. *Psychological Monographs: General and Applied*, 2(4), i-109.

- "Nice job"
- Choose the evening menu
- Rent a video game

This represents only a few of the wide range of possibilities of positive reinforcers. You will notice a wide variety of responses above that parents can use. Some are costly, some are free. Some take much planning, and some are spontaneous. Some are easy, and some are extravagant. Which ones work? They *all* do! Any of the above, if presented immediately after the desired behavior, will urge the child to do more of the desired behavior.

This begs the question: What happens if we do not reinforce good behavior? This answer is that the behavior will not be as strong, and may not be repeated at all. Consequently, we as parents clearly want to implement positive reinforcement, and we want to use it regularly- almost minute by minute.

What is the result of reinforcing unwanted behavior? Remember little Gracie? Mom *thought* she was doing the right thing since the candy bar stopped the bad behavior, but mom actually reinforced the child's whining, demanding, pleading, manipulation, and disrespect because a pleasant payoff was introduced just after the unwanted behavior. When parents do this it increases the bad behavior. What mom *should have* done early on is make the candy bar contingent on *good* behavior, i.e. "If you behave (clearly defined) while we are in Walmart shopping you may have a candy bar when we leave." If the child behaved badly then mom should follow through with no candy bar such that the bad behavior is *not* reinforced.

Considering the Walmart scenario more broadly and removing the candy bar from the equation...anything the child preferred could act as a reinforcer. If sitting in the larger portion of the basket is viewed by the child as better and preferable to the seat portion, this could be used as a reinforcer contingent on proper behavior. If the Gracie then acts up, she can be moved back to the smaller, seat area.

Let us consider next what might happen if mom had simply ignored the pleas.

Consequence Tool #2: Extinction

A second consequence tool involves doing something parents often find difficult and are skeptical of: *nothing*. Extinction is defined as giving no feedback and no reinforcers to a particular behavior such that the behavior decreases. **In simpler terms, ignore the bad behavior and it will go away.** This can be difficult because parents often feel as though they have to be doing *something* to address a bad behavior. Extinction runs contrary to common sense because you take no action. In fact, a parent may actually have to work hard at doing nothing. It is also difficult because parents find it hard to tolerate repeated displays of the same bad behavior while they wait for it to dissipate. Extinction takes patience and a high level of tolerance that a parent may need to develop. This is especially true if unwanted behavior has been rewarded for months or years without mom and dad realizing it.

One problem with addressing a behavior is that it constitutes attention. Attention is a powerful reinforcer and tends to strengthen or increase behaviors. Consequently, instructing a child to stop hitting his little sister is necessary, but can actually increase the bad behavior because attention is being given to it. These mixed signals can yield missed results and must then be considered by parents.

Extinction avoids this problem in that it eliminates all reinforcers. **This means that parents do not address a behavior, discuss the behavior, call the child down, or even make eye contact with the child.** They hold out and continue to ignore it for as long as the child engages in the behavior. Further, parents take the same ignoring approach tomorrow, the next day, and the next with the undesirable behavior. In other words, mothers and fathers must act as a team, consistently disregarding the bad behavior as long as it is present. I sense skepticism in you even as I write these words. In order to dispel doubts, let me convince you with an example and a few qualifiers.

As mentioned before, when our oldest child was about three years old she came home from school one day saying "f*** it!" Once my wife and I picked ourselves up off the floor, the action we took was......nothing. We did not correct or address it in any way. We knew she did not know what it meant. Any addressing of the behavior would only draw attention to it and further increase the likelihood she would continue saying it. After three days we never heard it from her again. We did alert the child care of the problem since we believed that was the source of our daughter's expanded vocabulary, but we took no other action.

Extinction *will* work to decrease unwanted conduct, however it is not good for all behaviors. **Defiance, disrespect, aggression, and anything that is dangerous must be addressed differently.** As parents we cannot allow rebellion of any kind, nor can parents tolerate verbal or physical assaults on anyone. If you have told Junior not to ride his bike on a busy street you cannot ignore it. Otherwise, you will be making a trip to the emergency room.

Second, the behavior must be ignored completely and consistently. If a child is throwing a fit (a good application of extinction) parents must outlast Junior. To some parents this sounds good in theory but almost impossible in practice. Dad may be able to ignore the fit-throwing five minutes, maybe ten, but his endurance begins to be taxed soon afterward and he shouts to the child, "You get up off the floor right now young man!" What this father did was interrupt successful extinction with attention, which reinforcers the bad behavior. If he had only held out and stayed strong. As parents, we must develop the patience to outlast our children however long it takes.

Third, we must be consistent and ignore the behavior every time it occurs. Inconsistent extinction will be met with inconsistent results, as well as confusion on the part of the child. If a parent will be diligent, future episodes of the unwanted behavior will become less and less frequent until it finally disappears.

Fourth, we must be mindful of outside reinforcers that fortify and pump energy into the unwanted behavior. For example, a young girl whines continuously. A mother may be doing a good job of extinction, ignoring the behavior consistently, but the little girl's actions are great entertainment for her older brother who laughs every time the sister moans. The brother's laughing acts as a reinforcer that must somehow be eliminated. Otherwise, the whining will continue indefinitely.

It is important to recognize that extinction is not indifference, passivity, or laziness, in fact quite the opposite. The intentional parent thinks through and decides what discipline practice most effectively teaches and guides the child. Extinction is intentionally choosing not to affirm or reinforce a particular behavior. By doing so the unwanted actions of the child are slowly eliminated.

Examples of When To Use Extinction:

- A child throwing a fit
- A child whining

- Any annoying behavior
- Attention-seeking behavior
- Pouting, sighing
- Storming off in a huff
- Bad attitudes

Many behaviors appropriate for extinction fall into the category of undesirable, but not correction worthy. Pouting, sighs that reflect disgust, and storming off are child behaviors that often ignite the wrath of parents. But, as previously stated, a parent's emotions are a poor foundation for actions. Ultimately these behaviors are best eliminated with extinction. At the same time, there may be other important issues the child or teenager is dealing with that may need addressing.

Extinction is a good remedy for attention-seeking behavior. But, parents must be cautious here in that sometimes this can be a sign the child is not getting enough attention. His actions, in this case, are a genuine behavioral appeal for necessary positive attention that he is unable to verbalize. Parents should look carefully at the situation, involving a counselor or psychologist to help if necessary. If parents are in agreement that the child is receiving adequate positive (non-disciplinary) attention, then attention-seeking behavior should be met with disregard. Parents must consider, however, that there may be legitimate issues in the child's life related to this behavior.

Lastly, extinction, as well as the warm bond previously described, works well with bad attitudes. This is another hot button that is frequently over-addressed by many parents and tends to ramp up in the teenage years. The problem is that attitudes are in a person's head. How can a parent intentionally change a mental process and how can a parent verify when it has been improved? Without any flippancy, I recommend allowing a child the freedom to have whatever attitude he wants. Remember: we are all in charge of our own happiness or the lack of it as we choose. But we also know that behaviors are often attached to attitudes. The *behavioral extension* of a bad attitude is a whole different matter. Disrespect, rudeness, sarcasm, or anger are all concrete behaviors that can be, and should be directly addressed. To summarize: we address any bad behavior related to the bad attitude, but not the bad attitude per se.

Back to little Gracie... extinction would probably have worked early when the problem was small. Months before the trouble started upon the first trip to Wal-Mart when the unwanted behavior was at a low level, ignoring it would most likely have stopped the pleading. At that time Gracie's requests had not yet been given attention or rewarded. If the whining was fruitless and no attention was given, little Gracie would have given up. What is currently happening is that Mom is initiating extinction but eventually gives in at each Wa-Mart trip. Now the child has learned that "no" really does not mean "no" and that she simply needs to outlast the parent. It will now take further action than ignoring the bad behavior to eliminate it.

Consequence Tool #3: Punishment

Punishment may be the tool most familiar to the reader. Sadly it is sometimes the one and only tool used by parents, not only excluding extinction and reinforcement, but omitting the close relationship, modeling, and other principles, which is a serious mistake. As already stated, punishment has a place in an overall discipline program. Used by itself, punishment somewhat works with younger children, but fails miserably in the long-term.

Punishment is defined as an undesirable consequence attached to an inappropriate choice or behavior. Like the other consequence tools, how we as parents respond to a certain behavior will predict its likelihood in the future. Like the other consequence tools, we can strategically use punishment to shape the actions of our children and guide whether it will show up again in the future.

Unlike positive reinforcement which *increases* behavior, punishment *decreases* behavior. Simply put, if used effectively, punishment gets rid of unwanted behaviors of all kinds. This is achieved by linking something unpleasant with the bad behavior. What happens chronologically in punishment is that the child's behavior is followed by the unpleasant response from the parent resulting in decreased bad behavior from the child over time.

Examples of Punishment:

- Take away television for two days
- Early bedtime in 10 or 15 minute increments

- Extra chores
- Timeout
- Take away cell phone
- No video games for one week
- Write 50 sentences
- No movie outing

In each of these examples, if punishment is introduced after the unwanted behavior, the unwanted behavior will be eliminated over time. As with the other consequence tools, the closer in time a parent can place the consequence to the infraction the more effective it will be.

Little Johnny colored on the wall one morning. His stay-at-home mother informed him, "You just wait till your father gets home" (which not only makes dad the bad guy but sends the message that she does not have the authority or backbone to deal with his behavior). Little Johnny was good as gold for the rest of the day. When dad got home at five o'clock he put the child in timeout. Was Johnny punished for coloring the wall that morning or for being good all day? It tends to be confusing for children, especially younger children with lower order thinking, when so much time lapses between the undesirable behavior and the punishment.

Additionally, when using punishment, punish with the goal of changing the child's behavior, not venting your frustration. The reality is that children push our buttons. They stir-up our emotions. They are a large source of our stressors. If we ventilate all of these feelings back on them we lose some of our discipline power and risk becoming abusive. If we use child punishment as our overflow valve we are likely to over-punish. This, in turn, will cause anger and relational problems in the child and establish an unhealthy model for venting anger for the child.

Consequently, **we as parents should never punish out of anger.** We must take the time to let ourselves cool down. Our punishment should be fair, reasonable, age-appropriate, and have the goal of instilling character through a change in behavior, not soothing our own emotions.

Also, punishments have a ceiling. **At a certain point, no amount more of the punishment teaches the lesson more effectively.** For example, a father assigns his ten-year-old son to write fifty sentences.

The dad may then think that 100 sentences will eliminate the bad behavior twice as effectively, or 200 sentences will work four times as effectively. With this logic writing a million sentences would ensure that the child would *never, ever* do it again. Once again, emotions of the of the parent may play a part in this line of thinking. The bottom line is that we must make the punishment reasonable, fair, and with character development at its focal point.

Further, it is important to remember that punishment does not teach the child what do to, only what *not* to do. Remember, punishment does not increase, boost, or enhance anything. *Punishment decreases!* Teaching the child *what to do* requires positive reinforcement and modeling. This again underscores the fatal flaw in using punishment alone as a discipline technique.

Lastly, **all of the consequence tools become increasingly more effective with the close relationship between parent and child described earlier.** While consequences work, we as parents can only dangle carrots in front of our children for so long. Eventually they will learn to get their own carrots. It is not just about behavior. It is about a foundation of great love for our children. It is about wanting the best for them, and this the child must feel! Teenagers lack the basics of maturity and insight, but they are surprisingly accurate in identifying motives. If a teen senses a father's discipline is no more significant than training the family pet, the child will soon rebel. Once rebellion ensues, character and positive behavior training quickly take a back seat, sometimes never to return. Our children *must* sense our love within, and as an extension of our discipline. We must give our children attention aside from discipline moments. Once again, the supreme importance and value of the warm parent-child bond emerges expressed through time and sacrifice. It bears repeating that with other aspects of parenting in place the need for punishment will be greatly decreased.

In the 1983 holiday classic *A Christmas Story* little Ralphie cursed as he spilled the lug nuts while helping his father change a flat tire. The child was later punished by holding a bar of soap in his mouth. As of the writing of this book the professional football career of Adrian Peterson hangs in the balance having used a tree branch to whip his son- something I also experienced as a child.[3] With these examples in mind, how far is too far in using this consequence tool? Punishment must be unpleasant to be effective. It must also be strong, but not severe. This excludes anything that is cruel, degrading, or more than

---
3 http://en.wikipedia.org/wiki/Adrian_Peterson

slightly physically painful. Punishments *cannot* cause physical injury! This should at least prompt caution in using a paddle, switch, or other implement to punish a child. Previous generations of parents had difficulty understanding the difference between punishment and abuse. Tough love was the preferred approach. While this book clearly endorses a firm approach to discipline, many times tough love is tough without the love.

A punishment can be the catalyst God uses to create a sense of guilt or shame, but should not be humiliating such that the *value* of the child is diminished. Remember, we target the behavior, not the child. Also, parents should avoid public embarrassment if possible. At times a child may force a parent's hand by acting up to the extent that Mom or dad has no choice but to address and control the behavior publically and often dramatically. Publically embarrassing a child is demeaning, damages the parent-child relationship, and is therefore counterproductive to the goal of parenting.

As we return to the Gracie scenario once more, would punishment have worked? Practically speaking, punishment would have been hard to implement since mom had to focus on shopping, they were in a public place, and the fact that Gracie needed to remain confined in the basket and supervised. However, in theory punishment would work in this situation. Logistically, reinforcement would be much easier to implement i.e. if the child behaves while in Wal-Mart she is rewarded afterward. Moreover, working from a positive position in teaching children is generally preferable to the negative nature of punishment. The particularly difficult aspect of Gracie's situation is not just that mom took the wrong approach- she took the wrong approach during *many* Walmart trips. Deeply ingrained ways of acting and thinking are a challenge. As with many long-term behavior problems, it will take significant focus and patience to correct little Gracie.

Using Timeouts Effectively

God loves us in a limitless manner that we cannot fathom. He loves us when we obey and when we disobey. He loves us when we love Him and when we rebel. Regardless of any other factor, God loves us immensely! **There are times, however when we are not in His favor and He cannot use us because of our own choices and behavior.** It is during this period that we are distant from God despite His continued love for us. God does not like this distance but allows it for our discipline. It is this (hopefully) temporary distance from God and its accompanying emotional pain that He intends to be a time of reflection, remorse, and reconsideration as we realign our will with God's. This scenario is demonstrated many times throughout Scripture. Samson, for example, found himself in this situation. It was the agonizing distance from God as well as its painful consequences that caused Samson to eventually recommit himself to the Lord and become useful once again. In other words, God put him in timeout.

Timeouts for children have been used in one form or another for many years, but have not been used to their potential. Fortunately, they have become more formalized and refined in recent years. A timeout for children is one of the most effective and universal tools that exists and can be used from young children to about 12 years old. Besides being useful for punishment or removal from a volatile situation, time outs are also good for a period of reflection, a calming of the child's emotions, instilling submission to authority, and encouraging self-control. Consequently, this technique achieves many different things at once.

A child who is unresponsive to time outs is rare and usually involves a poor procedure or inconsistency on the parent's part. As with *all* of the behavior tools, consistency is essential in achieving positive results. With young children Mom and Dad can begin by establishing an area of the room designated for time outs that can include a chair exclusively for that purpose. A chair tends to work best since it is a well-defined space and imposes limitations in the child's movement. Sitting on the floor or standing against the wall are not as well-defined and give the child some physical latitude that can result in playfulness and weaken the effectiveness of the time out. Parents can also give the chair a name if they wish. I have heard it called the power chair, the reflection chair, or simply the timeout chair

Timeouts work best under a tight, sure procedure in which the child sits in a chair one minute for each year of his age. He must sit in the chair properly without talking, clowning around, getting up, or asking is if his time is complete. Also, the child should not be entertained or distracted in any way (by television or an object in his hands for example) such that he can fully ponder his actions. Any violation of these requirements and his time should start over. Parents can use a timer or simply keep their eye on the clock. It is important that the child not be forgotten, and that parents inform him when time is up rather than the child determining or continually asking.

In homes with loose structure this procedure will initially create a clash of wills as Mom and Dad firm-up this technique. Obedience may be a struggle for the child in sitting for the prescribed time. **It is imperative that Mom and Dad outlast Junior so that this battle is won by the child's submission to the parents.** If the child gets out of the chair or violates another aspect of the timeout the time must start over. Not only will the child truly grow and learn at this point, but any battle early on will evolve over time into respectful compliance if administered consistently. A five-minute timeout may take forty-minutes or more. If parents will remain strong and keep standards high, it *will* get better. If this first timeout took forty-minutes, the next will likely only take thirty minutes, and the next twenty minutes. Typically within two weeks the child can willingly walk himself over to the timeout chair, sit himself down, and serve his time correctly and more independently.

Once a timeout has been properly served the child is allowed out of the chair. It is then important to engage in a *brief* conversation with the child that recounts the bad behavior and reminds the child that future misbehavior will lead to another sure timeout. Lastly, and very importantly, give the child a warm hug that assures the child that parental love remains in place despite any childish mistakes. This last step clarifies the confusion in some children's mind that "I was bad and daddy punished me so maybe he does not love me anymore." As with God, it must be clear that we have temporary withdrawn our favor, but never our love.

The Infamous Chart

Fifty yards from my counseling office is a highly tempting donut shop that I am certain is run by Satan! One of their irresistible schemes is to permeate the area with a sweetened smell that renders me helpless. At least that is what I tell my wife. I am pretty sure that I once bought sugar-coated sugar at this establishment! If that were not enough, they also gave me a card that promotes my behavior so that whenever I buy donuts they punch the card which eventually earns me a free dozen donuts! I highly cherish this card, buying whatever is necessary in whatever frequency necessary in order to eventually get my free donuts. With sweetened treats and a prized punch card as strategies I am certain to comply and buy most any sugary thing they want to sell me. And this is the point....

not only of this evil donut shop, but also of this section of the book. I have been effectively trained to buy more donuts with both an immediate reinforcer (sugary smell, tasty donuts, card punched) and a later larger (free donuts) reinforcer.

Charts have been used for years by clever parents since it is especially effective as a special emphasis in an area of behavior or to address a chronic problem. **Charts are also good when punishments have run their course and seem to have lost their effectiveness. Rather than continuing to punish for bad behavior, the idea is to reward for good behavior related to the same problem.** For example, rather than punishing a child for forgetting his homework, use positive reinforcement for *remembering* his homework. A chart simply formalizes that process in a visual, structured, and concentrated way.

A chart is technically called a token economy because tokens are earned by the child for desirable behavior. These tokens can be in the form of stickers, drawn-in stars, punches, checks, colored dots, play money, or chips. Once a certain amount of tokens are earned they can then be traded for something more tangible that the child wants such as a movie night, new toy, or a friend spending the night.

Years ago when our oldest daughter was about six-years-old she developed a chronic problem of getting out of the bed at night. A regular parent-child dance had established itself whereby we put her in the bed and she got out of the bed. We would then escort her back to the bed and she again would get out of the bed. This went on at times for hours some nights. We would scream, punish, and intimidate. The entire family was frustrated and losing sleep, including the child. Nothing seemed to work.

We then implemented a token economy system whereby she could earn a pink instamatic camera she had been wanting. We drew up a chart on a piece of poster board and explained how she could earn the camera. The chart was colorful and eye-appealing to heighten the interest. The poster board was divided into many boxes that represented days with the goal of filling up the boxes with stickers. She could earn a sticker by staying in her bed a certain length of time. In the first boxes (on the top left part of the poster board) was written a "5" indicating that she needed to stay in her bed five minutes to earn a sticker for that box: a relative easy and achievable goal. After five minutes we would go to her bedroom door and check on her. If she was in her bed she earned a sticker. Parent and child would typically make eye contact, giving her an immediate reward since she knew she was earning stickers toward the camera. The chart continued with five-minute boxes but then transitioned to ten-minute boxes. After six to eight ten-minute boxes the chart transitioned to fifteen-minute boxes, then thirty-minute boxes, and eventually several "all night" boxes in a final push. Each night we checked on her faithfully based on the particular box we were focused on. We then picked the efforts up again the next night with the next box, the entire chart taking fifteen to twenty days to complete.

With limited experience as a parent and only studying counseling at the time, I thought this system might work. Little did I know how effective it would be. From the very first night she never got out of the bed again. Like flipping on a switch, we went from dramatic battles that consumed the entire evening, to peaceful nights with miraculous cooperation from our daughter. And because her behavior and thinking had been gradually and systematically shaped, she continued to stay in her bed after the chart was complete and never gave us any further bedtime problems.

This type of token economy system can be adapted to many different areas of a child's life such as issues of school, bath time, manners, and morning procedure. It can be applied to a variety of age groups including teenagers. The target behavior should be specific and measurable, not simply "act better" or "get better grades." The chart can start slow and simple and gradually increase performance/behavior standards (as I did increasing the minutes), or remain constant throughout the chart. An important aspect of the system is the eventual reward. The privilege or material possession must be desirable enough by the child to generate strong incentive, but be affordable and achievable by parents. If not, it will compromise the system. **Also, parents *must* do their part and work the system consistently and faithfully.** A key component in the success of the bedtime token economy years ago in my family was the fact that we were willing to check on the child every five minutes faithfully and without delay. This meant that either my wife or I needed to get up, interrupt our activity, and check on the child as an expression of intentional parenting and willingness to invest for the good of the child. Our willingness to do this demonstrated that we were highly interested in our daughter's character development for the long-haul

Redirection

Young children and toddlers are very curious. The freedom to learn from this curiosity is an important part of the child's growth and will be for many years. The problem is that in the midst of exploring a young child can run into danger or destroy something important. Breakables in the home should be placed out of the reach of children of this age or the parents jeopardize valued items being damaged. The immaturity and curiosity of small children exceed their self-control and ability to be taught. Consequently, to expect a small child to show restraint and not touch grandma's antique tea pot is foolish. But, there is another useful approach.

Parents can take advantage of a child's curiosity and short attention span by using what is known as redirection. When a child becomes fixated on a particular idea or physical item that is not appropriate, parents can take the child's mind off the idea or item by introducing a new one that *is* appropriate. The parent may have to work up their acting skills and "sell" the new item to the child, but typically the child will be fascinated by the new item and quickly forget about the old one. This technique is especially useful when away from home or in public when a parent does not have the time to fully address the issue, or does not want to risk pointlessly become an embarrassing spectacle should the child throw a fit.

Parents must be careful not to use redirection beyond the young child period of life. What is beneficial in the early years is detrimental later. At some point around five or six years-old it becomes counterproductive to use redirection. This is because the child is now mature enough to begin regulating his emotions and accepting disappointment. At this stage in his development redirection stifles his character and emotional growth.

Spanking

As I work with families and the misbehavior of children, rarely does a day go by that I do not hear in my counseling office, "They just need to whoop'em more" as a remedy to behavior problems in children. I suppose spanking has been around as long as children have! As Adam and Eve anticipated their first child, they too must have pondered on the appropriateness of corporal punishment.

I frequently also hear "spare the rod and spoil the child" quoted as validity for parents to spank. However, from this literal interpretation it could be assumed that parents should buy a metal rod from Home Depot with which to whack their children. This is a passage (usually misquoted) from Proverbs 13:24 which says, "He who spares the rod hates his son, but he who loves him is careful to discipline him." The Hebrew word for "rod" is the same word used in Psalm 23 which reads "Your rod and your staff comfort me." Surely the Psalmist did not intend to convey that being struck with a rod would be comforting.

A rod, also known as a shebat, was the wooden staff used by shepherds to guide their sheep. The hook was used to pull sheep back into the fold as they naively left the flock. **The shepherd's rod was never used to beat the sheep, but was a symbol of guidance, leadership, and discipline, and to protect the sheep from predators.** It is these characteristics of God mentioned in the 23rd Psalm that truly comfort us.[4] This serves as a wonderful model for moms and dads in their parenting. Our purpose is not to beat children into submission, but to guide, protect, and discipline them into the highest of Godly character.

Most authors of discipline books (or at least the brave ones) offer opinions on spanking. This writer will be no different. But, unlike some, this book will attempt to address the topic in a balanced and practical manner. We will look at all sides of this, controversial topic.

Unless you just arrived on planet earth, spanking is a discipline technique that involves striking a child, especially on the buttocks. With the definition of punishment in mind, spanking is a strategy meant to decrease a certain behavior. Spanking may be the most common punishment technique used in our culture. It is extremely common. It is almost a staple of Americana. Some would even say we own the technique, which may account for its high frequency.

Both its effectiveness and ethical use remain a hotly debated issue despite many years of consideration. Factually speaking, spanking works as a deterrent to a target behavior because it is the sort of thing children would like to avoid. Some parents are skeptical of its effectiveness, but let me assure the reader that it will work to decrease a particular behavior if implemented immediately after the behavior. However, in my opinion it is overused for many reasons. Despite its effectiveness the use of spanking has problems. A parent who uses spanking will be forced to address other

---

4 http://hermeneutics.stackexchange.com/questions/1614/rod-and-staff-psalm-23

problematic issues along the way. Numerous side effects should cause the reader to rethink his/her use of this discipline technique.

Side effects from spanking:

1. *Spanking serves as a model for hitting.* A parent who hits will have a child who hits- guaranteed. Stopping the child's hitting will be challenging later. It will also be challenging to explain why Junior cannot hit but Mommy can hit.

2. *Spanking is often used as a means for the parent to vent anger.* An angry, red-faced parent with neck veins bulging while spanking is a common display in American homes. As stated earlier, this not only increases the likelihood of physical abuse, but it serves as a model for an inappropriate expression of anger.

3. *Spanking produces anger in the child.* The natural and universal reaction to being hit is anger, regardless of any other factor. A child is then likely to express/vent that anger in many possible ways- attacking a sibling, punching a wall, or hitting the parent back.

4. *Spanking can be used too often without forethought and too harshly.* Spanking is so easy it becomes automatic with many parents. It becomes nothing more than a reflex that encourages overuse. Spanking becomes the go-to technique that is used for big problems, small problems, and all problems in between.

5. *Children are often spanked based on the intensity of the feelings of the adult.* Rather than thinking through a fair, reasonable punishment that matches the behavior of the child, parents gauge punishment, and especially spanking, on the immediate intensity of their own feelings. This may also trigger the parent's own tendency to be impulse.

6. *Over time spanking becomes mindless and other alternatives are not considered.* The effortlessness and release of anger are self-reinforcing and promote yet more spanking. Parents can easily become caught up in excessive spanking without realizing it and over time put less and less thought into their discipline choices.

7. *Over time spanking ca reduce overall positive levels of behavior in the child.* Spanking will successfully reduce a target behavior, but it can also reduce broader behaviors causing a

once energetic and curious child to become not so energetic and curious. This is especially true if corporal punishment is used too often or too harshly.

8. *Spanking can harm the parent-child relationship.* Spanking physically hurts a child, bruises his ego, and threatens a once-formed emotional bond. A parent must then rebuild that bond and the trust that accompanies it.

9. *Spanking does not tell a child what to do, only what NOT to do.* A parent will never get more of a certain desirable behavior through spanking (or punishment more broadly). Spanking is limited to eliminating undesirable behavior. To increase good behavior, parents must use reinforcement in place of or in conjunction with punishment/spanking.

The analogy I use to clarify this spanking dilemma is that of the decision to use medication for emotional problems. Many people give careful consideration to the decision to take a medication to relieve suffering from depression, obsessive-compulsive disorder, anxiety, etc... As part of that decision the issue of side effects always arises. Medications of this type typically have a side effect, and often several. The question is how many side effects and how severe would the side effects have to be to abandon the medication? At what point, even though the medication is effective, would the potential harm become greater than the hoped-for benefits?

With eight noted side effects of spanking, this should initiate a thoughtful pause in the reader. It is not that spanking is not effective. It is that there are many side effects that go with it that parents must then deal with. Depending on the magnitude and extent of the side effects it may not be worth it, or at least requiring reevaluation. And though the Proverbs passage quoted earlier is typically misinterpreted, there are times when God takes very strong, dramatic action in cases of rebellion, or disobedience. **Consequently, I believe Scripture does allow for corporal punishment as a discipline tool.**

All things considered I recommend these four guidelines with regard to spanking:

1. *Use spanking wisely and sparingly.* Resist spanking as your first or automatic action- let it be your last resort. Let spanking be your "big guns," bearing in mind that no country pulls

out their big guns regularly or for every disagreement. Consider the consequence tools and seek out other alternatives that work as well or better than spanking.

2. *Spanking works best (one swat) with a child's willful disobedience, disrespect, or to gain a child's attention.* Multiple swats tend to indicate a parental release of anger or discipline that is dangerously close to abuse. Some behavior experts will include lying under the behaviors appropriate for spanking. I disagree with this, but long-term including or excluding spanking this under condition will make little or no difference as long as consequences of some kind are implemented.

3. *Never spank when angry.* The likelihood of excessive punishment or abuse while angry is very high and just not worth it.

4. *If you have anger issues of any kind, do not spank.* There are many other alternatives that work as well.

The Strong-Willed Child

The phrase "strong-willed child" has been around for decades. An internet search will quickly reveal that the popularity of the term has caused many child specialists to jump on the band wagon, lending their wisdom in how to handle this type of child. While these authors disagree on management of the strong-willed child, they do agree on its definition- A child with a tenacious, inflexible, immovable, stubborn, inborn personality trait.

In teaching parenting courses and soliciting a show of hands of parents who have a strong-willed child, I have been surprised to discover just how common this child trait occurs. More often than not parents report they have a strong-willed child. How could this supposedly rare phenomenon be so common? Or maybe it is not so rare. Maybe it is the norm. **Most, if not all children naturally display a stubbornness in getting their own way.** However, there could be another possibility in explaining this "rare" occurrence.

In talking to parents in my counseling practice and in the parenting seminars I conduct, I have discovered that children almost universally push as hard as they need to in order to achieve their goal. They may not have started out that way, as we might expect of a *true* strong-willed child. Over time, however, the child feels the need to increase intensity and determination to higher and higher levels in order to stay ahead of their parent's will so that they can "win." Because lower levels of intensity did not work, the child instinctively upped the ante. **When the child then "wins" there was a self-reinforcing effect establishing a link between his increased intensity and getting what he wanted.**

Six-year-old Juan used to pick up his blocks when told to do so until he figured out that by protesting his mother would do it for him. Mom eventually caught on to her son's scheme and began to hold him accountable. But, just as she took action Juan became more insistent and combative. Despite good intentions and much love for her son, she panicked, wanted a peaceful home, and continued to pick up the blocks. This dynamic persisted and in many different areas of parenting Juan. With each situation, just as Mom began to take the necessary action, her son would stay one step ahead of her and therefore able to get what he wanted. With Juan now sixteen, his mother longed for the simplicity of getting her son to pick up his blocks. This teenager now towered over her physically, regularly demanded the use of the car, cursed her and bucked up to her, and was clearly out of control.

With this description in mind it might be easy to label this child strong-willed. But remember, the true strong-willed child possesses this trait from birth. They are born that way! **What I have described here is a *learned response* not an inborn personality trait.** The above description is a process by which stubbornness is *acquired*. The child does not start out strong-willed, but still ends up that way because of the pattern described above. Because a parent may not have stood firm early on, it may seem like the child possessed this stubbornness from birth. It is this process that I believe is common, and which often leads parents to mislabel a child as strong-willed. More accurately this is a defiant, rebellious pattern of relating to adults and authority figures that is unknowingly reinforced and encouraged by parents. It is the sin nature allowed to grow combined with a conscious that is under-developed.

Battles of the will must be faced with courage and persistence while the child is young. Our fond feelings and desire for a peaceful home cannot supersede or replace our firm discipline. It is *imperative* that parents win confrontations early on. If not, subsequent battles become more difficult as the child becomes physically larger, more clever and selfish, and with greater willingness to manipulate parents.

What is the answer? The remedy is improvement in several areas of parenting that help a mom or dad regain control in the home, some of which have already been covered but are worth mentioning again:

- Establish yourself as the firm authority in the home. What you say goes.
- Refuse to argue since it assumes you and the child are equal in power and authority.
- Use the consequence tools to shape behavior.
- Think through decisions carefully with the child's best interest in mind.
- Enforce "no" by whatever means necessary.
- Never bluff. Follow through with *all* consequences.
- Take steps to insure your children's power always remains under control.
- Strive for the highest in character in your children.

Chapter Nine Discussion Questions:

1. Have you noticed someone in the behavioral or child development field avoiding the term obedience? Is that a word you are comfortable with? Which would you prefer, your child achieve (straight A's or accomplished athlete for example) or be obedient to you? How does this relate to 1 Samuel 15:22?

2. How would you define permissive parenting? Give several reasons a parent might be permissive?

3. How clear to your children are your instructions? Get the feedback of a spouse or trusted friend concerning the clarity of your instructions. Ask your children if your instructions toward them are generally clear or not.

4. What is the purpose of bluffing in a card game? How does this relate to bluffing in discipline?

5. Describe the concept of consequences in your own words. How are consequences Biblical? How does a sure system of consequences in the home prepare a child for adulthood?

6. List the three consequence tools. Give an example how each might be used.

7. Explain in detail an effective timeout procedure. What is the purpose of putting a child in timeout? Has God ever put you in timeout?

8. Describe a token economy or chart system. Is there currently a chronic problem with one of your children that a token economy would resolve? How would you use a chart for this issue?

9. Did your family spank you when you were a child? What ideas on spanking in this book differ from your family of origin? Name two problems with spanking cited in this chapter.
10. Do you have a strong-willed child? Explain how a strong-willed child might be created unintentionally by parents.

CHAPTER 10
Respect

It was originally written and sung in 1965 by Otis Redding, but it would be Aretha Franklin that would earn two Grammies for the tune that would eventually earn a #5 spot on Rolling Stones' list of all-time greatest songs. It became one of the feminist anthems of the 60's.[1] And what Karaoke fan has not sung R-E-S-P-E-C-T?

Like all character traits, respect (or the lack of it) is first taught in the home. We challenge our child in order for them to respect to us. Respect from child to parent is so universally agreed upon that a chapter on the topic might seem unnecessary. Despite being a basic requirement of any healthy relationship, there seems to be so little of it in our culture today. Further, it is a complicated subject, worthy of discussion since it has powerful repercussions in the lives of children. **Respect and honesty are the hallmarks of successful personal and relational functioning.** These characteristics are so important that the absence of either has the potential to threaten every aspect of a person's life. A violation of either respect or honesty by a child in the home should be considered a "deal breaker" and be met with swift, sure consequences.

But what is respect? It is one of those concepts that everyone knows about and understands, but find hard to put into words. Webster defines respect as worthy of high regard, to esteem or value. To respect a person is to look up to them or some aspect of their life. This is the relationship we must have with our children. They must highly regard us as parents. They must esteem and value us. They must look up to us. The behavior of children must reflect these ideas.

---

1 http://en.wikipedia.org/wiki/Respect_(song)

Why Should Children Respect Parents?

This may seem like an odd question, but as intentional parents we resist putting our brains on auto pilot. The short answer is that it is in our children's best interest to respect parents. Disrespectful, overly independent children tend to overestimate their ability to function in the world. Put bluntly, Junior does not really know what he "thinks" he knows. As an older child, this knowledge-confidence gap widens even more. He will not only dismiss true wisdom and knowledge, but he will place himself in danger of which he is unaware of. Because of this overconfidence, the child will make mistakes. If his disrespect is at a high level he will make *many* mistakes, and probably big ones. Because of this high level of disrespect, it will caused him to be un-teachable and un-protectable. He may learn life lessons as a young adult, but typically it will be through much pain and inconvenience.

The irony of a child respecting his parents is that it has nothing to do with parents. In reading the definition of respect (to highly regard or esteem) one might get the impression that parents must be arrogant, but respecting parents is completely about the child. It is about his relational actions toward the parent that build character, allows him to be taught and protected, and ultimately brings success to the child's adult life.

An important distinction is that of disrespect versus discontent. Some parents falsely believe that a child's disapproval of a parental decision, a child's feelings of dissatisfaction in the moment, or the absence of expressed love for the parent all constitute disrespect. We must remember, we need to give our children the freedom to feel what they want to feel, and have whatever opinions they have. *This is not disrespectful nor should parents be threatened by this.* In fact, the expression of these opinions or feelings is good! It shows open communication. At the same time we as parents are not likely to reverse a decision or should we attempt to change their minds, especially through a heated debate. We do, however, want the child to live in reality. This is achieved through regular, honest communication and through the warm bond referred to repeatedly throughout this book.

Why Children Do Not Respect Parents

In my observations of families, children do not respect parents for a number of reasons:

1. *The selfish nature of children.* There is a link between self-centeredness, power, and disrespect in children. As stated numerous times in the book, there is a natural selfish desire for children to want what they want- and right now! To achieve this they need to muster power and authority that exceeds that of the parent. Disrespect is a very common way that children attempt to increase power by lowering regard for and de-valuing the parent.

2. *Respect for others not modeled by parents.* The idea and incredible importance of modeling should be very clear to the reader by now. It is our single best strategy at teaching anything! Parents must examine themselves since it is often the case that the lack of respect for others that parents show is effectively absorbed by their children.

3. *Respect not insisted on by adults.* Like all other principles that are good for children, respect should be a standard in the home by which parents hold children accountable. If not, respect for others will not likely occur. And like other matters of character, respect should be non-negotiable.

4. *Behavior of adults not respectable.* Respect is both demanded and earned. Actions and attitudes of all kinds can affect a child's respect toward adults, even if it is insisted upon. Addictions, deception, emotional instability, angry outbursts, laziness, inconsistencies, immature behavior, and a friend relationship with your child are a few of the parental behaviors that will automatically earn disrespect from children. What best earns respect from children is when parents possess a combination of well-rounded personal stability, continued personal growth and achievement, as well a deeply demonstrated, sacrificial love of the child.

5. Weak parental authority. The reality is that children do not respect weak adults. The child may *like* the parent and manipulate the parent, but also view the parent as powerless, ineffective, wimpy, and spineless. Children instinctively smell cracks in parental authority if those cracks exist. The strong, authoritative position advocated throughout this book will inherently promote respect.

In some cases parents find it difficult to identify or recognize disrespect. They have some faint idea of the concept, but it is vague and undefined. Therefore, they are not certain if the behavior displayed equals disrespect. They feel that something is not right, but they cannot put their finger on it. In other cases a parent is caught off guard by a child's disrespect. It abruptly comes out of nowhere, and the adult is unprepared and taken aback. The parent is befuddled and confused, maybe even shocked at the unexpected contempt. Still other parents are apprehensive to confront disrespect because it promises a battle. Battles make many parents uncomfortable. Battles mean arguments. And worse, what if they do not win the battle?

I assure the reader that the battle is winnable. In fact, it is imperative that parents win the battle. The earlier a parent can begin winning the battles the better. **Parents must resist either a casual approach to parenting, or a well-meaning but unhealthy need to keep peace.** *We must accept the battles as they come and in the moment.* Avoiding a battle does not omit it, it simply delays it. Avoided battles grow over time so that eventually the parent will face a war. **Refusing to confront disrespect simply trades short-term peace for long-term bigger problems.** This is a dangerous trade-off. The better option is mild short-term instability and unhappiness in exchange for long-term peace. If disrespect is confronted as it happens and therefore resolved, the outcome will be a stable, respectful adult in the years to come.

To uphold effective parenting, we first must have a clear picture of exactly what disrespect looks like. We must recognize when a child has crossed the line *for their sake*. We also should not be surprised by disrespect, but in fact expect challenges to authority from our children. Their in-born selfishness makes disrespect predictable. Lastly, we must be prepared for it in the same way we would prepare for anything else that is likely or enviable.

How to Recognize Disrespect

As stated earlier, disrespect can be difficult for parents to recognize. The subjective and slippery nature of disrespectful behavior makes for a fuzzy evaluation of the concept. I suggest the following ways to evaluate disrespect:

1. *Specific words.* Any word that is insulting or derogatory; name-calling; verbal attacks of any kind; agitated criticism.
2. *A dismissive tone, word, or phrase.* Anything that puts you, the parent, at a lower place than a position of power and authority, or elevates the child's status. My personal favorite: "Whatever."
3. *A loud volume.* Children becoming increasingly louder and more intense should be considered disrespectful. This includes a child's eye contact that is more intense, or body language that leans inward toward you, bucks up to you, or is imposing in any way. This includes the child coming in close proximity to the adult for the purpose of intimidation.
4. *A belittling "you are less than" attitude.* Any behavior that says "I am looking down on you" or is generally condescending, demeaning, disparaging, sneering, mocking, sarcastic, scornful, annoyed, or patronizing; contempt of any kind.
5. *Demanding, elitist, entitled, or impatient behavior.* An insistent, selfish urgency on the part of the child for his convenience is disrespectful.

These behaviors should be met with firm correction, as well as consequences if it is a repeatedly problem. Children simply cannot be allowed to relate to adults and those in authority in a superior manner.

Firm Versus Harsh

Throughout this book a firm authoritative stance has been promoted as the position parents should take. For the most part parents operate under a calm reasonable baseline in volume and intensity. It is simply not necessary to exceed that. But, occasionally a parent's authority may be challenged or a child resists cooperating. It then becomes necessary to shift into "firm" mode.

Firm involves a slight raising of intensity to convey authority and intention to act. It is done respectfully, but alerts the child to comply immediately. This *slight* raising of intensity is elevated one notch, not ten. It is not yelling, screaming, or shouting. Additionally, a firm approach always maintains respect. It simply reminds the child who is in charge, and that unpleasant consequences are imminent.

The past willingness of the parent to follow through with consequences will usually achieve compliance at this moment and ensure that parental firmness is met with an obedient response. It is, again, worth repeating that ultimately it is not parental volume, threats, or coercion that gets compliance, but the willingness of mom or dad to take action.

Harsh, by contrast, also conveys authority but is absent of respect. It degrades the child with a high level of intensity and can include name-calling, cursing, threats, and intimidation. Because of this flawed parental approach, an explosive argument may evolve- the very outcome parents want to avoid. This is especially true of teenagers. The lack of respect by the parent gives the child implicit permission, a model, and a motive to reciprocate with disrespect. When this parent-child pattern persists for months or years the result is behavior problems and emotional damage to the child, as well as high levels of regular conflict. In short, screaming matches with children achieve little, and are damaging to everyone involved.

The curious thing about these two very different approaches is that both are likely to get results. The firm healthy approach will succeed, but the harsh method is also likely to achieve compliance. Let's face it, a child being screamed at will usually hop-to and do what he is told. This can give a parent a false sense of security causing mom or dad to believe they are going about their parenting appropriately. The problems are that this sends the message that harsh treatment is normal and appropriate parent-child interaction, as well as the fact this approach inflicts long-term emotional damage to the child.

Harsh will damage the relationship while firm maintains the relationship. Harsh is absent of respect while firm maintains respect. Harsh uses unrestrained intensity while firm uses minimal intensity.

Even when correcting a child it is important for a parent to maintain composure, control their feelings and words, and address the child rationally and calmly. In other words, be as pleasant as possible. I am not suggesting that when your daughter throws a ball in the house and breaks and window, or when your teenage son takes the family car without permission that they be addressed without the magnitude of the offense. In these examples the child needs to understand the extent of his actions. I am saying that we as parents must set a model for personal stability and self-control, think through our responses, and deal with a particular incident in a way that does not escalate the conflict and make things worse. Without this we cannot expect our children to act any differently.

Two-Way Respect

This brings us to an important related point. Decades ago children were subservient, invisible, and devalued. They were thought of as property and often exploited. It was the cultural model of parenting of that era. Old school thought is that children are to be seen and not heard. However, this flies in the face of many principles outlined in this book such as parents listening to their children, warm relationships with a children, and regular two way communication. The direct obligation and impact parents have on their children in training them to be stable, productive citizens with high character was grossly underestimated in past generations. Respect is not a one-way street. **Yes, children must respect parents. This chapter clearly promotes that idea. However, parents must respect children also.**

Respect comes in two forms-

a) Respect due another person as a human being made in God's image
b) Respect due a person because of their earned position in life

Children must respect parents for both reasons. Parents are a part of the human race, but parents also possess a God-given and society-given place of authority. Moms and dads are legally obligated to care for and provide for their children. With that obligation comes the financial responsibility and decision-making authority to raise them. With this position of authority comes respect.

Children on the other hand have no inherent place of earned respect or position. Children do not hold a position of authority of any kind. Consequently, that *type* of respect does not apply to children. But, children are members of the human race, and because of this are due that type of God-given respect. Matthew and Luke both record Jesus stating "Let the little children come to me." It was thought that with Jesus' high position he should not be bothered by small children, but He clearly conveyed that they would always have access to Him. This is the principle that escaped many of our grandparents and great grandparents. The respect between parent and child is mutual, but different. And hence, the basis and concrete expressions of respect they have for one another is different. Further, biblically, children are created in God's image. **Children are not God, but created *by* God and naturally deserving of certain respect.**

Dealing With Disrespect

By now the reader should be very convinced of both the necessity in the home of respect from children as well as the need to address the absence of respect in a timely manner.

1. *Prepare beforehand.* Given the nature of children we should not be surprised by disrespect….it *will* happen. Like all aspects of parenting we must think it through. We prepare through thoughtful consideration before the problem occurs. What is required for my child's best interest, and how can I promote that?

2. *Develop personal strength.* Some are born with an abundance of willpower, confidence, and natural authority. Others must develop this hutzpah. Whatever your case, you will need the determination and strength of will to stand up to the challenges of your child that are inevitable. It is a battle you *must* win for the sake of your child.

3. *Take on the small challenges promptly.* Do not excuse or dismiss a child's disrespect. It is not a phase. It is not someone else's fault. No one "caused" the child to act this way. Address disrespect the moment it occurs! When in the midst of a conversation and the child becomes disrespectful, immediately put the conversation on hold and address the disrespect.

4. *Take strong action.* At a minimum give feedback to the child, as in "You are being disrespectful" stated firmly and in a manner that expects immediate change. Except for the mildest forms of disrespect, command the child to "Stop being disrespectful." Another

effective phrase is "I will not tolerate your disrespect!" Remember the concept of firm? It may also be necessary to implement consequences for disrespect.

5. *As much as possible maintain the relationship.* The reality is that disrespect at least threatens, and may break the relationship. Ideally the child would be repentant enough to initiate and rebuild the relationship, but his selfishness and immaturity may prevent this. Parenting is often about meeting the child more than half way since we adults are the mature one. Consequently, the parent should initiate the reestablishing of the relationship if the child does not.

Chapter Ten Discussion Questions:

1. Describe how respect is linked to a parent's ability to teach and protect their children. Explain the irony of why respect toward a parent is not primarily for the benefit of the parent. How is this related to our respect for God?
2. According to this chapter, what are the two "deal-breaker" character traits?
3. Briefly describe the five reasons children do not respect parents. Do you think it is true that children do not respect weak adults? Give an example.
4. What is meant by "trading short-term peace for long-term bigger problems?" How diligent are you at confrontation of your children? To what degree are you comfortable with confrontation of your children, and does your comfort level matter?
5. How well do you recognize disrespect in your children? How prompt are you at addressing disrespect? What is the predictable outcome when parents do not address disrespect? In Galatians 6:7 we are told "God is not mocked". How does this relate to disrespect toward parents?
6. Compare and contrast firm versus harsh treatment of children.
7. Cite several reasons parents should respect children.
8. What recommendations would you have for a parent whose children are disrespectful?

CHAPTER 11
Responsibility and Accountability

On June 15, 2013 sixteen-year-old Ethan Couch stole two cases of beer from a Wal-Mart and drove away with seven passengers in his father's large, one ton pickup truck. One hour later near midnight the teenager drove seventy miles per hour without a seatbelt down a rural Texas road with a designated forty mile-per-hour speed limit. He hit multiple vehicles and overturned his truck. The accident killed four individuals, including a youth pastor with three children, and permanently paralyzed a sixteen-year-old from the neck down. He fled on foot from the scene while shouting to a friend, "I'm Nathan Couch…I'll get you out of this." Three hours after the accident Nathan showed a blood alcohol content level of .24, three times the legal *adult* alcohol limit. Valium was also in his system. At fifteen Ethan was arrested on two occasions for alcohol possession. His father was a wealthy business owner. His parents were divorced, both having also been arrested multiple times for various offenses.

Defense attorneys stated Ethan suffered from affluenza (not to be confused with the flu strain know as influenza), and was therefore not responsible for his actions. The term has received much publicity since this child's December 2013 hearing. Nonetheless the strategy worked as an unremorseful Nathan Couch received probation.[1,2,3]

It is tragic that such an offense be committed by such a young individual. Many red flags and missteps earlier in this child's life lead to gross levels of irresponsibility that went unchecked. Did this

---
1 http://en.wikipedia.org/wiki/Ethan_Couch
2 http://www.dailymail.co.uk/news/article-2521743/Ethan-Couch-crash-Drink-driving-teen-killed-spared-jail-hes-rich.html
3 http://www.thetruthaboutcars.com/2013/12/im-ethan-couch-ill-get-you-out-of-this/

child answer to anyone? Where was the guidance? Where was the supervision? And after the fact, what lessons can we learn from this related to parenting? Evidence suggests that both parents had issues and priorities of their own. While both parents would have likely verbally affirmed their love for their son, no one cared about this child enough to instill values in him and hold him accountability. As we might predict, Ethan Couch eventually achieved an age and level of power which exceeded his level of responsibility.

The online urban dictionary states that Affluenza is "A disease caused by too much money."[4] "The love of money is the root of evil," an often cited Scripture passage from 1 Timothy, appears to agree. Yet, many people have money and do not commit this kind of horrific deed. To label it a disease is to suggest the responsibility for the actions was outside of the teenager's control. Moreover, the child had no money- his father did. Further, the passage correctly is quoted is "For the love of money is a root of all kinds of evil. Some people, eager for money, have wandered from the faith and pierced themselves with many griefs" (1 Timothy 6:10). While some may point to a thing as the problem, evidence indicates that one's *attitude* and overall *character* are to blame for this kind of problem. We will never know if this tragedy could have been prevented, but we would all agree that parental influence had much to do with this young man's actions.

Other sources define affluenza as "A popular term for a dysfunctional family environment in which both parents work or have activities that decrease parenting time (causing) adverse effects, unsupervised kids/adolescents (which) may drink more, get pregnant, abuse drugs, or gamble online."[5] Jessie H. O'Neill started what she titles 'The Affluenza Project' writing and speaking on the topic. She describes the term as "a harmful or unbalanced relationship with money or its pursuit…the collective addictions, character flaws, psychological wounds, neurosis and behavioral disorders caused or exacerbated by the presence of or desire for wealth."[6] This definition presents the best clarity since it links money with the potential personality flaws and its accompanying outcome. **More than the money or possessions itself, this phenomenon is related to psychological and character aspects of the child- something parents have great control over as previously stated.**

---

4 http://www.urbandictionary.com/define.php?term=Affluenza
5 http://medical-dictionary.thefreedictionary.com/Affluenza
6 http://www.theaffluenzaproject.com/home/aboutjessie/

One tongue-in-cheek source suggests "though a cure has not been definitively established, affluenza is often treated by therapy which can include community service at a soup kitchen or homeless shelter."[7] This strategy, which takes the focus off self and money and onto character-building through serving others, could be more therapeutic than the writer realizes.

While most of us will never be affluent and therefore suffer from affluenza, this does not exclude our families from similar issues. A lack of responsibility and accountability is common. A child with too much power in our culture is routine. A family does not have to have money for the children to be spoiled or to internalize a damaging love of money.

Who Should Children Answer To?

Children who answer only to themselves do not develop properly and usually experience too much too soon. There must be a clear sense that your child answers to you, the parent, while allowing him to make only the decisions for which he is ready. The key is regulation and pacing, but there are some things universally inappropriate for children. For example, more than once I have had a misguided parent watch pornography with their child with the goal of educating the child sexually. Sex education in families is important but cannot be achieved with such vulgar, perverted means. The outcome will always do more harm than good.

In most cases it is not a matter of *never* exposing a child to certain information. It is an issue of timing. It is a matter of *when* to allow this information, privilege, freedom, or material possession, and to what extent is it tied to the child's age, efforts, and demonstrated maturity.

The term "parentified child" has been mentioned, but deserves referencing again. Relative to this chapter, this is this child whose parents provide inadequate support, who is at risk because he may be assumed to be more mature than actually he actually is. This child will often assume tasks and roles which Mom or Dad should fulfill, but because the parents do not, the child often fills the gap and undertakes them. Children do a poor job of raising their siblings, managing the family, or comforting a depressed mother, but they will usually attempt it and do their best. Consequently, a *willingness* to accept

---

7   http://www.urbandictionary.com/define.php?term=Affluenza

responsibility is mistaken for maturity. **It is this false maturity that is at high risk for emotional problems of all kinds, a codependent future, and experiencing much of life before he/she has gained the emotional, social, and cognitive development to process it.**

Taking Responsibility

Children seem to learn early that blaming others works. They either connect the blame dots as they see it modeled in other children or on their own they envision its effectiveness and figure it out on their own. James 1:14-15 tells us of the initiation of, temptation toward, and the progression of sin that can destroy us. Adults and children alike often make decisions grounded in their own desires, and based on selfishness and a false hope in a positive outcome. **A child will typically own up to what he did or act responsible when it is insisted upon him, but like most principles in this book he will only internalize it over time *if* modeling and a close relationship are included.**

Maturity is also an important factor. Years ago my mother had an antique wicker baby stroller. It was at least seventy-five years old, tattered, fragile, and irreplaceable. It was not to be played with because doing so would likely destroy it. It was only for looks, but with three daughters, each of whom loved playing with dolls, this became a temptation. When my family visited grandma's house, regardless of any rule or consequences, they were intent on playing with the stroller. When children are young and immature they are ruled by their impulses. These urges are an overwhelming pull to an action. It is here that we as parents must be understanding, especially with young children. As time goes on, however, children have more potential and ability to control these impulses. It is here that we must begin to insist they control their behavior and also include consequences if they do not.

Mothers and fathers must begin insisting children own up to irresponsible actions. **Even small incidents of escaped responsibility can initiate the pattern and set a poor precedent.** Parents must confront the child on issues of irresponsibility and cover-up, otherwise they may begin a successful lifestyle of deception. This, in turn, will negatively affect every part of the child's life in adulthood.

Earned Not Given

Children have many legitimate needs: food, clothing, shelter, medical care, education, and hygiene care. These are reasonable needs parents are obligated to meet that should not be tied to performance of any kind. Most everything else should be tied to earning and responsibility since this is how adult life works. This is especially true in the teenage years and as adulthood approaches. During these years the challenge to take greater responsibility for meeting his own needs must increase dramatically in order to prepare the child for adulthood.

Beginning even early on children must perform. They must learn that they have to *do* something- something creative, something that grows or teaches, something that produces, something that organizes and improves life, something that contributes to self or others, something that gets one active! It is a mistake for parents to take the approach that childhood is for having fun. Fun is not to be omitted. It too grows a child, especially younger children. But too often parents take on the domestic tasks that their children can perform. This is especially important since chores at home are an excellent opportunity to teach responsibility and accountability. Further, doing dishes, mowing the lawn, or vacuuming the living room teaches practical skills that the child can take into adulthood. As our children have gone off to college, it has been surprising how many of their roommates do not know how to wash their own clothes. This is the kind of skill parents must teach their children for successful adult functioning.

Allowances

Chores around the house also offer an opportunity for an allowance. A good rule of thumb is one dollar per week for every year of the child's age. Therefore a 10 year-old gets $10 per week allowance, but this is not set in stone of course. This assumes all chores are done and to a high level. Quality must also be taken into consideration, relative to the child's age and abilities.

Some parents take this allowance idea to the next level, particularly when the child is about 16 years of age. In this approach Mom and Dad give the child all, or a large portion of the money they would have spent on the child for living expenses over a certain period of time. The child is left with the responsibility of spending the money wisely on any number of things that may include entertainment, clothing, gas, haircuts and grooming, and prom expenses. The money must last the child for the time period, six months for example. Once the money is spent no more is given until the next time period. If six-months-worth of money is spent in five months, the child must then do without. This teach self-control, budgeting, cautious spending, and connects behavior with consequences. It also prepares the child for adulthood since this is the way adult life works.

William Bennett, former Education Secretary says, "We help foster a mature sense of responsibility in our children the same way we cultivate other traits: by practice and by example. Household chores, homework, extracurricular activities, after-school jobs, and volunteer work all contribute to maturation if parental examples are clear, consistent, and commensurate with the developing powers of the child."[8] I agree whole-heartedly.

I am convinced that a good work ethic is one of the most difficult things to teach children. With rare exception children are naturally lazy. They want to exert as little effort as possible in life, while receiving as many benefits as possible. The parents who have been successful in this challenge have probably done several things that encourage children and link effort with rewards. This includes monetary rewards, but also includes natural rewards of the satisfaction of a job well-done.

Clear demonstration by parents of a strong work ethic is where it begins. This modeling goes beyond simple avoidance of laziness to ambition and taking the initiative. Children should be taught beyond doing the minimum required in life. A good work ethic incorporates goals, determination, and is self-motivating. It also goes beyond simply responding to an opportunity to taking charge of one's life, planning for success, and making intentional career decisions.

Performance Versus Value

In our culture personal value is tied to many different things. Because of this there is a quest for significance that many people fanatically strive for all their lives. **This search for significance is often a thirst that cannot be quenched as individuals seek false sources of self-worth.** So many people simply want to feel important and will go to great lengths to do so. Teenage girls wear excessive makeup

---

[8] Bennett, William J., *The Book of Virtues*, New York, Simon and Schuster, 1993.

and revealing clothing in order to "feel" valued. Men obsess over making more money in order to "feel" valued. Others make multiple Facebook posts per day boasting of family achievements and displaying recreational pictures hoping to promote envy in order to "feel" valued. Money, material possessions, intelligence, talent, skill, position, and physical attractiveness are all tied to worth in a perverted value system. Lest the reader be confused, there is nothing wrong with materials possessions. Being attractive is not a sin. Having a high level of talent is a blessing, but **in a healthy individual there is a distinction made between being attractive and establishing beauty as a *basis* for worth.** There is a distinction between having money and believing yourself better or more important than others *because* of money.

This false basis even defies logic, as many have eventually found out. Even the best beauty, mental ability, or physical prowess eventually fades as the natural aging process plays out. Money can be earned and lost in an instant. Cars are destroyed in a mishap; houses burn down. Though tragic, an accident can occur to a young person and immediately end certain skills and abilities. These occurrences happen every day and are a testament to the uncertainty and brevity of life.

God's economy, however, is dramatically different. Our value is not conditional to God. Our worth to God is not provisional, as in "I love you if you…." What He thinks of us is not based on any human trait. We do not have to work or perform in any way, be intelligent, be thin, or have chiseled good-looks. If we eat Bon-bons on the couch and watch Oprah reruns for the next fifty years, God would not love us any less. Our worth therefore is not based on conditional actions or standards. God did not love Adolph Hitler any less than Mother Teresa. **God's love is based solely on the fact that He made us in his image.**

Any gift from God of talent or intelligence serves several purposes not tied to worth. First, it is a reflection of the gift-giver. Second, whatever abilities, knowledge, etc, we have has been given to us freely. We must be thankful and use it responsibility. Third, it guides us to the calling in life we are to fulfill. It does not determine our value in life, but our life direction. It does not determine our worth, only how God intends on using us. With this in mind, we should strive to develop whatever abilities, knowledge, skills, and influence given to us so that it can be used to its fullest. Even something we might consider shallow, such as good looks, can bring influence to a person and then be used for good. We must be cautious, however, that it not be a source of vanity, but a reason to deflect credit and give glory back to the creator, God.

I go into this lengthy explanation to highlight how we as parents are to view our children in light of performance. Far too many parents have difficulty separating this out. Their child's abilities take on a life of their own, void of any emphasis on character or balance. For too many parents, their children's abilities become a reflection of them. For too many parents the value conveyed to the child is consciously or unconsciously based on their child's straight A's, scoring a touchdown, winning a pageant, or playing a complicated piano number. While I believe that all of these, and many more, should be goals, they simply cannot be linked to value. **The child must feel loved and worthy regardless of grades, athletic ability, attractiveness, or any other personal characteristic.**

Self-Soothing

"I'm bored" said my 13 year-old son one day during his summer vacation. "Can I sleep in your bed" my wife and I were asked by each of our children at one time or another. "I really want some Dooney and Bourke shoes" my oldest child once said. In each one of these examples the child is essentially asking for the same thing- will you make me happy? Without realizing it adults often ask themselves the same thing- what external things, people, material possessions, sexual adventure, substance, or adrenaline-producing thrills will make me happy?

What is common in many homes is that the child is in a discontented state, wants relief, and holds the parents responsible for that relief. The question then becomes...it is a parent's responsibility to make a child happy? How does character development relate to happiness in children? How does this question relate to self-sufficiency within the child who will eventually become an adult?

As you may remember, one of the goals of enmeshed parents is that their child be happy. All things considered no caring parent wants their child to be unhappy, but to what extent are mom and dad *responsible* for that happiness? The way moms and dads answer this question has a huge effect on their parenting.

One of the things children must take responsibility for, but often approach with great resistance is the state of their own mood and happiness. This plays itself out in many different forms regularly in homes across America. Many adults have never learned this lesson and expect others to cheer them up. The basis of many singles looking for a mate is the same as the initial statements in this section- will you make me happy? And while we might expect it from a young child, this request directly or indirectly from a needy, unfulfilled adult can be rather pathetic. Our hypothetical adult is dissatisfied because of feeling stuck in life, but may not have the drive or internal strength to overcome his fear and pursue the self-development that would relieve his inner tension.

Self-soothing in children is the willingness and ability, relative to his age, to comfort themselves in times of distress. This distress can be large or small. It can be actual distress or perceived. Actually, almost anything can be a potential source of distress. In fact, almost anything *will* be a source of distress if not handled correctly by parents. Over time the many sources of distress then become limitations in behavior.

As parents we must provide the foundation for the ability of the child to soothe himself. Fear is a harsh controller. It dictates and drives many lives and many parts of people's lives. In so many cases it keeps individuals from fulfilling their potential and becoming all that God intends for them to become. Parents must model two things. First, moms and dads must control their own fears. For many, fear is a feeling that runs amuck, is over-focused on, and is the basis of decisions and actions. This process must be headed off early in the thought process, and therefore not be allowed to build in the person, thus ultimately control him. Second, parents must model "forging ahead" behaviors and attitudes, and take on challenges despite fear. Fear is universal! It is felt by everyone. But, the reality is that rarely do fears manifest themselves in the awful way we imagine. The outcome we imagine is almost always far worse than the reality. Often we have trained ourselves to engage in catastrophic thinking, never considering that the outcome might be good or envisioning the satisfaction from a particular challenge.

Parents then combine this modeling with encouragement. Moms and dads must act as cheerleaders, providing reassurance and inspiring the child to take small steps at first then graduating to larger challenges.

The willingness may be absent, especially in a reluctant child. Bear in mind that the characteristic of reluctance in children can be inborn or a learned behavior. It is the learned variety that we must avoid, lest we then have to unlearn the dysfunctional fear that has been learned. Parents must give Junior a gentle push in combination with the other character-building strategies in this book. As we start with very small, very easy tasks, and begin early on in the child's life, confidence is initiated and builds. The confidence at fifty years old to run a large company begins at eighteen months with picking up a single block and putting it in the toy box.

With this confidence and strategy toward fear, the foundation of soothing one's self is set. Now comes the opportunity and follow through. It is this area that parents may want to jump in and rescue. Parents may want to soothe the child because they do not want to see Junior struggle, and because they can help. Many people say, "I don't want my kids to have to struggle like I did." It is important recognize that struggle brings about perseverance and character. Removing the struggle does a disservice to the child since it removes that character-building element from their lives. Consequently, parents must restrain from over-supporting the child by allowing them to soothe themselves. **This is the essence of self-soothing- that children can solve their own problems, make themselves happy, and manage their own mood.**

This concept of self-soothing plays itself out early on as babies are allowed to cry in their crib as they fall asleep with a pat on the back by mom every five minutes. It continues as dad sympathizes and puts a band aid on a boo-boo, but does not respond to lingering whimpering by the child. Self-soothing applies when a mom does not respond to a child's whining for a new toy at Target, but tells him he can earn it by doing extra chores. It relates to a teenager daughter when a dad does not allow her to be disrespectful simply because she is in a bad mood. It plays itself out when a parent does not rescue a young adult in debt from irresponsible spending, though the parent has the financial means to do so. In each of these situations the request from the child is the same: will you make me feel better?

Children Sleeping With Parents

Family beds have become strangely popular. In this arrangement sleeping, or co-sleeping as it is called, involves a large bed in which the entire family sleeps, often involving multiple children of varying ages. The theory is that it encourages a parent-child and family bond. Infants almost necessitate same room sleeping arrangements because of frequent changing and feeding schedules, but not in the same bed since this can be dangerous with the potential for mom or dad to roll over and on top of the infant.

While only a minority of families intentionally implement the family bed idea, a child sleeping in the bed with parents is common. **For most parents, it ends up that way by default.** A child begs to sleep with mom "just one night," or the child comes into the bedroom in the middle of the night and the parents are unaware the child has crawled into their bed. In some cases Mom or Dad may know that the child is in their bed, but are either too sleepy or do not want the hassle of dealing with this issue at 3am. After one or two nights a precedent is set and habits begin to be formed. The once medium-sized hassle the parents avoided now becomes a bigger hassle in which allowing it is simply easier. Soon acceptance sets in and parents begin to rationalize the situation. "Maybe this isn't so bad" they think to themselves. "I enjoy cuddling with my children" Moms says to herself. Never mind that there is *no* room in the bed, that mom is sleep deprived, that the parents are periodically kicked throughout the night, and that sex has become non-existent. What seemed like a good idea at first has grown into an enormous dilemma with no easy solution. **Not only are there numerous problems here, but this flies in the face of intentional parenting.** If your child sleeping in the bed with you has reached the intolerable point the best solution is to implement the token economy described in chapter nine.

In typical homes masked requests made for soothing are commonly made by children wanting to sleep with parents. Perhaps nowhere are parents more obliging. As with other direct or indirect requests to "make me happy" parents must think it through carefully and refrain from participating when not appropriate. Ultimately this does a disservice to the child because it sets a pattern of looking externally for happiness and elevation of mood. Some parents are able to set guidelines that achieve the best of all worlds. The children sleep in their own beds, but are occasionally allowed to sleep with mom and dad. The family sleepover may be done spontaneously or it may be done every Friday night, for example, as a special event. Still, there's that loss-of-sleep thing.

Also, parents must be keenly aware of their own motives for allowing (or promoting?) the child to sleep with them. The question becomes: does this meet my child's need or my need? Many parents if they were honest with themselves would admit that *they* receive comfort and emotional support from their child sleeping with them. This becomes a dangerous reversal of roles that will be detrimental to the child.

Then, there is another issue to be addressed- suppose the child is sick or scared and wants to sleep with Mom and Dad. Suppose they are *pretending* to be sick or scared to manipulate the parents. How to you tell the difference and do you handle manipulative sickness different from real sickness?

I will offer what we used in my home. Mind you it is not the bedtime utopia and does not solve all aspects of the problem, but it seemed to solve the majority of them effectively for our family. We never let any of our five children sleep in the bed with us. We viewed it as a boundary issue and an issue of requiring our children to soothe themselves at bedtime. Therefore, a clear distinction was made between their sleeping space and our sleeping space. Because sleeping with parents was never started in our home, it never had to be fixed and children reoriented back into their bedrooms- which can be an enormous task. If our children were legitimately scared (parents can usually tell the difference) or sick, they were allowed to sleep *beside* our bed for one night. After the one night, they were required to go back to their own beds. Because the child had only been out of his bed for one night, and since the carpeted floor provided limited comfort, migrating back to their own bed was easy for the child. Allowing the child to be close to the parents during the one night also provided some emotional comfort in a situation in which he or she justifiably needed the consoling from legitimate sickness or fear.

Children and Power

Power has been defined as "the ability or capacity to perform an act effectively."[9] Despite our instincts regarding children, power is not inherently bad. In fact, we want our children to be capable of "performing acts" effectively. How else will they succeed in life if they are not able to perform? **The problem is not children having power; the problem is children with too much power- power they cannot handle- power they are not ready for- power that exceeds their parent's power.** That changes our focus as parents, not to withhold power, but to *regulate* a child's power. It must be given to the child in the right amount and at the right time. In giving children power, timing is everything. Give too little power to the child, and his growth and opportunities will be stifled. Give too much power, and he will find himself over his head in situations he cannot handle. Since the former is rare, we will discuss the latter.

A child's power and wherewithal naturally will increase as he gets older. As a child becomes more mature, more intelligent, and gains more knowledge, the potential exists for the child to use these traits

---

[9] http://www.thefreedictionary.com/power

to make decisions and engage in behavior that is harmful. It is here that parents must step in to prevent such decisions. In doing so it is imperative that Mom's and Dad's power *always* exceed the child's. Parents must take great steps to monitor any means by which the child's power becomes disproportionate. As long as this dynamic exists between parent and child, the child can be kept safe and teachable. Consequently, personal and relational aspects of the child must be kept in check such as freedoms, privileges, isolation, and a general disconnect from family.

As previously stated, there is a natural tendency for children to desire power since it is often the means to their fondest desires. In holding children accountable it is important that children not acquire power that exceeds either a) their own level of responsibility, or b) their parent's power. If either of these states occur the child is in danger. We have discussed this idea relative to freedoms and privileges. But what about objects of power?

Tools of Power

Objects or tools of power are very sought after by children in our culture. Thirty years ago these tools barely existed. Consequently, they were minimally considered by parents. **Technology has provided a wealth of devices with which children can increase their power to the point of being detrimental.** Various devices now available allow a child to conceal information from parents, communicate with wayward or dangerous people, disengage from the family, provide an excessive focus on entertainment, and allow pornography and other inappropriate material into the child's life. These promote drama, or provide an avenue to unhealthy relationships. Electronic devices and apps allow much potential for harm, or at least the squandering of time by children. And with each passing day more electronic devices and apps are invented. Examples of such include cell phone, home phone, video games, computer and internet, CD's, Facebook, YouTube, Instagram, and Snapchat. Other non-electronic concerns include money, privacy, a car, and a credit card. It is the misuse or excessive use of all of these means that has potential for great harm if not regulated by parents or in some cases omitted completely.

Cell Phones and Children

As previously stated, any object or device that increases a child's power must be either regulated, or in some cases eliminated until a certain point in time when the child is more mature or trustworthy. Nothing falls into this category more than a cell phone. **Cell phones deserve special recognition in the category of "tools of power" since they are so versatile as communication and elaborate entertainment devices.** The power within a cell phone is roughly equivalent to giving a child the keys to the city in many cases. This is precisely what makes them so desirable by children who begin insisting on a cell phone in elementary school and touting its communication benefits for the parent. Further, many parents focus on pleasing their children at the expense of thinking through such decisions especially since all of the child's friends have one. Let's face it, a cell phone makes a great Christmas gift! And what parent doesn't want to see that twinkle in their child's eye on Christmas morning. But, the happiness of the moment often vanishes in the struggle of the crisis a phone can bring. In their defense, cell phones do enable parents to keep in touch with children in regard to after-school pickups and other activities. In our 21st century way-of-life cell phones are almost necessary for an individual to function. But, believe it or not children can function without one.

One rationale I often hear from parents that buy their teenager a phone is that it helps them keep track of their child. They give permission for the youth to go to a friend's house or to the movies, for example, but require the child to periodically check in using the phone. However, **a child can be doing anything, anywhere, with anyone, and a phone will not prevent it or notify a parent of it.** A child may report that he is studying at the library when he is actually with friends smoking pot or busting out car windows. A call from a child verifies nothing except that he currently alive. Consequently, **a cell phone provides a false sense of security in parents, and often further enable children's deceptiveness.**

The same aspects of a cell phone that make it convenient render it potentially harmful. The same ease and efficiency of communication between parent and child also allow the child to communicate with anyone, at any time, and in any frequency via voice mail, email, or text. Add to this internet capability, camera capability, gaming capability, movie watching capability, and song storage and listening capability, and the potential for misuse (even by good kids) increases dramatically. They can easily be used to deceive, distract, and obsess over. **Cell phones feed into the most immature aspects of children- to play.** Given a child's nature and the open potential of a cell phone, problems are almost inevitable.

Many a parent has regretted giving their child a cell phone because it increased the child's ability to deceive them, and/or became an object of obsession by the child. To many parents, a cell phone's primary and most useful feature- communication- becomes a vehicle for many harmful aspects to the child. Parents can monitor cell phones to decrease its improper usage, but regular checking of the child's phone and provider records are limited and time consuming. If a parent must invest thirty to forty-five minutes per day toward these accountability measures, the cell phone is probably not worth it. Moreover, most of these strategies by parents can be circumvented by tech savvy children. Simply put, is extremely difficult to thoroughly monitor a teen's cell phone usage.

The bottom line is that parents must have a sense of the child's maturity and trustworthiness, and refuse to allow a child a cell phone until he has proven himself. A history of honesty, responsibility, and maturity are the best gauges of whether the child is ready for a phone. Even then a phone with minimal capability is a good place to start. To trust a young or untrustworthy child with a cell phone is foolish and has predictable results. There are simply too many loop holes and too much temptation for most children, especially preteen and younger. A more detailed description of the problems of children and cell phones is in the appendix of this book.

Stratagies for Dealing With Lying

It is not uncommon for all children to lie at one point or another. Lying is one of many shades of deception in which parents *must* hold children accountable. This can include misleading, stealing, misrepresenting, omitting information, cheating, trickery, telling a little white lie, circumventing the truth, or distorting information. How each of these forms of deception are handled by parents will determine if it continues. It is imperative that deception be addressed promptly such that it does not become a habit that evolves into a lifestyle in adulthood.

One of the often overlooked attributes of God is that he understands. He recognizes our weaknesses, our humanness, our lack of maturity, our vulnerability to our own selfish desires. Not that He tolerates sin, but that He understands. Lying is so severe and offensive that it is easy to become harsh or overly punitive. **Deception of all kinds must be taken seriously, and the importance of honesty must be conveyed to the child.** However, a desire to help them with the problem is also essential. This does not absolve the child of responsibility or mediate any consequences, but it does recognize the temptations and life obstacles of childhood.

Regardless of the child's age, strategies for squelching lying include modeling, prevention, detection, investigation, accountability, and consequences.

Specific strategies:

1. Parents must role model the utmost in honest behavior in every aspect of their lives. Again we see how powerful modeling is in the home. Honest parents are more likely to have honest children.

2. Reduce the likelihood of deception by limiting the freedom and power of the child so as not to exceed his character level and maturity. A child with excessive power or excessive tools of power is more likely to deceive. We cannot tempt children beyond their ability to maturely handle the decision and expect positive results.

3. It is *imperative* that parents have the ability to immediately identify whenever the child is untruthful. Gross deception and rule violations often go unnoticed right under a parent's nose. Parents must be in touch with their children. We must be aware, alert, sharp, attentive, perceptive, and knowledgeable. We must keep our eyes and ears wide open so that we can recognize deception.

4. Launch an investigation if necessary going to whatever lengths required to uncover the truth. Anything that does not add up should be checked out. Stories that are sketchy, chronologies of time that do not make sense, money that is inconsistent with purchases, accounts of events that are illogical, and information from the child that varies from other sources must all be investigated. As parents, we cannot let these inconsistencies go without probing to uncover the truth.

5. The child answers to the adult who holds the child accountable for his actions. Children must answer for whatever deception they have spun, and at the magnitude they enacted

it. The child should also correct the deception through restitution that may include going to the offended person and telling the truth.

6. Lastly, provide unpleasant consequences that act as a deterrent to future deception. Punishment of some kind, and the anticipation of punishment are important in decreasing deception in the future. The punishment should fit the crime.

Summarizing the principles to responsible behavior:

1. *Model the desired behavior.* Parents should display the most dependable, conscience, trustworthy, appropriate behavior and attitudes possible.
2. *Insist the child take ownership his actions and decisions.* Children cannot be allowed to skirt responsibility or blame others from their actions. Parents must hold children accountable to owning up to their every behavior.
3. *Require work of the child.* Work is not negotiable- it is mandatory. Tasks that are assigned or regular chores should be required beginning in toddlerhood or soon thereafter.
4. *Tie work to rewards.* A link between efforts and pleasant returns is the goal. Conversely, no effort should yield few or no rewards in the home.
5. *Limit behavior.* Firm and clearly understood boundaries to behavior should be the family expectation with accountability and a willingness to follow through with enforcement.
6. *Regulate power.* Personal authority should be allotted based on maturity and trustworthiness. Freedoms, privileges, material possessions, and tools of power must be controlled lest the child's power exceed the parent's.

Chapter Eleven Discussion Questions:

1. What examples of neglect or absent parenting have you heard of or witnessed recently either personally or in the news? What was you internal response to the example you gave? Do you think affluenza is a chronic problem in America? Why or why not?

2. How can we as parents help children understand that they are accountable to God?
3. How is a child who blames others related to Adam and Eve and original sin?
4. How would you define entitled? Why is it important to connect effort and rewards in children? How will this connection help your future adult child? Are allowances for children a gift?
5. What is the difference between promoting effort versus a performance-based value system? What are the dangers of a performance-based self-concept? In what ways do we have to perform to be accepted by God? See Ephesians 2:8-9. However, does God have a specific task for us all in which He wants us to be passionate about? See Matthew 28:19.
6. Describe self-soothing? How well do each of your family members self soothe including adults? What is the difference between requiring a child to soothe himself and neglecting the child?
7. What are some positive aspects of co-sleeping? What are some negatives? What does the chapter state is the best solution to eliminating a child sleeping in his parent's bed?
8. What are some tools of power or influence your children currently possess? According to the chapter, is it bad that children have power? Are any of the tools of power your children currently possess and mentioned in this chapter, beyond your child's maturity, level of responsibility, or that exceed your power? How have you successfully regulated and supervised cell phones in your family? What specifically have you done to achieve this?
9. How is lying tied to the nature of children? How is a child with excessive power linked to lying? Describe an investigation of a child in your family related to deception. What are some possible outcomes in children if lying goes unchecked or unaddressed?

CHAPTER 12
Self-Development

No growth ever takes place without opposition. Muscles do not develop without lifting heavy weights. Cognitive development does not take place without mental strain. Neither does social development take place without knowledge, practice, and social risk. The previous four challenge chapters emphasize this opposition and resulting growth. This chapter will also stress challenging children within the two-component parenting system of challenge and support.

As we again think about the concept of challenge, it is important to consider the elements that are conducive to the child accepting the challenge. It is one thing to introduce the challenge. It is another for the child to accept it, and then another for the child to internalize it as a comprehensive way of operating long after he has left the home.

Guaranteed Results

An alarming number of children are being prescribed psychotropic medication today. Anxiety, depression, impulsivity, aggression, hyperactivity, and distractibility are significant issues in children as young as two-years-old who are under a doctor's care in order to control the symptom. **The increased medicalization of these problems are a testament to the quick-fix nature of our culture, as well as the reluctance of parents to reflect on their own influence on their child.** Pills are not only easy, they often yield immediate results. Most people recognize the appropriateness of medication in some situations. For most children, however, a better solution that is in the child's long-term best interest is in a change in one or more aspects of his environment.

In the preface of this book the power that parents have was put forth as a foundational assumption. This includes the power parents have of almost complete control over the environment in which our children exist. In the early years, we decide what the child eats, where he sleeps, when he bathes, when and how much he is stimulated, and who holds him. Until the child begins school we have virtually 100% of the influence over our child. We as parents make every decision, large and small, that affect the child. Once the child is of school-age, our power slowly tapers off and we begin to hand some of the reigns of control over to the child and others. What has been internalized from the child's environment begins to manifest itself soon in childhood. **We must begin to see a strong connection between our children's behaviors and attitudes, and the environment in which we control.**

Before the reader becomes frustrated and uses the book as a fire starter, understand the difference between control and outcome. We have 100% of the control over the environment, but this does not give us a 100% guaranteed outcome. The child's inborn personality, as well as his own decision-making ability, should also be taken into account. These other factors contribute to the final product as our children become adults. Nonetheless, the right parenting approach gives us a high level of confidence of the outcome. No, the results are not guaranteed, but the probability is high! In fact, the link between approach and outcome is so high that the style and methods of parenting, good or bad, are often multigenerational in their effects.

Security In Children

The old saying goes, "you can lead a horse to water but you can't make him drink." There is some application to that in children. A parent can apply the right techniques, but the child does not have to buy into them. This especially applies long-term as children become adults. This book has described direct discipline techniques, relational strategies, regulating cultural influences, how to supervise children, and respect strategies. One thing has been omitted thus far, however, and that is cultivating teachability through a secure environment.

While we might be quick to believe that a high quality environment is a result of being wealthy, income is only a small part of this concept. One aspect of an adequate environment is that there is enough financial resources to meet the *needs* of the children, not shower them with lavish gifts. Security has nothing to do with a privileged upper class existence, a cushy life, or an easy lifestyle. In fact, these things can provide a lifestyle that is *too* relaxed and stress-free, and does not provide enough challenge.

Security is an overall feeling of well-being in a child that is determined by his environment. The extent of a child's security is derived from everything he sees, hears, and experiences, both past and present. It is the collective sum of everything the child has experienced thus far in his life. If we consider everything a typical ten-year-old has seen, heard, and experienced, it would already be enormous. The body of information that this would represent would be mind-boggling- every word spoken, every person the child ever met, every song the child ever heard, every television show the child ever watched, every visual image the child ever saw, and more. This is what greatly determines his character, his view of the world, and the level of security. It is this security that determines his receptiveness to your relationship, modeling, and direct discipline. It is also this level of security that determines the child's functioning socially, academically, behaviorally, and practically.

Security is not a black and white idea, but a continuum. The level of a child's security is graduated with each point along the scale typically producing certain results. Because we want the best result in the outcome of our children, we must provide the most secure environment.

What Consitutes a Secure Home?

A child's security is primarily grounded in the stability of his home. **This means that as much as possible we must provide an environment that provides for the reasonable needs of the child and establishes consistent, reliable, calm, and emotionally and physically safe surroundings.** This includes many different factors, too numerous to list specifically. Generally, this begins with the child's own parents who are emotionally stable, provide for the needs of the child, generate adequate income, and discipline appropriately. If married, the parents display a solid relationship with good conflict resolution skills. There is adequate stimulation of the child relative to his age, educational considerations, and opportunities for social interaction. It includes the safety and stability of immediate family members, extended family, and friends. It also consists of the physical home which should be safe, adequate, and with the utilities on. It includes comprehensive consistency and predictability in the child's life with a high level of routine.

Couples living together have been the trend for decades. While it raised eyebrows once, cohabitation has achieved an accepted, legitimate place in the culture today. Scripture is clear in the confines of sexual activity relative to relationships. Cohabitation simply takes it one step further with some sense of validity in the couple's minds. The long-term relational and personal costs associated with laissez-faire sexuality often get unnoticed in focusing on the immediate pleasure and romantic bliss couples seemingly enjoy in living together. These costs are especially important when there are children involved. **That fact is that cohabitation represents a weak or temporary commitment to a partner that promotes insecurity in children.** A couple living together with halfhearted dedication to each other, and hence the child, is detrimental to the child. There may be some superficial security that additional finances or protection affords, but the limited (or in some cases absent) dedication to a strong, healthy family that cohabitation represents is ultimately counterproductive to a child's development and character. While children will often embrace a father figure they have not had, it also creates insecurity as the child senses this boyfriend may not be around very long, nor does he have to. The boyfriend has no legal or social obligation to his partner or the child- and this is the problem. The child forms an emotional attachment to the male which later is ripped apart when he leaves, scaring the child emotionally. Many versions and definition of "family" can meet a child's needs and provide security, but the most secure child is the product of two emotionally healthy, stable, and highly committed biological parents.

An Insecure Home

What makes a child feel insecure? In many ways this is an easier question since the bad is easier to identify. Let me answer this question with some examples I have observed over the years:

- Frequent moving
- Marital conflict
- Unambitious family
- Inconsistent discipline

- Divorce
- Regular community violence
- Enmeshment
- Dad's gaming addiction causes neglect
- Utilities turned off periodically
- Alcoholic father
- Spiritual apathy
- Educational indifference
- Mom's Facebook addiction that causes neglect
- Older brother who bullies siblings
- Live-in uncle with anger issues
- Dad arrested for domestic violence
- Pot-smoking friends of dad
- Mom's spending issues
- Sexual abuse of children
- A spoiled child
- Interfering, domineering grandmother
- Single parent with many romantic partners
- Yelling and cursing in the home
- Disorderly, wild adult friends
- Poverty through laziness
- No bedtime routine
- Mom abuses prescriptions
- Food money spent on lottery tickets
- Father's repeated infidelity
- Rules without a relationship
- Disorganized home
- Permissive parenting

SELF-DEVELOPMENT

In each of these examples there is something in the child's world that threatens his personal stability. In each example there is a component the child is exposed to that creates insecurity. In each example the parent has failed to meet the needs of the child in some way. These are examples of family issues both large and small. It makes sense that sexual abuse would cause problems in adulthood, but would the reader predict that no bedtime routine would threaten a child's stability and affect him long-term? Granted, this issue will probably produce a very minor issue in the child in adulthood, but how small is small, and how much family instability is acceptable? Children are of such high value that little of a parent's poor lifestyle is acceptable when it affects the child. Consider what quality of parenting would the reader have preferred when he/she was a child?

The more the incidents that threaten the well-being of the child, the more insecure the child will become. **Why is that a big deal- because insecurity brings behavioral and emotional problems, developmental obstacles, and threatens the long-term stability of the child into adulthood.** This contradicts the very purpose of parenting and the goal of this book. Moreover, it is possible that many cases of medicating children are a result of insecurities from family system problems that could be remedied by correcting the family issue.

Associations

One of the most influential aspects of a child's life is his associations. Associations include anyone he comes in contact with regularly. These associations will not only have modeling effects on Junior, but put direct pressure on the child to conform to the behavior and life philosophies the person possesses. These philosophies may be clearly stated, or may be simply displayed with the unspoken expectation of conformity from your child.

Associations would include many possible people- immediately family, extended family, day care workers, teachers, coaches, friends of both parent and the child, and neighbors and neighborhood children. Each of these individuals must be monitored to guard against extreme or harmful influence. Differences of opinion or lifestyle differences that are minor will only challenge the child's thinking, but not threaten his functioning.

If the family unity is strong, with the warm bond previously described, and hearty structure and discipline, outside influences will be greatly reduced. In other words, with the right atmosphere in the home parental influence easily trumps friends, even in teenagers. Nonetheless, associations must still be chosen wisely. We must strive to protect our children, but not insulate them.

I recently ran across a Facebook cartoon in which a young child was eating a gigantic chocolate bar. The caption reads "grandparents be like, one little snack before you go home." This may not be far from the truth. There is a fine line between a grandparent occasionally loosening the standards on one hand, and repeatedly spoiling and indulging to the point of affecting character on the other. Some Papas and Memaws believe they have unrestricted liberties with their grandchildren. The unspoken assumption in some families is that because you are a blood relative you get a free pass in terms of influence. This is especially true since grandparents are close in the blood line, enjoy elder status, may have limited time with grandchildren because of their age, and seemingly deserves respect. On this basis parents may be tempted to lower or even eliminate any standards that would apply to other people in terms of their associational influence on the children. But, **the duty of parents to protect and care for their children supersedes any obligation to grandparents or other relatives**. Parents must maintain high standards when it comes to who impacts their children. This can be dicey and may require tactful but firm diplomacy with grandparents.

Indicators of Insecurity

How do we know if our children are insecure? Is there a blood test? Maybe an x-ray. How about a brain scan. What if we simply ask the child if he feels insecure? Unfortunately it is not that simple. This last suggestion comes closest to practicality, but it too has flaws. Children will rarely initiate a conversation in which they admit feeling insecure. Even if asked, few are able to comprehend the question accurately or the concept. Children just do not have the analytical abilities or verbal skills to communicate this idea.

The issue is somewhat grey and any test is bound to be somewhat subjective (but so is the "test for ADD that is heavily relied upon). Nonetheless, it does provide a guideline that can help parents in assessing the need for environmental change. As stated earlier, **children cannot verbalize insecurity, but**

SELF-DEVELOPMENT

they do *act* it. The day-to-day behavior of a child is the best yardstick of insecurity in children. Below are a number of behaviors and attitudes that are possible indicators of insecurity. Carefully go down the list and check off any items that you have observed in your child:

- anxiety
- hyperactivity
- acting out
- fears that are irrational or excessive
- reject comfort
- problem sleeping
- excessive talking
- sad affect
- preoccupied with romance
- worrisome
- clingy
- regression
- rebellion
- school problems
- whiny
- anger/aggression
- low energy
- self-harming
- isolation
- social problems
- impulsiveness
- physical complaints
- attention-seeking

- bed-wetting beyond five years old
- excessive crying
- self-loathing
- addictions (FB, internet, gaming)
- obsessive behavior
- resistant to try new things
- scattered thinking
- poor boundaries
- trust issues
- excessively shy
- excessive emotionalism

The reader may be thinking at this point, "Don't all children have these traits? Don't all children act out sometimes? Aren't all kids whiney? Isn't this just part of being a kid?" The answer is *yes*. Childish selfish and immaturity manifests itself in many ways including the list above. Most or all children display these behaviors at one time or another. So, how do you tell the difference? Where is the line between normal conduct we might expect from any child, and behavior that parents should be concerned about?

I suggest three criteria in distinguishing the difference. If any one of these criteria are met a change is probably necessary within the family environment in some area.

1. *The Magnitude.* How big is the symptom? Virtually all children throw fits, but a nuclear meltdown that lasts for hours is very different. Likewise, any teenager can earn a bad grade in a course, but straight F's are an indicator of a much bigger problem. Any symptom of large magnitude must be addressed.

2. *Consistency.* Has the symptom lasted for more than two weeks? Both children and adults become sad occasionally. Being rejected by a friend, a bad hair day, or just adolescent moodiness are to be expected, but a despondent child for days on end is beyond normal and must be addressed.

3. *Number of symptoms.* Are there four or more symptoms? Any child, regardless of age, possesses adjustment issues in a few areas. The resolution of these areas is part of the growth process. This criteria allow for flexibility while offering an objective standard. It is not uncommon for a child to be angry when he does not get his way, but fighting at school, regular angry displays at home, hanging out with the wrong crowd, and distancing himself from parents are a clear indicator that there is a more serious problem.

As a final caution, it is important to note that these criteria hold true regardless of other factors. It is often the case that one of these three criteria fit a child who appears otherwise stable. **Children who are high achieving, socially competent, mature, get good grades, or are talented or athletic, are equally as vulnerable to insecurity and its harm as their lower functioning counterparts.** These traits, however, have a way of masking the indicators of insecurity. In the mind of many adults, these traits cancel out negatives ones- *they do not*. Consequently, as parents (or anyone who works with children) we must be careful that we do not adapt a false sense of confidence in the child when there are symptoms of insecurity but positives traits as well.

The Cycle

As stated earlier, the problem with these characteristics of insecurity is that they negatively affect development. The effects are often hard to recognize, especially early on in the child, but the more time goes on the more of a cumulative effect manifests itself and the more difficult it becomes to repair the damage, especially if there are a large number of characteristics of insecurity. At a point in time this underdeveloped child approaches adulthood, along with the accompanying overconfidence, strong desire for independence, and (sometimes grossly) inadequate preparation because of the family environment. Mistakes by all young adults are common. But, **a toxic combination of many environmental problems such as the ones listed, almost guarantees significant mistakes in life and multiple crises that can include legal problems and incarceration, drug or alcohol addictions, relationship mistakes and crisis pregnancies, general low functioning, or severe poverty.**

Families are often locked in to this mode of operating and have great difficulty escaping. The host of dysfunctional ways of thinking, behaving, norms of life, expectations, and life philosophies, are programed through their families, and can often be traced multi-generationally. The cycle begins with one or more environmental problems in the family such as the ones mentioned. This causes insecurity in the child. The insecurity leads to emotional and/or behavioral problems the parents are ill-equipped to deal with or unwilling to address. In fact, the parents may not even recognize that there is a problem, believing it to be normal childhood issues. Because the environmental problems are never resolved, the child now becomes an adult with many emotional and adjustment issues. He finds adult living difficult since he is unprepared with poor insight and a lack of maturity. Because of cultural influences he/she is also likely to buy into the American romantic ideology. This, combined with the fact that romance and sex elevate one's mood, distract from personal issues and generally offer affirmation, now ushers in relationship mistakes, crisis pregnancies, and other generally poor decisions. Ill-prepared parents with a baby initiate the cycle again with environmental problems and a child who will likely experience insecurity in a plagued generational pattern.

Damaging to Development

Typically there is a strong cause and effect to the family system. **The future stability outcome of the child is usually commensurate with the environment in level of problems and length of time the child is exposed to those problems in the home.** This threat to development happens in two ways, either or both of which can occur.

First, the child abandons normal development and switches to crisis/survival mode. When there is an environmental problem, such as one in the example list, the child's internal functioning shifts. Whereas normally the child would be thinking about building tunnels in the sandbox, dancing to a Cinderella video, or going to a basketball game with friends, his thinking is now modified. The most primitive part of the brain automatically switches to ensure survival. This can be a slight shift or a radical and comprehensive shift depending on the extent of the environment threat. If there is constant yelling and cursing, the child perceives this as a threat and his brain shifts. Similarly the child switches to crisis mode with inept discipline, inadequate food in the home, or an abusive older sibling.

A second common source of insecurity in the home is that of a parentified child. As previously mentioned, this occurs when a child is given adult levels of authority and responsibility. Parents in this case place too much on a child either out of weariness, or out of inadequacies, addictions, or emotional issues of their own. A child placed in this position will almost always accept it. It gives them an identity, a purpose, attention from the parent(s), and power. Moreover, they often believe it to be the norm. My experience has been that girls are more often parentified since they tend to be more natural care-givers who value family.

Parentified children are put in the position of cooking, cleaning, getting siblings up in the morning, discipline duties, and emotional support of parents. In some rare cases they are even depended upon to generate income, which can include illegal activity such as delivering drugs or shoplifting. Children, especially young children are typically quite inept at these domestic duties or emotional support, but will give it their all. Over time the child feels a twisted sense of obligation and responsibility. He or she may willingly take on additional tasks, which pleases Mommy very much. The child takes ownership of the parental role with little sense of how inappropriate or damaging this role is. Meanwhile, the age-appropriate tasks, the childhood milestones, and the developmental objectives that will serve as foundations of personal functioning in adulthood are being skipped over. An opportunity to develop social skills is substituted with doing the family laundry. Jumping rope is substituted with making the siblings supper. And joining the Future Business Leaders of America club at school is substituted with comforting a lonely mother.

There is a maturity in this child that is impressive to outsiders. More accurately, it is a pseudo-maturity since it is not true development. **The adult-like actions, however, mask internal issues that are mounting since key steps in development are being omitted from the child's life.** Those steps are difficult to detect in a young child since they are few, and since they are masked by a child who seems grown up. But, there is a cumulative effect. The older the child becomes the more the issues multiply, the more the developmental milestones are missed, and the more the likelihood of issues in adulthood

Breaking the Cycle

The reality is that life itself brings incidents of insecurity. Parents lose jobs. Houses burn down. A sibling dies. Mom is hospitalized for three months. Floods come. Fathers go off to war. Life is full of events that threaten the stability and security of children. If they occur from an external source they tend to have minimal effect on children. In fact, these outside disturbances usually build resilience in the child and may even *better* prepare him for adulthood. If, however, the source of the traumatic event is internal and therefore under the conscious control of the parents, the result is increased insecurity. A father can be laid off of his job, or dad can get angry after two weeks of new employment and walk off the job. The difference between an outside happenstance versus an in-house decision determines control and responsibility that children usually recognize. Once again, this underscores the power that parents have in determining the outcome of their children.

The good news is that at any point in time corrections can be made in the home to establish a calm, stable, consistent environment that meets the reasonable needs of the children. At any point in the cycle described earlier parents can make changes in the family system and correct elements of insecurity. When this is done it quickly shores up the child and enables him to thrive. The bad news is that there is no time to lose! With each passing day opportunities are lost and children elude small points of development that will add up and affect them later. And though the reader may assess his family functioning above most, even small points of personal, marital, or family issues that go unresolved will have an effect on children.

Drama!

In an effort to address additional issues of children relative to development, I have included several sections of common issues parents face in older children. Drama is a term adapted fairly recently in our culture, but one in which all generations have become familiar. It consumes enormous amounts of time and energy in children, and, in my experience, is an accurate predictor of poor adult functioning. No one likes drama- or at least that is what people state. What I find is that those who criticize it most harshly often unknowingly participate and create the most drama.

Though we all understand what it is, drama is difficult to define. There are many characteristics of drama in teenagers that can including:

1. gossip
2. unnecessary competition
3. possessiveness of friends and boyfriends/girlfriends
4. jealousy
5. attention-seeking
6. excessive conflict
7. formed alliances for political power
8. mean-spiritedness
9. well-masked neediness
10. involving themselves other's conflict
11. exaggerated emotions

12. thriving on crisis
13. a hyper social lifestyle
14. reactionary tendencies
15. superficial friendships believed to be deep
16. a disliking of solitude and peace.

In part, drama is about stirring up dissension, of which Scripture has much to say about. Drama is defined by making unpleasant hostility out of a peaceful person or situation. A primary aspect of drama is inciting ill feeling, anger, and conflict where there was none.[1] If asked, a drama queen is likely to say she (or he) dislikes each of the above traits, especially in others. The individual can often even recognize these traits accurately in another person, but be blind to the same characteristics in their own life.

Electronics and social media have rocketed drama to a new level in recent years. Now the means by which drama is promoted has become more efficient, and private conversations and disagreements can now become public, and therefore others can be pulled in. Now gossip, conflict, and friendship politics attract more attention and generate a bigger audience. **This makes monitoring of electronics and social media of children by parents imperative.**

The reason for this dysfunctional pattern of relating depends on who you ask as many theories abound. I believe that it is caused by one or a combination of:

a) melodramatic parental role models
b) a lack of relational security as a child
c) a legitimate need for attention that was not met in childhood causing deep adult insecurity, avoidance of abandonment, and other issues from which drama serves to distract, and self-care or self-soothe at which they are ineffectual.

In short, the child has reasonable needs in which he/she frantically attempts to get satisfied. But, because these needs are not met, it sets a pattern of relational and personal instability. Consequently, the

---

[1] Proverbs 16:28, Proverbs 16:21, Acts 24:5, Romans 16:17, Psalm 140:2.

seeds of "drama" behavior are sown in childhood. These characteristics emerge behaviorally beginning as early as six or seven years old with a fixation on friends, excessive image consciousness, and heightened emotions. An exposure to the culture (music and the media especially) that is beyond the child's years increases the effect. Hormones and increased independence then complete the picture in adolescence. By the teenage years a strong pattern is set that is difficult to alter and usually persists into and throughout adulthood. In extreme cases it involves multiple romantic partners and/or marriages, friendship and career instability, and emotional highs and lows that are intense and uncontrollable. As with all human traits, a genetic factor cannot be ruled out. But, I believe the home environment is powerful enough to supersede and guide any child into either a positive productive life or a life filled with drama and lack of fulfillment. In other words, **there may be some propensity toward "dramatic" behavior in a child, but without the other environmental factors mentioned above, a drama queen is not likely to emerge.**

It is again imperative that parents provide a healthy, stable, well-disciplined environment for their children since it will strongly determine who they become. Parents must address dramatic behavior and attitudes as soon as they begin to emerge in the child since these traits will affect virtually every aspect of the child's future. Steps to address/prevent drama in children:

1. Model healthy personal behavior. Emotions that are properly controlled, friendships that are stable, and conflict that is resolved will encourage the same in children.
2. Maintain a stable marriage. If not married pursue romantic relationships extremely slowly and cautiously. Any excessive romantic focus or dependency will teach children the same.
3. Promote reasonable expressions of feelings that are equal to the event. Give feedback and correct excessive emotional displays promptly.
4. Punish, at least mildly, the traits of drama mentioned above. Begin early while the problem is small.
5. Eliminate or regulate avenues that provide opportunities for excessive communication and gossip, such as Facebook, texting, Instagram, and email.
6. Teach and insist on proper resolution and avoidance of conflict.
7. Keep the child's social life in check and in balance.

Mothers and Sons

It goes without saying that mothers play a key role in any child's life, including a son's. Her nurturing and other contributions cannot be overestimated, but there comes a time when the mother-son relationship changes and her role must be modified.

It has been said that a mother can raise a boy, but it takes a father to raise a man.[2] At some point during the early teenage years males changes. His physical appearance changes dramatically. Not only does his voice deepen, but his shoulders broaden, his muscle mass increases, and he takes on a growth spurt the likes of which he has not seen since toddlerhood.

Secondly, hormones begin to surge through his body. Testosterone flows through his new physique prompting increased aggression and high risk behavior. Television shows abound of teenage males skateboarding off houses, playing with fire, and jumping over moving cars. Thanks to male testosterone, the emergency rooms are guaranteed a steady stream of customers doing absurd stunts females would never think of.

Thirdly, an interesting psychological metamorphosis occurs. During this period a young male will evolve into a mindset of protector. A sense of bravery, tough-mindedness, leadership, intensity, and gallantry emerge. This change is in preparation for the protector and provider role he will one day need to have a successful family.

I am very cautious to establish a parallel between animals and humans, but in this case the analogy can help us understand the potentially destructive force of teenage male behavior. Many animals run in packs and have a clearly established hierarchy. The powerful male leader is known as the alpha male. This male is respected and followed, and gets first claim on food. He also fends off any threats to his pack and ensures the hierarchy is maintained. This benefits the entire pack, such that roles are clearly understood and the pack is kept safe.

I describe this to help mothers, both married and single, to understand and prepare for this change. Teenage boys do not like to be told what do to. However, children of this age and stage still need much supervision and guidance. Consequently, a mother disciplining her testosterone-filled, unruly son who stands a foot taller than she does can be tricky. **It is here that a father can more effectively stand up**

---

[2] http://www.thisisyourconscience.com/2011/06/fathers-are-necessary-because-a-woman-cant-teach-a-boy-how-to-be-a-man/

to a teenage male's defiance, achieve submission in the child, and re-establish the family hierarchy that is in everyone's best interest. In fact, it can be beneficial for mom to defer to dad more during these often tumultuous years. The family alpha male, who is physically large and possesses testosterone of his own, must exert himself, keeping the overconfident teen male in check. If the power of the teenager is left unrestrained, the results can be disastrous. If no father is available, an uncle, grandfather, coach, or other male close to the family can suffice. I, myself had an uncle who played this role. And though I was taller and larger than average, my six-foot five-inch uncle who was a former William and Mary basketball star put me in my place, the result of which was a more stable, submissive teen.

To Tattoo.....or Not to Tattoo

Alternative looks have become more popular in recent years and in some ways more mainstream. Tattoos were once brandished by sailors and bikers to warn others of their machismo. Today tattoos are common and worn by many of both genders and include brightly colored innocent imageries. Skulls and flames are still popular, but have also been replaced with butterflies, crosses, and unicorns. The high level of talent in some elaborate tattoos often goes unrecognized. Other similar body art, radical hair modes, unusual clothing, or alternative looks are commonplace as well. The question is whether we should allow these looks in our children.

First, young children are not mature enough to make these decisions and therefore should not be allowed to make them. By the mid teen years, children can begin to make a few of these choices. Hair colorings can be considered, but funded by the child and generally discouraged by Mom and Dad. The positive aspect of hair is that it can be changed back, grown back, or fixed in whatever ways are necessary. This is not so with other decisions. Tattoos and piercings should be considered permanent. Forever is a long time to display an impulsive decision, brief fad, or short-lived preference decided upon when young. Most if not all states require an individual to be eighteen years of age, or signed for by a parent to receive a tattoo or piercing. Again, I believe children are not mature enough to make this permanent decision and as a parent I would never approve of it. Once the child turns 18, legally and otherwise all bets are off.

A second issue parents must consider is that these kinds of alternative looks can indicate adjustment or emotional problems. It is not necessarily the case, but a possibility. Self-expression, identity, conformity to peer norms, expression of angst, affiliation with a particular group, or to commemorate an event are common reasons to get pierced or tattooed. Some of these reasons can be normal and appropriate, but can also be the foundation of personal issues not yet resolved. **While rarely identified as such they can also represent self-hatred, self-mutilation, or self-punishment.** If such issues exist they should be resolved.

A third issue is that of limiting opportunities. In some cases alternative looks are a self-sabotage of success. I generally encourage self-expression in teens and young adults, but with parameters, because, depending on the degree of extremeness in the look and the long-term goals of the individual it may limit opportunities. Teens and young adults must understand the reality that people in positions of authority have opinions about looks. Right or wrong, if an interviewer does not like an alternative look you will not get the job. Right or wrong, people tend to assign lower character to extreme appearances. A supervisor or business owner is looking for employees that represent him well and will not offend customers. Also, depending on the field the teenager wants to pursue, they may not be taken seriously or trusted if they display an alternative look. This is true especially of professional or higher income jobs. In our culture we expect professional individuals to dress and look in a prescribed way that give some amount of predictability to their focus in life. Making good impressions is an important aspect of life that opens doors. A neck tattoo, facial piercing, mohawk, and multiple chains hung from black baggy pants will likely limit an individual to a minimum wage job at Hot Topic. **It is this limitation that alternative looks afford that should be conveyed to our children.** By in large, it will be the natural outcome of these expressions that will play out and cause the young adult to rethink his appearance rather than any parental controls.

An Eschewed Perspective

One of the most practical things a family can instill in their child is perspective- not just the broad categories of life and right from wrong, but the small nuances of everyday functioning, judgment, knowledge, and how a person conducts himself. This is another aspect of the environment that is sometimes omitted in families.

This eschewed perspective is not noticeable in early childhood but becomes apparent in the elementary years. The child feels odd and other children begin to relate to him differently compared to others. Since social skills are a large part of personal success but are lacking in this child, some ostracizing make occur. In adulthood the differences can be dramatic. A whole host of life skills geared toward high functioning may be absent. Ironically he may end up displaying minimal functioning and act as a loner.

One of the primary aspects of a personality disorder is that they "are associated with ways of thinking and feeling about oneself and others that significantly and adversely affect how an individual functions in many aspects of life."[3] This adverse effect results in predictable life difficulties, mistakes in judgment, relationship problems, and is often the foundation of adult personality disorders. It is for this additional reason that parents must provide the most stable, calm, predictable, supervised, structured, disciplined, supportive environment possible.

Chapter Twelve Discussion Questions:

1. What is the link between a child's development and his environment?
2. While admittedly there is a place for medicating children, why do you believe some parents are so quick to medicate their child?
3. How would you describe the feeling of security in children? What is the connection between security in a child, the family environment, and the child's development?
4. How does God make us feel secure?
5. Compare and contrast the homes of a secure and insecure child.
6. How does permissive, inconsistent, or ineffective discipline contribute to insecurity in children? How do poor associations of either the parent or child contribute to insecurity in children?

---

3 http://www.dsm5.org/Documents/Personality%20Disorders%20Fact%20Sheet.pdf

7. How do children convey that they are insecure? Name five behavioral indicators of insecurity in children. How might these indicators pass for normal childish behaviors? How does a parent tell the difference between normal and abnormal childhood behaviors?

8. Describe the generational cycle of family environmental problems.

9. Describe a drama-filled event you have witnessed recently? What does the book say are the roots of drama in a child? How do social media and electronics fuel drama? How does drama consume time, ill manage relationships, and hinder goals?

10. What general approach does the chapter recommend for mothers of teenage sons? Do you agree or disagree? Why?

11. Describe an optimal family environment for a child to feel secure, thrive, and develop. Must family environments be perfect for children to turn out well? Explain.

CHAPTER 13
Putting It All Together

One of the best loved sitcoms of all time is *Everybody Loves Raymond*. It chronicles the life of the Barone family and showcases the opposite of virtually every positive principle in this book. The dynamics displayed in this show are enough to make any family feel better about their own family struggles.

Marie is the matriarch with two grown sons and possessed high support low challenge in her former parenting. Her favorite cooking ingredient is "love" of which she has ample to go around. This love manifested itself as enmeshment when her sons were young which has kept them immature and dependent throughout the years. As other family members have pointed out, Marie possesses a psychological hold on her sons and manages much of their lives to this day. No doubt she was overly involved in her son's lives when they were young. Rather than "working herself out of a job" Marie has invested much energy in *maintaining* her parenting job with her sons. As an enmeshed parent Marie had low expectations, soft discipline, and plenty of coddling. She had a distant husband and an unfulfilling marriage which prompted her to get her needs met through her children. Marie has successfully managed to keep her sons geographically close to her so that her needs can continue to be met. She was (and still is) especially fond of Raymond with whom she enjoys secret alliances and who at times becomes an emotional surrogate husband. As such, Marie conveys a superior and competitive relationship with Ray's wife of whom she is highly critical. Many episodes and parts of episodes are devoted to Marie fixing her family's problems whether they want her to or not.

Frank is the detached husband and father of the adult sons where he implemented high challenge low support parenting. He sees no value in relationships and enjoys being thought of as the "tough one" by his peers. Frank is harsh, self-absorbed, and displayed rules without a relationship toward Ray and Robert. He saw children as an intrusion into his life rather than a blessing. His two approaches to correcting behavior problems were punishment and ridicule, often challenging his son's masculinity by calling them "Nancy" to which they are still highly sensitive. Frank's opposite challenge/support tendency from his wife caused much family conflict and confusion in the sons, and was never resolved. Though he loves his entire family, he curses, yells, makes crude remarks, is sarcastic and globally disrespectful, and is therefore potentially the poorest role model of the family. As such, Ray and Debra should considering limiting contact between Frank and their children.

Robert is the older of the two sons. Now in his 40's, he is single and still lives with his parents. Despite his towering height he has difficulty asserting himself, remains heavily dependent upon his mother, and is extremely indecisive. The chaos in his family of origin is the root of his insecurities and neurotic tendencies including the need to touch food to his chin before eating it. The lack of parental unity years ago in combination with a doting mother and disconnected father has yielded a confused and immature adult son. A divorced man, he expresses romantic confusion throughout many episodes, usually dating stronger women to whom he has difficulty committing. The continued enmeshed relationship between Robert and his mother often prompts her to rescue and fix his romantic dilemmas.

Raymond is the younger sibling with a wife and three children. To some degree Ray broke away from the excessive closeness with his mother. But, his continued enmeshment with Marie is the foundation of poor boundaries with her and spouse-like loyalty toward her. Raymond learned manipulation from both his parents and frequently uses his sports writer job as an excuse to watch television or go out with his friends. He is a responsible bread-winner, but a mediocre husband and deplorable disciplinarian. Ray married a strong domineering woman since that was the role model in his childhood, and because consciously or unconsciously she compensates for his irresponsibility. Raymond does nothing domestically and rarely helps with the children. He loves his children but often selfishly goes golfing instead of engaging in a family activity. He is less emotionally dependent than his older brother, but is still excessively attached and subordinate to both his mother and his wife. These two women often use guilt to manipulate Raymond. In defense of Marie and Debra, guilt-inducing is the only thing that moves Ray somewhat toward responsible behavior. Both Robert and Raymond often act like children, whining and in need of guidance and nurture by a female. A major theme of Ray is his strong need to be liked. This trait permeates his friendships and parenting, and prevents him from taking a stand on anything. As such he is a permissive disciplinarian since a focus on fun ensures his children will like him. Raymond has occasional good judgment in directing his children but does not follow through with enforcement. Ray is low on support and absent on challenge.

Debra is Raymond's wife and in some ways the most stable member of the family, offering high support and high challenge parenting. She is responsible and mature, taking her role as wife and mother seriously. However, she often enables Ray, even encouraging his irresponsibility without realizing it. She and her husband are not unified in parenting and the children occasionally exploit that division with various manipulation strategies. Like her mother-in-law, Debra enjoys being the martyr since it affords her the right to complain as well as increased power in the marriage. Her parenting is far superior to her husband's, but her reactionary displays can undermine otherwise effective discipline. Debra continually attempts to make Ray a tough-minded, responsible husband and father he should be, while Marie continues to coddle and enable him. In one episode entitled *The Sneeze*, Ray brings to the attention of both his wife and mother that he does not feel good. Detecting his typical neurotic, hypochondriac behavior, Debra is skeptical that he is sick. To her annoyance, however, Marie quickly begins to nurse her son back to health with chicken soup, bed rest, and excessive mothering. This eventually becomes a showdown between the two ladies in which Marie declares she loves her son and is giving him "what he needs." To which Debra accurately declares, "No! You're giving him what *you* need....a sick little boy to take care of."

Since *Everybody Loves Raymond* is a sitcom it is intentionally humorous. To their credit there are adequate resources and the adults are productive and hardworking. In real life, however, this family would self-destruct due to the personal issues and selfishness of every member. If this were an actual family they would experience even higher levels chaos, high conflict, resentment, multiple divorces, and probably wayward children in Ray and Debra's family. The gossip, family secrets, under-handed alliances, indirect communication, and interfering would cause perpetual riffs between family members. The neglect, enmeshment, favoritism, passivity, unnecessary control, unmet needs, relationship mistakes, permissive parenting, interfering, personal insecurities, and regular harsh insults would have ruined the Barone family. Moreover, the generational effects would be enormous.

The Cost of Waiting

Fortunately we can learn from this fictitious family in the ways outlined in this book. We can make personal changes and become intentional parents. Even if previous generations have not done family well, we can. **We can do nothing about our ancestors. We can do much about our offspring.** But, we cannot wait. With each day that passes an opportunity is lost to instill character and ensure stability in our children.

It has been said that the best time to plant a tree was 20 years ago. The second best time is now. There is a window of opportunity with our children. At birth the window is wide open. With each day, that window closes a minute amount- an amount so small we do not even notice. And that is part of the problem- a single day is such a miniscule portion of 18 years that we under estimate the power to influence that each day presents. We tend to believe there is plenty of time to correct- plenty of time to get it right. It only occurs to us as we order the cap and gown that the end is near. The window that was once wide open is now almost closed. It was closing all the time we just didn't notice. Like the parents of the troubled 17 year-old in the introduction of this book, we can become comfortable, preoccupied, or believe that the parenting task will take care of itself. We can also innocently become overwhelmed with the business of life. This is especially true of parents who have multiple children.

We must refocus and reprioritize. Moms and dads must get a clear picture of the window of teaching opportunities that will one day be eliminated. **Parents must grasp that the power and influence they have over their children will have an end point.**

New Challenges

One does not have to go far back in history to see a very different America in which children had few options. Whether it is athletic, entertainment, recreational, or electronic, most present-day opportunities did not exist just one or two generations ago. This has produced more job options, more technology options, and more options in our down time. Though debatably an improvement in the quality of our lives, it also has made for a broader spectrum of problems we parents must cover. Cell phones, the internet, video games, and their accompanying problems did not exist at one time. We have become almost obsessed with entertainment causing Hollywood and Nashville to meet the demand and bombard our children with options. School dilemmas of drugs, violence, or shootings were unfathomable. Television had three channels and PBS- and all of it turned to white noise and snow at midnight. Moreover, we could not have imagined nudity or cursing on television. We parents have *so* many bases to cover and *so* many pieces of our family to hold together.

The answer is to live with our families on a deserted island- or so it would seem. The other alternative is to set priorities. Over the years as a family therapist I have seen moms and dads place high importance on many things.

Misdirected Goals

I have watched The Learning Channel show *Toddlers and Tiaras* several times with fascination. Middle to low income families invest large amounts of money and time in a child, teaching her to walk, dance, and present herself in a glamorous and polished manner. The children are regularly pushed to preform past the point of a breakdown. Many of the girls (and sometimes boys) do not appear genuinely interested and therefore must be coaxed into doing a pageant. Pageants often include toddlers who have no clue what is happening. Oddly, the parent is often the only one watching her own child during the performance. The small fortune necessary to participate often puts the family finances in jeopardy. After considering these obstacles, what has been the benefit to the child and at what price? Many would ask what long-term goal is being served and do the benefits match the costs? In interviews with pageant parents they state they are building confidence in their child; or they are starting the child out on a career, but will their pageant experiences truly be a catalyst to confidence in other areas? Some of the children look anything *but* confident. They looked frustrated or bored. Still others adapt a hyper-confidence that is sassy, arrogant, or bratty. Further, one would question the wisdom in building an individual's career beginning at two or three years old.

Lest the reader think I am picking on pageants, these are question we as parents must ask of every activity, every piece of electronics, and every entertainment and recreational possibility we face. In fact- every decision! My point in the pageant illustration is that we as parents can become side tracked in many ways that serve various purposes that do not serve the best interest of the child in the long run. Moreover, even in beneficial activities and projects, we can miss the ultimate goal- character.

PUTTING IT ALL TOGETHER

Parents must ask themselves how a club, project, organization, activity, etc... contributes to their child. What are we trying to achieve. And does this decision meet *my* need or my child's need.

This book has now come full circle. We began with the same proposed goal to which we will now return. Let me suggest that the bottom-line goal is to build character. With that as an overall goal, this means that every aspect of the child's life should in some way support that goal. **Either directly or indirectly, every part of the child's life must contribute in some way to building character.** If not, then it may be counterproductive and therefore detracting *from* character, or at least squandering time in which better character-building might be achieved.

This requires that we as parents scrutinize every one of those parts with our character criteria. Depending on the age of the child, this can include the child's day care, extracurricular activities, volunteer activities, sports, scouting troop, marching band, and the magazines he reads. Every element in the child's life should directly or indirectly support the goal of building character. If it does not, parents must reconsider that aspect of his life.

A nobler venture, but one that can possess the same potential for being misguided is the pursuit of goals, achievements, education, and church involvement. These activities, or sources of activities are in theory linked to strong character, but these sources are still in need of scrutiny. Why- because the same goal can be missed. Do not confuse the goal with the means to the goal, or parts of the goal. Achievements are an aspect of hard work and character, but can be completely void of character. Church involvement seems like an endeavor that is part of character on the surface, but can be an extension of selfish or impure motives. Consequently we must evaluate the specific family activities and the motives behind the activities with honesty.

We must also ensure that the home is the primary teaching source of high character. Other groups, clubs, teams, etc... are only secondary sources. These secondary sources *supplement* the primary source, but should not be relied on excessively. A major parental mistake is believing that a secondary source of character development such as a club or sports team can override the modeling or teachings from home, or a poor family environment. Rarely is this the case. **As parents we have been mandated from God as the primary instrument to instill character, stability, and preparation for our child's calling.**

Small Changes Can Make a Big Difference

By now the reader may be feeling overwhelmed. It is this controlled chaos that parents to some degree must accept, especially if there are multiple children in the family. It has been likened to herding cats. There are a variety of logistical, financial, and physical limitations that must be considered while accomplishing the goal with an often uncooperative and melodramatic set of individuals known as parents. Nonetheless, it can be accomplished with a realistic perspective and the right tools. This book has attempted to provide specific strategies and techniques with which to achieve the goal of high quality parenting.

Any one strategy that is implemented will improve family functioning. However, it should be realized that all areas work in conjunction with each other. Replacing almost any component of a car will usually improve the entire car, but the reality is that all parts of the vehicle work together- the components depend on each other to function as an efficient unit. Evaluate. Start small. Get coaching. Find a support group. Enroll in a parenting class that concurs with the principles in this book. Re-read sections of this book.

As parents we must think of the whole child, and hence every aspect of the child- his friends, his media exposure, his education, and his spiritual development. We must also think of the broader principles that apply. Eliminating a violent television show is beneficial, but the broader principle is the modeling it represents and the desensitization toward violence that would likely occur.

As with all principles outlined in this book- the earlier they are implemented the better. Having seen teens in counseling for years and having five of my own, I think they get a bad rap. Yes, they have minds of their own and are often overconfident. But, often a teenager's rebellion is an extension of the chaos or poor parenting practices of the family that began many years earlier. In some cases, a fifteen-year-old male sits in my counseling office for reasons related to changes that that needed to be made in the home many years earlier. **Compounding this goal is the fact that kids are not evenly teachable throughout their childhood.** They are extremely impressionable early on, less so in the middle years, and become minimally teachable as youth. In musical terms of dynamics, they begin as an *fff* in teachability and end up as a *ppp*. Consequently, we cannot waste the early years. We as parents must make the most of the young childhood years since our influence will wane eventually. With that in mind, my hope is that parents of younger children read this book and take advantage of this crucial time in their child's life.

Lastly, our original premise was that high levels of both challenge and support are the most effective approach in parenting. As the reader now has an understanding of what constitutes challenge and support he or she should do much personal reflection. The natural tendency is to favor one or the other. The reader and spouse (if applicable) should also do a family evaluation. Remember- to the greatest extent family issues are a result of inadequate challenge, inadequate support, or both. Therefore it is imperative that each parent examine himself or herself for sufficiency in both areas. Once again, it is not my goal to induce guilt or bring shame on the reader. Parenting tends to be naturally guilt-producing as many parents feel inadequate, but an evaluation for the purpose of improvement is a worthy goal that will likely produce dividends in family stability in the long run.

Grace is a Wonderful Thing

I look back at some of my parenting and cringe- especially with my first child. I was young, had a poor role model for a father, and largely winged it. I desperately could have used this book. No parent gets it all right- even the best ones. But we parents cannot make big mistakes. Those almost guarantee problems in behavior and security in our children. My own father was unstable and neglectful. This lead to a divorce when I was five years-old. Because of little or no child support from my father we lived in poverty. These family issues trickled down to me and my two sisters who all had significant adolescent struggles. **We simply do not have the right to heap emotional baggage onto our children because of our poor decisions.**

I say this cautiously, but I am convinced a mom or dad can actually make a fair amount of mistakes and still come out with a good kid. This is the grace aspect of parenting- something we all need. Most moms and dads are good parents who love their children. They are parents who are doing most things right, but would improve their child's behavior, character, and thus future with some adjustments. By making three or four changes in the way they discipline or relate to their children, most moms and dads can take their parenting from good to great.

Being a parent comes with a lot of automatic baggage- namely guilt. I find that parents everywhere feel inadequate, have regrets, and are saturated with self-doubt even when they have done their best. As mentioned previously, the reality is that most parents are doing a good job- in fact, a better job than they think. So rest easy. Forgive yourself if you have made mistakes. Ask your child for his forgiveness regardless of his age. It will heal and reconcile.

With all of the recommendation in this book, there are no guarantees in parenting. In some cases responsible adults come from families who are negligent and wayward young adults emerge from the most stable, wholesome families. At a point in time all children will choose for themselves their life path and have the option to choose away from the positive things they have been taught. But, these examples are rare.

My point is that no parent is perfect, but we cannot use this as an excuse for a half-hearted effort. Love does cover a multitude of sins (1 Peter 4:8), but the temporal consequences, resulting emotional and behavior problems in our children, and the legacy we leave for future generations will remain.

Once you've assessed your family and chosen a challenge item and a support item, go back and re-read the particular area of focus. It can even be a sub-area, such as moving from harsh to firm within respect. Many times small changes make big differences in a specific child and in the family functioning. Whatever the case be brave! Take yourself on! Grow as a parent! And encourage your partner to grow also.

Chapter Thirteen Discussion Questions:

1. To what extent can you identify with the Barone family? How so? Which character in this sitcom do you personally identify with the most? Why?
2. Do you agree that in real life the Barone family would self-destruct? What evidence do you have to support your conclusion?
3. Explain the planting tree analogy. Do you agree?
4. In what ways are raising a child easier and harder than when you were a child? Be specific. How have electronics affected raising children positively and negatively?
5. Have you ever had to move because of the negative influence to your family from a community or extended family? What was the outcome?

6. Write a mission statement for your family. Use company mission statements as an example if necessary. Make it brief and to the point. Then list all family activities, clubs, organizations, etc..., and carefully evaluate the extent to which each activity supports the mission statement.

7. How does a mom or dad evaluate their parenting and acknowledge mistakes that may promote improvement, yet avoid getting bogged down in guilt or feel overwhelmed and therefore not make the changes they need to?

8. Despite a parent's best efforts, there are times when moms and dads must simply endure the day. Describe a time like this. How does grace play out in this situation? What principles in this book might decrease this kind of day?

Appendix

What Wrong with Children and Cell Phones?

1. **An Object of Status Contrary to Character:** The pursuit of status for status' sake is contrary to, and threatens high character. Cell phones often indicate to other students "I'm better than you." This especially true with newer, more expensive phones. Frequently this is intentional and used to counter the many insecurities, moral confusion, and immaturity of children. In addition, cell phones can fill emotional voids, elevate mood, and distract from emotional issues that need to be addressed.

2. **Expensive Electronics Vulnerable to Damage**: Children are naturally careless because of maturity they have not yet attained. What if we assigned our child to pass back and forth at school, and generally handle multiple times per day an expensive piece of Waterford crystal? The outcome would not be good. And yet we do the same with a delicate piece of electronics expecting it to be safe. Damage to a cell phone that the parents paid possibly hundreds of dollars for is highly likely with children. Moms and dads often then become angry at the child concerning a preventable and predictable mistake that parents could have controlled.

3. **Phones Feed Into Electronic Obsessions:** In our 21st century, children are extremely fixated on electronics generally and cell phones specifically. Any parent who has taken away a cell phone from a teenager can attest to the strong emotional reaction from the child as if they undergo phone separation anxiety. Because of this obsession, when children lose

their phone or leave it at home they frequently have an unhealthy response akin to a panic attack.

4. **Phones Squander Large Amounts of Time:** A 16 year-old male in my counseling office recently told me he texted over 1000 times per day. Second only to the phone itself, is the obsession teens have with entertainment and friends, of which a cell is the vehicle to. While once simple telephones, the cell phones of today are elaborate entertainment devices that can contain thousands of songs, numerous games, thousands of pictures, or full length movies. It is not uncommon for children to spend 6-8 hours per day in entertainment or communication activities via their phone, which often include late hours of the night. This is time that would be better spent in sports, music, hobbies, chores, homework or extra-curricular activities. Talking on their cell phone, texting, Facebook, Instagram, ask FM, twitter, Snapchat, Kik, various music and game apps, and many other apps all squander time in unproductive and often unhealthy activity. Besides wasting time, many of these phone activities increases teen conflict and drama, and enable the child to get over on parents. Recreation and social development have a legitimate place in children but must be balanced with productive efforts and personal development that do not encourage immaturity and superficiality.

5. **Unregulated Internet access:** Phones today are internet capable and therefore allow children unregulated access to any web site. This can include web sites that promote hopelessness, negative attitudes, teen drama, gossip, and pornography.

6. **Tech Savvy Teens**: Technology advances so fast these days that parents find it difficult to stay current. Because of extra time and interest, savvy teenagers often have technological knowledge that surpasses his parent's. This knowledge enables the child to evade accountability. This, and other aspects of a cell phone put Junior's power and authority at a dangerous point that may even exceed mom's and dad's power and authority.

7. **False Sense of Security:** If a child is in danger or doing something he should not, and cell phone can neither prevent it nor notify a parent of it. Yet somehow parents feel better when their child has a cell phone. Parents sometime require their child to 'check in'

periodically...but this does little or nothing to ensure safety or wise decisions from the child. It's as if moms and dads believe a cell phone is a 24-hour security guard standing watch to prevent bad choices of their child. Consequently cell phones give parents a false sense of security and often cause them to let down their guard, thereby actually INCREASING harmful possibilities.

8. **Insuring Children are Happy:** In most households children begin as pre-teens or earlier begging for a phone. Genuinely loving moms and dads want their child to be happy. Furthermore, cell phones make for a great surprise at Christmas and on birthdays. But, parent's desire for their children to be happy often exceeds their willingness to fully evaluate of the effect the phone will have on their child. The myriad of deception, security, and obsession possibilities are not considered by otherwise good parents.

9. **Inappropriate Media and Contacts:** Children often download music, pictures, videos, or movies to their phone that are harmful or inappropriate that parents are unaware of. This is also true of associations. Various friends, strangers, and stalkers that parents would never allow their child to associate with now have free access to their unsuspecting son or daughter via a cell phone, and parents frequently have no idea of these often unhealthy or even dangerous associations. There are now apps that are specifically designed to help children's texts, pics downloads, etc.., go undetected by parents.

10. **Difficult to Monitor:** Cell Phone communication and activity of a child can be monitored by daily inspections or getting online and checking records with the provider. But this is extremely time-consuming, assumes the child's texts have not been deleted, and has limitations in identifying a contact. Parents can check the internet history, but children can delete that history. As previously stated, the sole purpose of many apps today is to better enable children to deceive parents. Parents can insist children delete inappropriate apps, but they can easily download it again. Consequently, even at best, parent's ability to monitor children's phone activity is limited.

11. **Pseudo Communication:** Because of electronics, and cell phones specifically, quality face to face connection has been minimized in our post-millennium world. Now we frequently

APPENDIX

plan, resolve conflict, have conversations, express our love, and generally communicate excessively through electronics. While often efficient, it represents substandard and impersonal communication.

12. **Interferes with Family and Other Relationships:** Because of the supreme importance we place on cell phones and the need for immediate gratification, most children (and parents?) have their phone with them, have it 'on' at all times, and MUST answer it when notified. This includes during dinner, while driving, during a conversation, or in class at school. Individuals in our presence are rudely ignored because so few have any phone etiquette. Children are compelled to answer emails, texts, and calls immediately. This causes children to miss a relationship opportunities and encourages them to isolate themselves from their families.

Made in the USA
Charleston, SC
09 December 2015